Warman's

Costume Jewelry Figurals

Identification and Price Guide

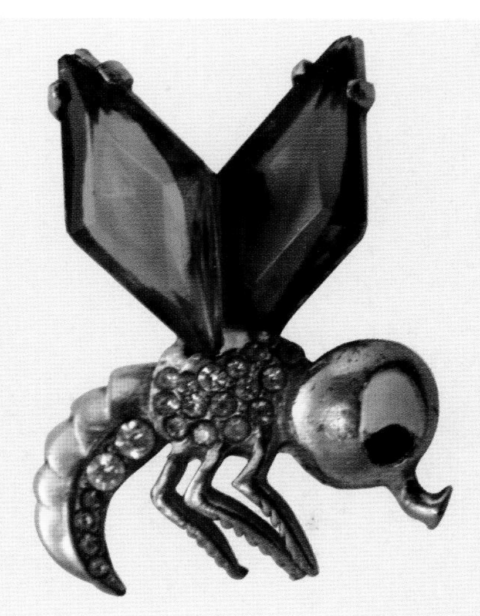

Kathy Flood

Published by

700 East State Street • Iola, WI 54990-0001
715-445-2214 • 888-457-2873
www.krausebooks.com

Our toll-free number to place an order or obtain
a free catalog is (800) 258-0929.

Library of Congress Control Number: 2007922997
ISBN-13: 978-0-89689-562-1
ISBN-10: 0-89689-562-9

Designed by Wendy Wendt
Edited by Kristine Manty

Printed in China

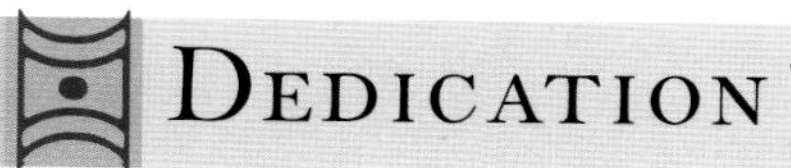

Dedication

For my favorite figurals,

Thomas and **James**

Acknowledgments

Photographer Tom Holzhauer persevered through some nail-biting events to come up with pictures of the pieces in this book. Capturing a large quantity of even beautiful or interesting things can turn into an experience fraught with tension, so as much as his talent and efforts, man did I appreciate his absolute cool. It was almost fun.

Enthusiastic jewelry devotees backed up his lead with photography of their own when shipping wasn't in the picture. For bolstering the book on that front were real gems named Dennis Scheer, Nathalie Bernhard, Valerie Gedziun, Henry Dale House, Dianna Flanigan, Neil Cuddy, Iradj Moini, Nicole Bernhard, Gail Crockett, Brenda Forman, Scott Reifsteck, Pat Smith, Erik Yang, Yelena Zhilo, Brenda Duff, and that multi-flavored lifesaver, Ann Mitchell Pitman.

Crucial interviews with key industry figures included the brilliant Elliot Handler, Karl Eisenberg, Ruth Kamke, Kenneth J. Lane, Marge Borofsky, Paul Verrecchia and the late Robert Mandle.

For sharing their most intriguing pieces up close and personal, this group gets serious grazias from the author: Myrna V. Seale, Ian St. Gielar, Michelle and Bettina von Walhof, Lisa Corcoran, Karen Parnella Workman, Lynda Bagley, Liza Amidon, and above all, my friend Susan Radosti, whose genius contributions enhanced numerous chapters. Without her, the book would be a lot less fun. Without my husband, Greg, the book wouldn't even be a reality.

Finally, two sparkling wits of the jewelry world, Joan Vogel Elias and Carol Spigner, women we all miss very much, may have helped keep me awake many late nights, chattering in either ear as I wrote. They were early jewelry pals. So are the always-generous and informative Patsy Seal and Bobye Syverson: great early guides for greenhorns. And to every person at Krause Publications who contributed their care to the creation of this book, I tip my beret.

Contents

Introduction

When jewelry-club members meet in homes or space, getting together to gush over gorgeous, gem-encrusted parures they're going to wear for upcoming special events, a separate set of club members also acts enthused. They pretend they are going to wear such treasures too, but in fact feel guilty and wonder if they really love jewelry after all. They wring their hands because…they have no rings.

They don't even own a necklace.

The fretful ones are aficionados of figural jewelry.

Figurals, like miniature art sculptures, are designs in the form of flora and fauna, people, places, things. As entertaining to look at as to wear, figurals sometimes spend their pampered lives in dark, velvet-lined drawers and see sunlight only when their owners open up the jewelry chest to gain the great pleasure of a peek at them—because their owners don't actually wear jewelry.

That's a slight exaggeration, but the extreme view rings true, too. Collectors of glimmering bracelets, earrings and necklaces have a relationship with themselves, a usually healthy vanity that drives them to adorn, decorate and bring light to their faces. Figurals collectors develop relationships with their figurals, coming to love the pins like friends or pets, and appreciating them as individual works of art.

Thus, the aesthetic appeal of a figural is often different from the allure of a flashy ring, complicated necklace or shimmering bracelet. A figural exudes character and often *is* a character, whether anonymous enameled heads or the exact likeness of Charlie McCarthy – or our cover girl, Vivien Leigh. It may commemorate history (the Moon landing), symbolize a hobby (flower gardening), stand for a passion (cats), capture a fad from a bygone era (a dancer doing the Peppermint Twist). You name it: If something happened, there is jewelry to note it, from elaborate, enameled Pearl Harbor scenes to rhinestoned Twin Towers and every event in between, joyous to tragic.

Charms are obviously the most recognized figural form, but the spotlight here is on brooches. Like many charms, though, some figural pins are mechanical: They move and do things, open and close. Some play music. Other figurals are as glamorous as any jeweled bracelet and swim in faceted or cabochon stones. From fabrications of plainest plastic or wood to heavy sterling, figural brooches may be all about the medium (when beautifully cast or carved), or cause a commotion when splashy and decorative.

Rarity provides the extra luster.

Some collectors and dealers focus on figurals with the most personal appeal, whether that means they adore an aspect of history (British monarchy, American patriotism, ancient myths) or are simply partial to a general form: exotic faces, poodle dogs, trembler birds, fur-clip fruits. Incredibly, virtually any theme can be found, if not in profusion, enough quantity to be collectible. That goes for, you name it: Can-Can dancers, organ grinders, gargoyles, ladies with fans, ladies with mirrors. Choose a common theme instead, such as ballet, as your field of pursuit and the chase can continue for a lifetime.

How lovely then that figural costume jewelry isn't just where the fun is. It's also where the lucre lies.

If someone asked you to show them the money on Internet auctions, steering them toward diamonds might prove disappointing, for those often sit like wallflowers at a dance getting nary a bid to tango. Costume jewelry, on the other hand, is often the most popular girl at the prom. And all it takes is two ardent suitors for her self-worth to spiral out of the stratosphere.

How zany is it that base metal and rhinestones, if packaged cleverly and creatively in the motif of a moody sailor by Trifari or big-mouthed fish by Eisenberg, may far out-fetch karat gold and diamonds? That fact always prompts a now-familiar story told about European collectors who leave precious jewels scattered about the bedroom, but keep their best costume stuff locked in the safe lest a burglar break in.

The most heartfelt reason most collectors become impassioned about figural jewelry, though, isn't merely amusement or money. Rather, figurals—be they seahorses, snakes, cherubs, butterflies, queens, hearts, ballerinas (or whatever floats one's boat, including boats)—get under jewelry lovers' skin because they are wonderful works of art, portable and wearable sculptures that may tell a great story to boot.

Sometimes that story harks back to a world we never knew, and a figural pin is a touchstone to it—one reason figurals hold great appeal for history buffs. Sometimes the story suggested by a brooch reflects our own personal histories: our love of travel or cooking, architecture or making music. Then the figurals become personal-identity jewelry.

Author's first figural; gift from Great Aunt Mae.

Figural brooches may be brawny and bursting with jewels, or humble metal creations with a touch of enamel, but many are so deeply steeped in culture or history, they hold us fascinated whether beauty or beast.

The memory of a summer day is still crystal clear when, as a young girl, I discovered my first wishing well while out exploring. An older kid said no matter how hot a day got, you could pull fresh, cold water out of it in a bucket, and that kids sometimes fell into wells and mean boys threw cats down into their dark interiors. I read in an encyclopedia that mystical creatures entered netherworlds through wells—or you could toss a penny in, make a wish and it would come true. For the rest of the summer, all I could think about were wishing wells. Obviously I wasn't the only one intrigued, for the wishing well is a familiar costume jewelry figural motif. Just seeing such a pin prompts remembrances of childhood past, or the good old days for all who decorated grassy lawns with quaint, kitschy cottage wells.

Some figural jewelry is made to honor or recall major historical events, from somber ones (bloody battles, sinking ships) to celebratory occasions (the new Millennium, coronations, royal weddings).

Figural jewelry is unbeatable when it comes to self-expression: Steiff lovers favor Teddy bear pins; flower pins grow on gardeners' lapels; Christmas tree pins have grown popular as festive keepsakes all year long because collectors can't get nearly enough Noel in December.

Literally, the jewelry world holds something for everyone. Reading about Krause Publication's book on collectible *Little Golden Books*, I wondered if the author knew there were Little Golden Books figural pins.

If the thousands of jewelry houses that created this world of wearable art hadn't employed such talented designers, figural jewelry would be far less exciting and compelling. If you asked someone dull to design a romantic heart 100 different ways, she wouldn't be able to. But few dullards worked at the houses of costume jewelry, so every figural motif you can conjure up can be found in at least 100 different witty variations. If someone made me guess the first time I saw a Christmas tree pin how many different tree designs could possibly exist, I would have speculated 50. Today I'd guess 5,000. *How* is that possible? It requires imagination beyond imagination.

It's the scope, the sheer variety of figural jewelry that makes it so appealing, so addictive. But it's the unique interpretations that make it art.

It's not easy to name a costume jewelry maker that created no figural jewelry, so the breadth of what's out there seems infinite at times. And countless vintage figural creations exist that we have yet to lay eyes on. That realization is thrilling beyond measure in the collectibles world.

Costume jewelry created in the likeness of every living thing does attract collectors who have no intention of ever wearing those pins on their lapels. For these undecorated minimalists, their pieces really do compose an art collection, and rather than requiring a museum for display, 100 fabulous finds require only a few drawers. (Size is another major consideration when it comes to jewelry collecting as an increasingly popular hobby. For the most part, it doesn't require rented storage space.)

It's also hard to ignore the fact, even if there isn't a mercenary bone in your body, that figural brooches live in neighborhoods where big bucks are traded. All over the world, people sit intently at computers waiting for search engines to tell them an original Staret Liberty torch or Boucher phoenix or Hobe bandora, Eisenberg femme fatale, Coro Chinese emperor, Reinad swan or Trifari jelly-belly-winged bird can be theirs for the bidding. Those determined, single-minded collectors know they'll have to shell out considerable clams to snag the special object of their affection.

But Bargains Still Abound

The great news is, clever figurals are for sale for as little as a dollar in antiques malls, backyard sales and even on the Internet. The resale profit involved can potentially come in handy for everyone, from high-school girls saving for college to seniors scrimping to pay for pricey prescriptions. Finding figurals makes sense for anyone, both in terms of fun and finances.

What to look for depends whether you are collector or seller. Overall, here are the 10 biggest bargain areas and where to find them.

1. **Go small**. If you like and appreciate tiny things, then a fabulous collection of figurals can be built quickly and cheaply. The truth is, most collectors prefer pins with presence, meaning at least 2 inches high and preferably 3. If 1- to almost-2-inch pins hold charm for you, you can make out like a bandit, nabbing even the best for less: exquisitely crafted Trifari minis or even some diminutive DuJay brooches. Petite pins often go bid-less or buy-less in Internet auctions or Web shops.

2. **Shiny objects**. One collector of figural pins said recently she is all about glitz, shine and flash. If that's true for you, if you don't need vintage or antique jewelry with all the history and the handsome patina, you'll be able to build a collection quickly and inexpensively. The older jewelry is, the rarer it usually is, and that costs more. If razzle-dazzle rocks your world and the 21st Century holds as much appeal for you as anything from 1940, fun's on the menu. But don't expect monetary appreciation. A garish and glittery 4-inch bird being cranked out in China is part of a very large flock.

3. **Origin unknown**. Most collectors can't help being signature snobs because unsigned jewelry is riskier for possible resale, so they balk at paying a bundle for unsigned pieces. Pins, when originally made, went unsigned for all sorts of reasons, none of which was that they were chopped liver. If you don't need a mark, you're way ahead. Obviously, if you're hunting for a certain motif, whether crowns or cats, the design is the key and a mark is secondary. Not to say you won't come to covet a gilded-sterling silver signed Trifari crown bursting with liquidy cabochons, or a signed Hattie Carnegie big cat lurking in the grass. But an equal passion for the unsigned has huge rewards. The difference between, for instance, a signed Mazer mask and an even more elaborate mask only attributed to Mazer may be hundreds of dollars. There's your answer to the question, What's in a name?

4. **Humble names**. The classic example in this category is Jonette. A jewelry company in business for almost 70 years manufactures so much merchandise, it is taken for granted. Jonette jewelry figurals were always reasonably priced, too, so it seems every woman in the world bought some during her lifetime—and it's all still out there. The very fact of its breadth and ubiquitous availability made J.J. specimens wildly affordable. After Jonette shut its doors in 2006, its quotient of sex appeal immediately started rising, even if slightly (a bitter irony). But a collector could spend decades searching for reasonably priced J.J.s and never find them all. Vintage J.J. pins are bargain gems; some are beautiful creations, full of surprises. Modern designs are witty, and the product of active imaginations. Other "unsexy" names that send chills up too few spines include Gerry's, Sarah Coventry, Monet, Art, Avon, and many others. It's not to say these names aren't found on fine costume jewelry. Mainly, there is simply a lot of it. (Contrast these with the "hot" names in the Treasure Aisles section.)

5. **Weird & Wacky**. For every 10 collectors intrigued by a fabulous floral pin or glamorous heart, only two might desire a kooky or freaky specimen. If you have a penchant for the offbeat or can develop one, you'll be able to build a collection much more cheaply.

6. **Flea Market & Antique Mall Trends**. Parts of the collectibles business experienced a slowdown in 2006, and the costume-jewelry market wasn't fully immune. One trend that resulted was price-busting by dealers who went so far as grouping merchandise on shelves by cost, all $1 or $3 or $5 or $10. Buyers appreciated the opportunities. These dealers decided to be wisely flexible, still able to make their case rents, while others who stood firm during the slowdown packed up and left altogether after too many months of losses. The low fixed-price trend has been a gold mine for savvy collectors who gobbled up the bargains for keeps—or plan to sit on their finds till the big picture is peachy again.

7. **Fixer Uppers**. Learn how to repair jewelry in order to buy great bargains in damaged goods or "injured beauties." Replace missing stones, solder pin back findings, touch up enameling and you can revitalize jewelry that's been degraded. Obvious cautions are to stay away from heavy corrosion and verdigris, or brooches with stones so unusual they may never be replaced. Also, if you're buying to resell, many potential buyers will hesitate before purchasing your re-dos. If the jewelry is for you, though, go for it. I found the most corroded, unsightly lady brooch in an

antiques mall and despite her sad appearance, she remained recognizable as a real dish. Hard times had left her hideous. This was before I knew of the Calvaire Debutante pin—and she was a vintage version of the signed specimen. A professional repair person performed a major makeover, putting the overhauled babe back in business, rescued from an ignominious life in that case, or the trash heap.

8. **Books**. Most collectors with a fixed or limited budget find it hard to funnel precious funds away from jewelry into anything else, and that includes books. It's not that collectors don't appreciate enlightenment; they just can't pass up a pin. Instead, buy as many books as you can afford, for they're worth their weight in gold and will pay off in every way, informational to monetary. Consider putting yourself on a forced-purchase program: buy a jewelry book at least every month. Experience suggests you'll learn crucial facts from every single one of them. You'll buy duds for sure, and run into dead-wrong research, but overall, books will become best friends. One off-hand sentence may send you deep into a passionate love affair with a new subject.

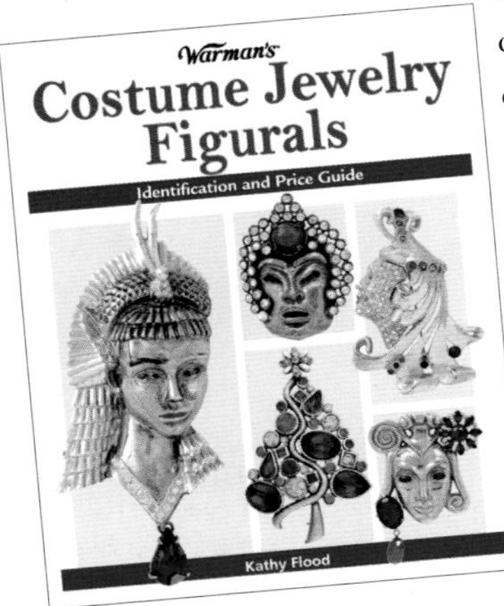

9. **Reproductions**. If you're certain you'll never be able to afford the rarest thousand-dollar figurals even if they present themselves to you – but you love the designs – consider making a collection of reproductions. Repros are bad news when their true nature is hidden or lied about. When it's clear they're new or newer copies, they become many collectors' only opportunity to own the great gems of costume jewelry history. One of the best-known recreators of famous figurals refers to its production as recasts. They've brought back everything from the Eisenberg Original mermaid to the Staret Liberty Torch, which has gotten pricey itself. Another more affordable direction to take is in vintage unsigned versions of famous designs. The shame of reproductions comes when scoundrels make copies and pretend they're originals. The sham is most shocking when it befalls companies still in business. Sharpies have the nerve to rip off designs by current famous makers, changing one minor detail and having thousands of pieces made in China. People involved in such activities scoff at the notion that what they're doing is dishonest.

10. **Speak up**. Good things come to those who yak. Shyness never pays when out hunting. See a dealer and ask what else they have. Call out at crowded flea markets and ask if they have what you're looking for. Get to know antiques mall owners or managers; casual chit-chat may lead to treasures. I was talking with one woman who ran a small mall and after some fairly boring banter, she mentioned as an afterthought her ex-son-in-law's grandmother had a huge collection of very old Christmas tree pins. Suddenly, the conversation seemed scintillating. Another time, the owner of an antiques shop remained entrenched with another customer and we were about to walk out the door when I decided to interrupt them. The dealer turned out to own a figural collection I never would have imagined. Leave shyness and reticence at home every time you embark on a search mission.

The Flip Side: Treasure Aisles

You can't help but pay serious attention to the figural costume-jewelry category when an unsigned metal-and-plastic King Neptune pin that's merely *attributed* to Hattie Carnegie sells for $600-plus, or when the Boucher Octopus sells for more than $14,000. If they hadn't been figurative motifs, but merely ravishing circle pins or rhinestone razzmatazz, they wouldn't have sold anywhere near those figures, if at all.

With that in mind, here is a treasure-laden scavenger hunt to enjoy, spotlighting 64 prices realized. Who doesn't love a list like this, and an assignment that's at once challenging and rewarding. This abbreviated treasure tracker's guide to desirable goodies is fun whether you want to keep the loot or convert it to cash. Almost all the sales amounts noted are actual sales results, prices realized, from eBay auctions, a better barometer than "prices asked" on Web sites because it's not always possible to determine actual sales figures from Internet stores.

Remember these dandies when you're out (or in) scouting. (Prices rounded to nearest dollar.)

1. Eisenberg Original dolphin fur clip, pink jeweled fins, **$939.**
2. Staret jeweled lion face pin, **$775.**
3. Reinad unicorn pin, **$495.**
4. Eisenberg Original stretching leopard brooch, **$632.**
5. Eisenberg sterling vermeil flower fur clip, fuchsia baguettes, **$775.**
6. Trifari Sinbad the Sailor pin, **$1,195.**
7. Unsigned plastic and metal King Neptune pin, **$633.**
8. Eisenberg Sterling lady duck pin, **$1,295.**
9. Corocraft coach fur clip, **$416.**
10. Trifari fierce bird fur clip, Lucite wings, vulture or eagle, clutching baroque pearl perch, **$5,407.**
11. Eisenberg Sterling vintage mermaid pin, aquamarine-colored beads and stone, **$1,540.**
12. Unsigned man on hands and knees in dog house, wearing top hat, **$386.**
13. Hattie Carnegie primitive ram pin with tall horns, **$440.**
14. Unsigned mechanical pelican brooch with movable mouth, **$399.**
15. Eisenberg Original buddha head with pink-red jewels, **$675.**
16. Vendôme brooch with birds after Georges Braque, **$512.**
17. Eisenberg Sterling galloping horse brooch with enamel and rhinestones, **$514.**
18. Trifari sterling and Lucite jelly-belly sailboat brooch, **$762.**
19. Hattie Carnegie anteater, **$376.**
20. Eisenberg Sterling pair of fighting cocks, **$610.**
21. Trifari sterling frog pin with cabochon-center body, **$430.**
22. Eisenberg Original lady in profile with long tresses, fur clip, **$875.**
23. Boucher Mandarin fur clip, **$910.**
24. Chanel Novelty flamingo pin, **$449.**
25. Eisenberg Original Egyptian man (or Waterbearer), emerald rhinestones, **$537.**
26. Trifari black enamel and faux-gems tree brooch, **$1,924.**
27. Trifari Lucite sterling jelly belly Airedale fur clip, **$1,625.**
28. Trifari ear of corn pin, **$810.**
29. Trifari moonstones bird brooch, **$567.**
30. Unsigned jelly-belly elephant pin, possibly unsigned Trifari, **$622.**
31. Trifari sterling jelly-belly orchid pin, **$462.**
32. MB Boucher pink-enameled octopus pin, **$14,100.**
33. Trifari frog brooch on Lucite jelly-belly lilypad, **$5,207.**
34. Hobe Oriental Bandora pin, **$432.**
35. Bakelite scarce black cat face pin, **$691.**
36. Trifari jeweled horse head pin, **$372.**
37. Eisenberg Sterling Medusa fur clip, **$500.**
38. Silson drunken tiger with goblet, fur clip, **$510.**
39. Har reclining fortuneteller genie, **$411.**
40. Eisenberg gilded sterling vase with sapphire rhinestone centerpiece, **$615.**
41. Eisenberg sterling Can-Can dancer fur clip, **$499.**
42. Har standing genie, **$449.**
43. Karu Bakelite WWII Be Alert! Pin, **$908.**
44. Trifari glass mosaic Christmas tree pin, **$350.**
45. Unsigned DuJay lady fur clip, **$2,500.**
46. Trifari large fruit-salad bird pin, **$1,084.**
47. Eisenberg Original king and queen fur clips, **$1,200.**
48. Iradj Moini parrot head pin, **$861.**
49. Rare Bakelite frog pin, **$910.**
50. Eisenberg Original jardiniere, **$770.**
51. Trifari fruit-salad flower cart pin, **$405.**
52. Bakelite hat shaped pin, **$560.**
53. Eisenberg Original big-mouth fish pin, **$639.**
54. Bakelite cigarettes and matches pin, **$425.**
55. MB Boucher paved preying mantis pin, **$900.**
56. Bakelite pears cluster pin, **$459.**
57. Trifari jelly-belly snail pin, **$444.**
58. Vintage Bakelite and brass large floral bouquet pin, **$899.**
59. CoroCraft Sterling double fish pin set, **$362.**
60. Bakelite large, carved, painted Indian Totem Pole Pin, **$1,259.**
61. Trifari KTF rhinestone cat pin, **$338.**
62. Unsigned chubby-swami fur clip, **$688.**
63. Trifari jelly belly eagle-bird, **$7,300.**
64. Boucher 1940 enamel and rhinestones parrot pin, **$513.**

So Surreal it's worthy of Dali or Schiaparelli, this 1940 fur clip signed PJ Co. has a design patent credited to Scotsman Samuel MacNeil and features a celestial-themed, fruit-face cocktail pitcher, **$1,295.**

CHAPTER 1  Pin on a Famous Face

Glitterati

Imagine jewelry counters at Saks and Macy's stores stocked with the lookalike countenances of stars such as gorgeous George Clooney and Angelina Jolie. If this were the mid-20th Century rather than the early 21st, fans might be able to buy such celebrity brooches.

The most recognizable faces 50-plus years ago cast not just in films but in pins was a trend back then. Some directors, most notably Cecil B. DeMille and Alexander Korda, are affiliated with multiple movies' related jewelry. The deals must have been successful enough that licenses continued to be requested.

Vivien Leigh, first encountered on American shores as Scarlett O'Hara, proved a green-eyed moneymaker when it came to affiliated premiums sold in her likeness or name. Leigh won an Academy Award for her portrayal of the definitive Southern belle as steel magnolia, but she also won the pocketbooks of fans who wanted some keepsake of Leigh in her most renowned role.

So no wonder a clever costume jewelry company jumped on the next opportunity to profit from Scarlett-turned-Queen of the Nile when Leigh won the lead female role in Gabriel Pascal's presentation of George Bernard Shaw's "Caesar and Cleopatra."

Vivien Leigh as Queen of the Nile, from the film version of George Bernard Shaw's "Caesar and Cleopatra," 1946, Providence Jewelry Manufacturing, unmarked, gilded metal with rhinestones, 3" pin, **$1,200.**

Jewelry from this 1945 production (not released in America until autumn 1946), billed as "The Most Lavish Picture Ever on the Screen," included designs based on characters and icons from the film, as well as designs actually worn in the picture. Because this line of jewelry went unmarked, pieces still remain unidentified today. No one has definitively assembled the full panoply included in the 15-piece set. However, Italian jewelry collector-historians Carla Ginelli and Roberto Brunialti first identified the "head," as Leigh's Cleo brooch was called, in the book *A Tribute to America.* They found the jewelry documented in an old advertisement in *Women's Wear Daily.*

The Providence (R.I.) Jewelry Company manufactured this bust of Cleopatra in the actual likeness of Leigh. When it comes to celebrity movie-related jewelry, it's "Possibly the Finest Costume Piece Ever Produced." Quality metal plating, strong resemblance to a major motion-picture star, and excellent depth of casting (more sculptural than most figurals) make it extremely desirable. (The decorative, dangling ruby navette is usually missing.)

Adding to the drama surrounding this movie, Leigh miscarried her child with husband Laurence Olivier during filming. Despite all of this, the Cleopatra brooch is a rarity today, meaning it must not have sold well at retail. (It's hard to imagine the creation easily thrown away if many women actually did have them, so more should have turned up if sales were successful.)

Vintage photograph of Vivien Leigh as Cleopatra.

A vintage 1946 full-page magazine ad for Gabriel Pascal's 1945 production of George Bernard Shaw's "Caesar and Cleopatra."

Vincent Price as Baka, from Cecil B. DeMille's 1956 production of "The Ten Commandments," Joseff of Hollywood, 2" pin, **$75-$100.**

Carmen Miranda brooch, painted, glazed pottery, unsigned 1940s Elzac knock-off, 3-1/4", **$50.**

A savvy businessman and jewelry manufacturer named Eugene Joseff was justifiably known as "jeweler to the stars." His work was probably featured in more major motion pictures than anyone else's, and movie stars wore his creations in their personal lives too.

Killed at age 43 in an airplane crash, Joseff was already deceased in 1956 when Cecil B. DeMille remade his own epic 1923 silent film "The Ten Commandments." His wife Joan Castle Joseff was at the helm of the company when the classic DeMille remake debuted.

Joseff and Castle frequently created jewelry from sketches by a film's costume designer, whether Walter Plunkett or Joe De-Young. In the case of 1956's "Commandments," the costumers were award-winning Edith Head with John Jensen, Ralph Jester and Dorothy Jeakins, so the scowling brooch of Vincent Price as sadistic Egyptian slave driver Baka may have been rendered by one of them and then cast by the Joseff of Hollywood firm.

The furrowed brow and brainy forehead of Tinsel Town spookster Vincent Price, as cruel "Ten Commandments" builder-architect Baka, are deeply cast into this figural brooch of burnished golden metal. It is signed Joseff in script italics, reproducing the designer's own autograph. While handsome and interesting, the pin is all metal and off-putting, but of interest to movie buffs, connoisseurs of the actor, and collectors of curious face figurals.

While it's easy for 21st-century collectors to understand the timeless allure of a Vivien Leigh or even Vincent Price, that's less true of other hot properties of the past. Two examples: Charlie McCarthy and Carmen Miranda.

Some jewelry companies that never made another celebrity look-alike in their histories did create Carmen Miranda pins. (Elzac is just one such name.) Miranda, the Portuguese-born "Brazilian Bombshell," strikes modern observers as so over-the top and caricaturish, her sex appeal so in-your-face, it's practically impossible to believe she was one of the highest-paid entertainers in America during the 1940s—and probably the highest paid of all in 1946.

Granted, her tutti-frutti hat was colorful and exotic and lent

Charlie McCarthy pin, plastic, unsigned, 1", **$10-$75.**

Charlie McCarthy fur clip, enameled metal, mechanical, Cohn & Rosenberger, 1", **$75-$150.**

itself to fanciful brooches, but that wouldn't have been enough to put her on the lapels of such legends as Joan Crawford and Lana Turner. Carmen Miranda needed real star power to become so fashionable—and she had it.

From her Broadway beginnings in 1939's *Streets of Paris* at the Shubert to raves in such Forties vehicles as "Weekend in Havana," "Down Argentine Way," "Doll Face" and "That Night in Rio," Miranda worked her bananas to the bone: In the 13 years between 1940 and 1953, she made 14 movies. The camp entertainer sold millions of records, and Saks Fifth Avenue made a fortune off licensed accessories related to the outlandish Latina. Carmen Miranda died in 1955 at age 46, and even Bugs Bunny had paid tribute with a cartoon impression of her. Countless products were sold in her likeness, and that includes many costume-jewelry pins.

Although David Letterman made ratings hay with "Ventriloquists Week" promos in 2006 and 2007, most people today can't possibly comprehend the craze stirred by Edgar Bergen's dummy Charlie McCarthy, also known as actress Candice Bergen's older wooden brother. The wise-cracking, smart-aleck, human-like puppet, who dressed better than most mortals in a tux and top hat (not to mention the monocle), cracked audiences up coast to coast on the pair's "Chase and Sanborn Hour" show at NBC, which ran for a whopping 11 years, plus three more on CBS with Coke as sponsor.

Jewelry companies created two different pins in the image of chatty dummy Charlie McCarthy. One is unsigned and unattributed, a plastic pin of small proportion. Also petite, another pin, actually a pronged fur clip and the virtual twin of the plastic version, is a more elaborate design: Licensed by Bergen to Cohn & Rosenberger (Coro) for manufacture in 1937, the lavishly enameled cast-metal clip is mechanical. A lever in back operates Charlie's jaw, so his mouth opens and closes as if he's talking.

Specimens with both the enameling and monocle intact do appear, so if this clip is meaningful for a collection, it might be best to hold out for fur clips in near-perfect condition.

One putative "Josephine Baker" figural head brooch, enameled metal with rhinestones, 1940, unsigned, 2-1/2", **$50-$125.**

Marilyn Monroe pin, painted ceramic and rhinestone chain, 1988, Clay Art San Francisco, 2", **$25.**

The story of a young African-American woman from East St. Louis, Illinois, who moved to France and became the toast of Paris in the Twenties and Thirties isn't only fascinating; it prompts jewelry collectors to imagine her likeness in any pin that even vaguely resembles her.

One of the most notorious and celebrated characters ever to grace the City of Light, Baker was renowned for her *joie de vivre,* charisma—and style without equal.

Most people know about the topless banana-kini of her stage presentations, but her flair in costuming extended to the street, where she was the last word in chic.

Josephine Baker would be flattered that jewelry lovers see her everywhere. The girl with skin so sensational Frenchwomen felt required to bronze their own with nut oils caused such a unique commotion in her bananas and bare breasts that the luster lingers on after all these years.

The talented cabaret star made movies (such as 1934's "Zouzou"), sang ("J'ai Deux Amours" was perhaps her most popular ditty), set trends—and created a huge family around the orphans she adopted.

If a seller can convince a potential buyer that a figural brooch is indeed La Josephine, the price automatically goes up.

Another Baker, Norma Jean, shows up in a number of pin permutations, and there's not much doubt when it's her. If there are degrees of recognizability when it comes to icons, Marilyn Monroe is way at the top. The ultimate Blonde Bombshell captivated everyone from Dimaggio to Warhol, and the world in between.

One jewelry company captured Marilyn in her skirt-blown pose over a subway grate, and another representation, licensed in 1988 by Monroe's estate, looks as if it's about to utter a poop-poop-e-doo. With beauty mark notable above smiling red lips, Marilyn wears a faux diamond necklace and heavily lashed bedroom eyes.

Pablo Picasso, Self Portrait pin, plastic-encased metal, signed Ives, 1980s, 2-1/4", **$50-$100.**

Barbie pin, woods, marquet and inlay, unsigned T. Breeze Verdant, 2000s, 2-1/2", **$125-$150.**

The greatest artist of the 20th Century surely deserves immortality as a brooch. Pablo Picasso himself finally was made into jewelry in the 1980s, as a dimensional, layered, plastic-on-metal pin by Ives.

It's fitting that the pin portrays the artist's 1907 Cubist self-portrait rather than earlier ones.

To add interest to this modern production, Picasso's head is cleverly doubled and raised higher than his shoulders and the background base. It emphasizes the dark lines and makes the face more intense.

It's unlikely any other artist has been reproduced as a pin, so this is one more example of the Spaniard's unique charisma.

One of the most famous faces in the world belongs to Barbie Roberts, a.k.a. Barbie doll. The teenage fashion model from Willows, Wisconsin, didn't look much like a high-school co-ed in her earliest incarnation, circa 1959, with those trademark eye brows (pointed arches) and knockout figure, not to mention the killer wardrobe of haute couture. And Ruth Handler's brainchild still had some of her exotic Euro 'Bild Lilli' heritage showing through on that unique countenance.

In jewelry, designer Stuart Freeman created perhaps the most exclusive and collectible line based on Barbie, all sterling, capturing everything from her extreme torso to her tony pumps, but the face he focused on was California-cool Malibu Barbie, not the original. Artist T. Breeze Verdant did a small-edition jewelry rendition of No. 1 Barbie in marquetry–in effect painting with woods, miniscule pieces perfectly set to form her familiar facial flamboyance.

Employing woods native to such disparate locales as Nigeria and Switzerland, Breeze made the Barbie brooch as international as Barbie herself.

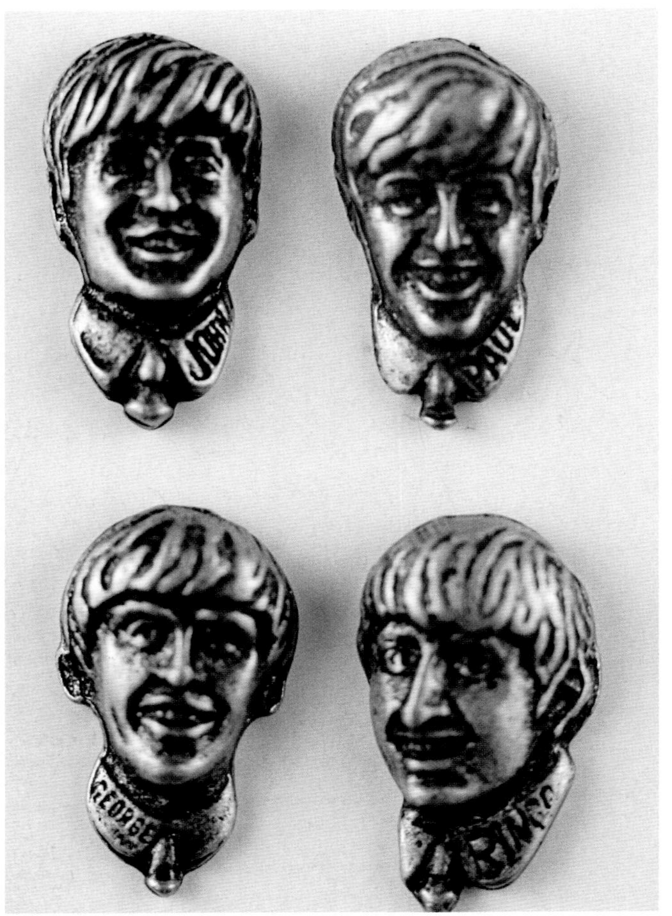

The Beatles, four 3/4" pins, cast metal, signed NEMS, 1964, **$25.**

Charlie Chaplin pendant, enameled metal, unsigned, 1970s, 5", **$50-$100.**

In the music world, neither Sinatra nor Streisand were transformed into pins, but The Beatles were. Somehow they're just more wearable than Ol' Blue Eyes or Babs. And in the Sixties, girls needed the Fab Four as close to their hearts as they could get them.

John, Paul, George and Ringo measured an 8.0 on the youth quake's Richter scale and stood at the forefront of the British Invasion of America. The mop-heads turned up in all variety of pins, often accompanied by guitars. Perhaps just their faces are most desirable of all, though.

One company, probably Coro, designed a series of enormous figural pendants in the Seventies, each one of them articulated and bold. The scarcest and most coveted character is Charlie Chaplin, complete with cane, bowler, and loads of comic insouciance. Charlie can be posed this way and that, so he's more fun to keep on a desk than wear dangling around the neck. Very likely, this homage to the Little Tramp was created during a surge of popularity after movie-house revivals of his films, especially "Limelight," "Modern Times," "The Great Dictator," "City Lights" and "The Gold Rush." Or it could have been marketed after Chaplin's Christmas-Day death in 1977.

CHAPTER 2  WINGED THINGS FOR AVIAN AFICIONADOS

The Birds

Hitchcock did for our feathered friends what Glenn Close did for new acquaintances. Suddenly, they could be very, very creepy.

In fact, bird figurals are most captivating when they hold the power of emotional symbolism from fable or myth. Contrast that with early birds, from the Art Nouveau and Victorian periods, which were merely lovely (because birds are beautiful, after all). The Bird of Paradise could be displayed with its lavish, swooping tails, and peacocks with their colorful egos on full display, with feathers of jewels and enamels. Flamingos are tall and regal whether pink or just jeweled in general.

But the swan became wildly popular because it had a back story, not just aesthetic appeal, whether a tragic affiliation, as with *Swan Lake*, or a happy ending to a tale, as in *The Ugly Duckling*.

The oddball penguin? Pure Art Deco, with that sleek, spare body and cool, impassive demeanor. Its natural coloration suggested a tuxedo, so penguins were further treated in pins to top hats and canes, symbols of the nightlife-and-cocktails culture, all that puttin' on the Ritz of the pre-war years. (Years later, Anheuser-Busch managed to make the penguin creepy in its beer ads and that hint of menace made penguins magnetic all over again.)

Parrots and other tropical types perched on lapels warn of wanderlust and are symbols of our love of travel to exotic locales. The common canary and parakeet were rehatched as brooches because it seemed every American home in the Fifties had one or the other in cages in their kitchens.

Cardinals took wing as a figural choice because of their radiant coloration, and were a staple in Jonette's jewelry, for example. Turkeys, not so much, even if Ben Franklin did want toms as the national bird.

As for lovebirds, the meaning of the classic pairing was obvious and simple, so these cooing couples were an obvious choice for sales success among jewelry companies. It's the lovebirds created after Tippi Hedrin purchased a pair and brought them along to a seaside town that put a different spin on the lovey-dovey slant.

Two of the most successful birds of all, though, are the eagle and the rooster.

The eagle is a symbol of strength in almost every culture, Aztec to Zuni. The bald eagle got the nod as America's bird in the 1780s because of its majesty, power and longevity. It

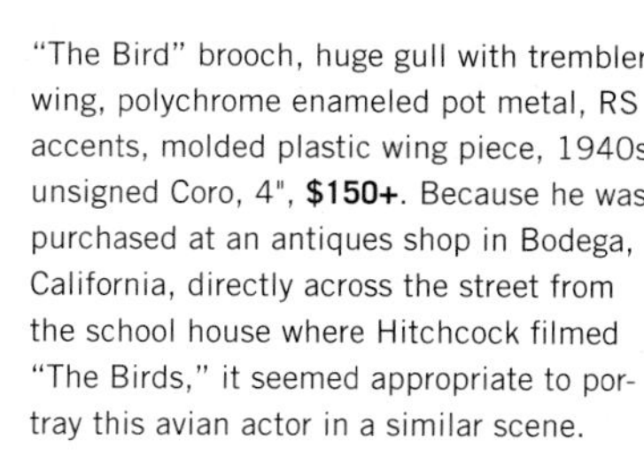

"The Bird" brooch, huge gull with trembler wing, polychrome enameled pot metal, RS accents, molded plastic wing piece, 1940s, unsigned Coro, 4", **$150+**. Because he was purchased at an antiques shop in Bodega, California, directly across the street from the school house where Hitchcock filmed "The Birds," it seemed appropriate to portray this avian actor in a similar scene.

Another view of "The Bird."

also signifies freedom in every aspect—and the average American's fabled love of it. When the decision was made after the Revolutionary War to develop a great seal for the United States, what better to portray the nation than this bird of unquestionable might (well, except by Audubon and Ben Franklin). The bald eagle's accoutrements—shield, scroll, arrows and olive branch—meant to say this was a country that welcomed peace, but would defend its freedoms whenever it had to.

Even in jewelry the golden eagle is sometimes portrayed mistakenly instead of the bald, meaning white-headed, eagle. Whatever eagle is cast, though, as America's national bird it clearly reached new heights of meaning during WWII, when it was as *de riguer* on lapels as a V for Victory or Old Glory, the Stars and Stripes. Often huge and bejeweled, the Forties eagle might be swooping in with talons bared, showing the power of a nation fighting a war on two fronts, or perched with dignity holding a pearl, in solemn recollection of Dec. 7, 1941. As a motif showing off a place's martial prowess, the eagle brooch also met its opposite in another bird, the dove, symbol of a nation grateful for peace.

If eagles ever went out of style post WWII, they regained fashion strength in the early Sixties (which was still the Fifties in spirit), smaller in size but packed with the same old-fashioned sense of Americana.

Lovebirds pin, glittery rhinestone-encrusted pair, 1940s, unsigned, 2", **$25-$50.**

Jelly Belly Lovebirds pin-pendant, silvery metal lovebirds imbedded in large Lucite "cage," embossed metal accents creating fancy-cage illusion, unsigned, 1960s, 2-1/4", **$50.**

As for the ever-alert rooster, Teddy Roosevelt had a one-legged pet that never made an appearance as costume jewelry, but any serious figurals collector knows how many roosters have been cast as pins. Flocks. Even though the rooster is to France what the eagle is to America, and even though the powerful god Abraxas has a rooster's head, and even though Chaucer put Chanticleer the rooster in *The Nun's Priest's Tale* and Barbara Cooney's 1959 book *Chanticleer and The Fox* won the Caldecott Medal, it may have been the Leo Burnett Ad Agency's 1957 design of Cornelius the Rooster for Kellogg's Corn Flakes that really imprinted that bird on the American psyche. It caught on as such a colorful design element in American kitchens (or more appropriately, kitschens) that antiques malls are flooded with the discarded roosters of passions past.

Not so in costume jewelry, though, where roosters remain a cock o' the walk. Most of the big names in jewelry made redheaded boys who strut their stuff—and symbolize ego.

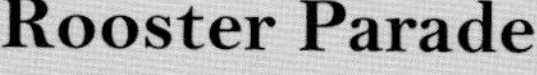

Rooster Parade

Maybe most jewelry makers created roosters at some point in their designing lives because it's hard to resist the cocky attitude and color possibilities invited by such plucky birds. Here's just a handful of rooster motifs, contemporary to vintage.

Bettina von Walhof, 2006, **$950.**

Unsigned Adolph Katz design, 1940s, **$50.**

ROOSTERS OF RENOWN

Which famous and infamous persons should wear rooster brooches or cufflinks as assigned by Chinese astrology? Helen Mirren, Cate Blanchette, Catherine Zeta-Jones, Steve Martin, Eric Clapton, Larry King, Michael Caine, Yoko Ono, Ivanka Trump, Jessica Alba, both Nathalie Portman *and* Hayden Christensen, both Paris Hilton *and* Nicole Ritchie, Ellen Degeneres, Beyonce Knowles, Britney Spears and, at the far opposite ends of the spectrum, peace activist Cindy Sheehan and terrorism mastermind Osama bin-Laden.

Reinad, 1940s, **$250.**

Vendôme, 1950s, **$50.**

Ian St. Gielar for Stanley Hagler N.Y.C., 2006, **$175.**

Staret, 1940s, **$150.**

Bird Watching

Here is a small, desirable flock list of birds for collectors to find. Look hard and pounce if spotted. These fine-feathered favorites fly off fast—into the cages of other collectors.

Trifari: Lucite-winged bird on pearl perch by David Mir; jelly belly swan, rooster head, parrot and heron; Ming bat, swan and Royal swan; flying heron; stork; fruit salad bird, firebird.

Hobe: huge starry eagle necklace.

Eisenberg: eagles and fighting cocks.

Boucher: gryphon, pelican movable, swallow, lovebirds, pheasant and phoenix.

Coro: mallard, parrots, cockatoo, toucan, screech owl, blue-jay Duette, giant pheasant, bird of paradise.

Reja: Lyre bird, duck and peacock

Mazer: hummingbird

Schreiner: penguin

Staret: trembler songbird, parrot, turkey, Pearl Harbor eagle

Iradj Moini: parrot

Nettie Rosenstein: fighting cocks

Chanel (Reinad): turkey, bird of paradise, gryphon

Silson: owl

Elzac: Freshie the Freshman penguin

... and many others.

David Mir's design-patent rendering of the most spectacular fantasy bird, for Trifari.

Des. 129433 1941 Adolph Katz for Coro.

Des. 137201 1944 Alfred Philippe for Trifari.

Des. 145272 1946 Alfred Philippe for Trifari.

Des. 129535 1941 David Mir for Trifari.

Des. 121403 1940 Victor Silson for Silson Bros.

Golden Feathered Friend fur clip, gilded metal, 3-D, turquoise bead eyes, unsigned, 1950s, 2-1/2", **$50-$100**. Its identical twin has turned up in karat gold, signed Erwin Pearl.

Kissing Peacocks pin, gold-plated metal, large crystal chaton, signed Mosell, 1950s, 3-1/2", **$75-$150.**

Peacock King Chatelaine pin, strange crowned bird pin mimicking actual chatelaine with charm attachments on ends of chains, four birds surround peacock, paying homage; base metal with amber cabochon, probably European, unsigned, 1915-25, 5", **$50-$100.**

Crazy Cubist Birds pin, gilded metal, look as if sprung from Picasso's imagination, unsigned, 1950s, 3", **$50-$100.**

Mammoth Dove of Peace triple fur clip, white-enameled gilded metal, so large it has three clip mechanisms (including one under each wing), signed Authentics, 1946, 8" when wings are fully extended, **$250+.**

Penguin pin, sapphire RS belly, dusty blue enamel, unsigned, 1930s, 2", **$50.**

Mother and baby penguins pin, enamel and pave RS, unsigned, 1970s, 2", **$25.**

Father and son penguins, enamel, unsigned, 1970s, 1-1/4", **$25.**

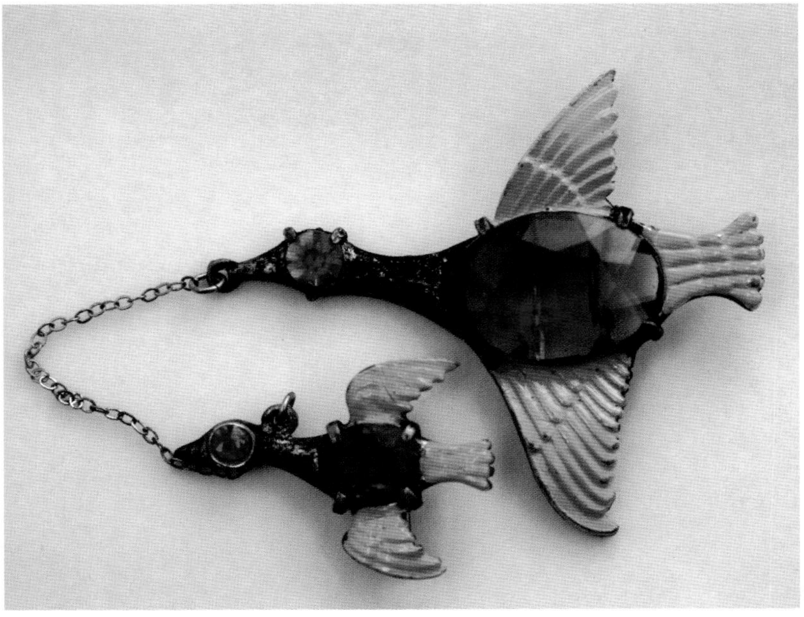

Baby & Mother fur clip chatelaine, pink-enameled pot metal, faceted glass bellies in emerald and sapphire, colored-chaton heads, 1-1/2" and 2-1/2", unsigned, 1930s, **$50.** Still has original store tag with price, stamped 17 cents.

Partridges...in Pear Trees

This unsigned vintage pin played a key role in an "All My Children" soap-opera plot during the 2006 holidays, **$50.**

Jonette Jewelry made its fetching featherling in a number of colors before it closed in 2006, **$10-$25.**

Cadoro Topiary, **$50-$100.**

Nettie Rosenstein's sterling jeweled masterpiece is a hard-to-find old fur clip, **$225.**

Unsigned but typical of the Beatrix gaudy Technicolor metallics, **$50.**

The most-produced partridge-in-pear tree of all, this version by Lianna in minty pastel green, **$50.**

Beatrix Jewelry made this design in several permutations, including a stained-glass version, **$50.**

Classic Cadoro, **$50+.**

Corel was so confident of its castings, it didn't even feel the need to enamel or be-jewel, **$25.**

Golden Pears Cadoro, **$50+.**

Original by Robert creations are some of the most desirable of all, due to that unparalleled enamel work and affinity for unique designs, **$150+.**

Vero's entry in the partridge-pear sweepstakes features luscious fruit and gold-metallic oiseau, **$50.**

Taller Cadoro, **$50-$100.**

Collection Spotlight

Pot-Metal Peacocks

Pot metal probably never looked so posh as on the bejeweled beauties that belong to Dr. Brenda Forman. After a long career in government and the aerospace industry, she teaches jewelry courses and pursues a lifelong love of jewelry—as well as these fancily plumed peacocks.

"I'm pretty sure they date from the mid- to late 1930s to 1942 at the latest," Forman figures, based on the metal employed. She's collected vintage costume jewelry for six years but isn't certain when this thematic menagerie began being gathered. "I have the gorgeous Boucher peacock, a couple of knockoffs of it, and the equally gorgeous Jomaz, but somewhere along the line, I got intrigued by these humble pot-metal guys. They all have the same form for the body, and then feature endless variations on the tail. I don't even remember which one was first, but he now has many near-twin brothers."

Forman knows them inside and out: They are never signed, always made of pot metal, and the pin mechanism may be horizontal or vertical. Their tails determine overall size: peacocks with a single row of rhinestones in the tail are 3-1/4 inches x 2-1/4 inches, while two rows of rhinestones dictate a size of 3-1/2 inches x 2-1/2 inches. Peacocks with alternate tails vary in dimension, but never by much.

Asked her best guess on whodunit, Forman personally doesn't believe a "name" designer is behind the peacocks. "The fact the same form is used over and over, and the fact the arrangement of rhinestones in the tails so often looks as if someone simply grabbed whatever colors were left over that day, well, that ain't what Boucher or Eisenberg would *think* of doing," the doc declares. (We personally might guess Reinad. As for the wild variety of stones, they would certainly promise to match many clients' "costume" colors. Maybe this peacock was simply a raving success.)

Differences in the peacocks—or call them *les paons* for the woman who translated Henri Vever's 1906-1908 three-volume landmark study, *French Jewelry in the 19th Century* from the original French—include not only the design of the tails, but also slightly different enamel colors on the birds' bodies, notably on the wing edges. "An elderly woman in Tucson owns one with a double row of gold-colored rhinestones in its tail. She bought it when she was a young woman, maybe circa 1940. She said it was an expensive piece considering her budget then, but whether that means it was a high-end piece for most people, I don't know."

As far as values go, Forman says, "... These peacocks' prices have been climbing in the past year. When I first started accumulating them, they were dirt cheap, from $12 to $30. One with a double row of rhinestones would have been a little under $100. But they're going up, although they haven't hit the $300 level yet," says Forman, who was featured on the Discovery Channel program, "The Hope Diamond," part of its "Unsolved History" series.

Maybe Discovery could do a show on Forman's fabulous flock.

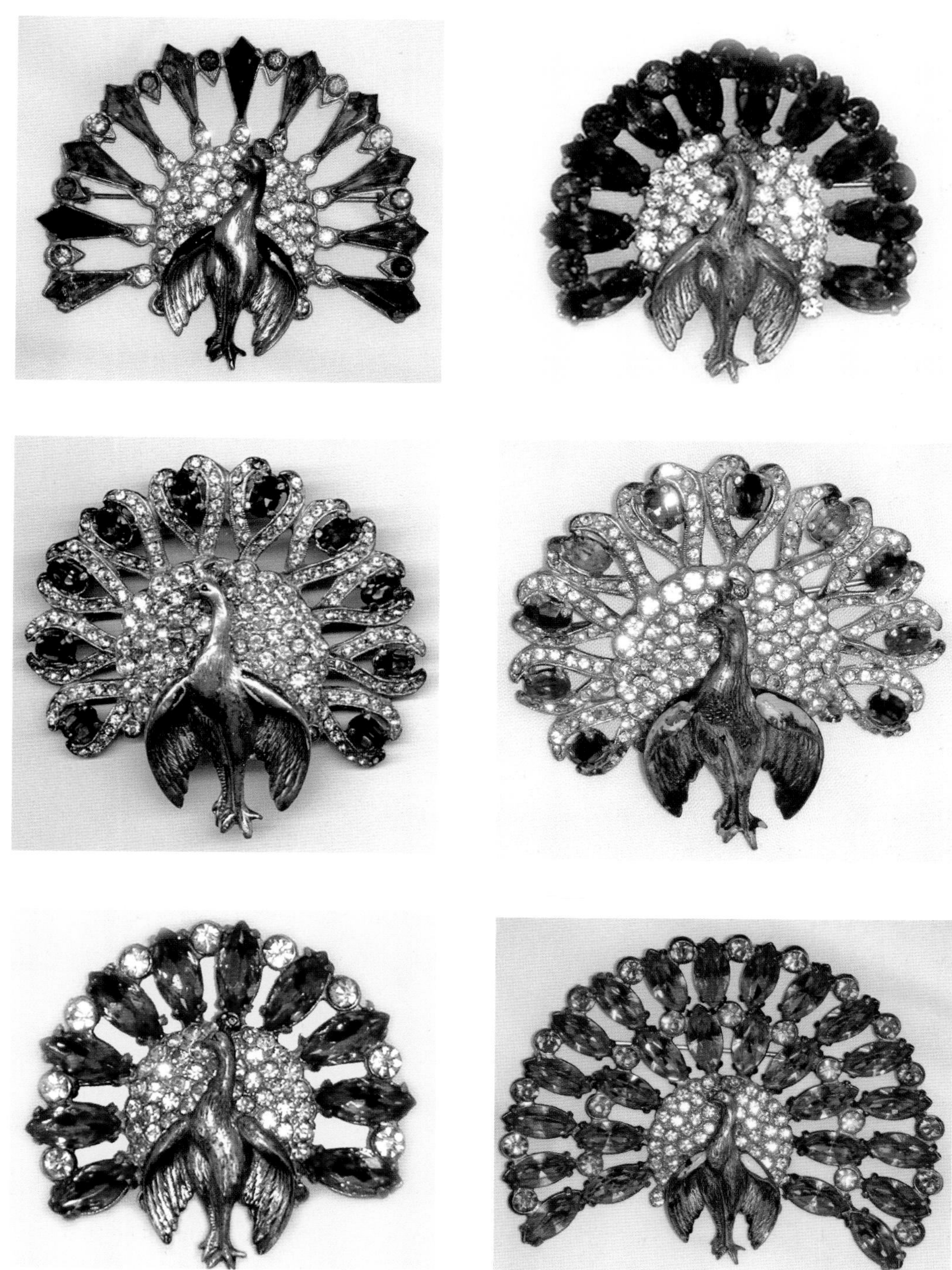

Eisenberg

After a softening in the market for vintage Eisenberg figurals, which reached its nadir in 1999-2002, the category slowly rebounded and has returned to almost robust health. The bad taste of reproductions soured collectors on this historically desirable name that, like most costume jewelry, peaked in the 1990s. For example, Harrice Simons Miller valued Eisenberg figurals in the 1994 second edition of her costume jewelry book at between $1,400 to $2,500 for figurals including the fly, mermaid, pave-winged angel, horse head, basket of flowers and large duck. In her 2002 third edition, those values had dropped considerably, as represented by knock-down prices in auction results. The range fell to $150 to $1,700 for fighting cock, various birds, fish, zebra, ballerina, Can-Can dancer and even the mermaid (in the highest range).

Most notably in 2006, Eisenberg Original and Eisenberg Sterling figurals really began to regain their historically strong footing. A few sky-high sales gave collectors renewed confidence they would not be throwing money away if they threw it at a fur clip or brooch with the coveted signature.

The allure of Eisenberg is due to the flamboyance, beauty, size and rarity of its figural pieces. Compare their scarcity with the plentiful availability of Elzac's figurals, the company's bread and butter. One thing the contrast demonstrates is that women were less willing to pay a lot for novelty figurals. They could purchase large Elzac brooches for as little as $2. Not so the huge metal Eisenberg pieces, and on top of that, many fewer were made.

The most famous designer for Eisenberg, long-time Fallon & Kappel superstar Ruth Kamke, explains that four collections a year were created for Eisenberg and usually only two figurals were included in each collection. (Some collections did include additional figural designs, but only up to a maximum of four.) So, not only were initial designs scarce to start with, but the figurals actually produced enjoyed poorer sales success compared with the glittering non-figural jewelry. That rarity naturally drives even higher interest today.

New collectors are always surprised when they learn this major name in costume jewelry began as a successful dress company. In fact, most fashionable women traveling between New York and California on the Twentieth Century or El

Star Lady fur clip, dramatic bronzed finish, emerald RS marquise eyes, emerald cabochon star centers, crystal chaton accents, articulated earring, signed Eisenberg Original, 1940, 2-3/4", **$1,200.**

Capitan stopped on their journeys in a city famous for fashion, Chicago. Just one reason women disembarked there was to order the latest dress wardrobe from the Eisenberg Company.

While Eisenberg's delicious crepes were carried in 500 stores across the country, an actual stop in the Second City for the very latest, designed by the eccentric Miss Irma Kirby, was even better.

The heyday of the Eisenberg dress was 1936-42. The bonus accompanying each chemise? Jeweled clips of colorless paste adorning the dresses. The tale of those jewels has been recounted a million times: Women took such a fancy to the rhinestones, retailers told the Eisenbergs their customers swiped them right off the dresses.

Those words echoed in the ears of Jonas Eisenberg, who'd founded the company in 1914, and his son, Sam, and nephew, Harold, when the dress market softened. As aviation curbed train travel, the women who used to stop in the Windy City began flying over it. The dress companies' new union partners cut deeply into profits, and the labor market dried up as factory workers' children became business people. The men realized that all that glittered just might make a huge difference in the bottom line. And so they went into the jewelry business in earnest.

The line proved an immediate hit. Eisenberg's presence in stores grew from 500 to 2,000 retailers because jewelry emporia now carried the brand, not just clothiers. The quality of the pieces was exceptional as well, for Eisenberg counted on the most talented designers, mold makers and finest Swarovski paste. Remarkably, by 1958, Eisenberg had stepped out of the dress business entirely.

Ruth Kamke was still a 15-year-old teenager when she became an employee of Fallon & Kappel during a high-school work-study program. F&K designed and manufactured jewelry for the biggest names in the costume jewelry world, including Eisenberg. Moving quickly up the ladder due to her diligence, hard work and innate talent, she was still young Ruth Wortmann (Kamke became her married name upon wedding in 1944) when she designed such fabled costume-jewelry pieces as the Hattie Carnegie unicorn and the outrageous Eaves/Eisenberg "Piggy Goes to Market." The special talent Kamke had, what admiring collectors today most appreciate in Kamke without realizing it, was her ability to conceive fantastical figurals mold makers could actually execute. If she were only a great artist but could not come through with designs that translated into jewelry, then the gargoyle leaning on a stone, the brawny Puss 'n Boots, the bizarro scrubwomen and the rather ugly men with bejeweled Chanel beards would not exist.

Asian Princess brooch, gilded base metal with crystal pave RS, ruby navettes and cabochons, faceted crystal AB briolettes set *en pendant*, signed Eisenberg Original, date unknown, 5-3/8", **$500.** (This is a Reinad for Eisenberg figural, dating it to pre-1942, but chandelier crystals are coated with aurora borealis iridescent film, dating it to post-1955. Eisenberg specialist Bobye Syverson believes crystals may be elaborate replacements for old faux pearls.)

When metals turned scarce under wartime restrictions, Eisenberg and Fallon & Kappel signed a contract of exclusivity in about 1942. Thus Kamke stopped creating pieces for other clients, such as Hattie Carnegie. It is worth mentioning here that before the firms sealed the deal of an exclusive arrangement, another manufacturer making intriguing Eisenberg figurals was Reinad, a New York metal house.

Two of the most spectacular creations by Reinad for Eisenberg are the Oriental Princess and the 1941 so-called African Mask, also described as a jewel-cheeked Flapper in profile—or yet another Josephine Baker look-alike. Intrigue built surrounding those pieces because they also turn up marked HC for Hattie Carnegie, as well as marked Reinad (in the case of the Princess) and Chanel (in the case of Josephine). It's likely Reinad made both the notorious ladies first for Eisenberg (the Eisenberg Original version is the most elaborate), and then reassigned them when Eisenberg said bye-bye.

New collectors who develop a passion for Eisenberg jewelry find they must come to terms with a variety of markings and confusing dates to match. The mark changed over the years. The hotly pursued Eisenberg Original mark graced figurals in the Thirties and early Forties. Sam Eisenberg, Karl Eisneberg's father, copyrighted the Eisenberg Ice name in 1935, but it was actually featured as a mark on jewelry much later. They employed the letter E mark in the 1940s as well. Eisenberg in block capital letters marked figurals such as the classic first Christmas tree during the Seventies. In the 1940s and 1950s, the script signature was stamped into pieces. From 1970 until today, Eisenberg Ice on an oval is soldered on to the back of a pin. Before 1953, stones were always prong set.

Karl Eisenberg himself marked 55 years in the business in 2006. When it became clear in the 1990s Eisenberg's three children would follow their own career paths, Eisenberg merged with a company that supplies jewelry to chains such as Kohl's.

Eisenberg jewelry is first in many collectors' hearts, but the company was also first in other areas: first to advertise costume jewelry in magazines, from *Ebony* to *Cosmo*; first to feature an African-American model; first to feature a nude model. What an interesting trip it's been.

"Josephine Baker" fur clip, gilded pot metal, large topaz roses montees set into cheek and headdress (faded), topaz lozenge briolette set *en pendant* as earring, signed Eisenberg Original, 1940, 4-1/4", **$750-$1,500.**

Marilyn Monroe bust dress clip, dramatic bronze finish, inset faceted crystals, dimensional and sculptural, signed Eisenberg Original, 1940, 2-1/4", **$300-$400.**

Eisenberg Original King and Queen fur-clip chatelaine together, **$1,200-$1,400.**

Neptune or Poseidon King of the Seas fur clip, signed Eisenberg Original and 3, gilded metal with black-enamel accents for beard and hair, turquoise beads lining crown, large ruby ovals and chaton RS in diadem, 1940, 2-3/4", **$500-$600.** Side bale attached to reverse for chains that held his partner queen nearby, but he's currently single. Note: Typically known only as a king, a nearly identical roi is featured on an Eisenberg Original scarf, making it more likely this king is Neptune too.

Jello-Mold Floral dress clip, pot metal, RS accents, large molded ruby glass dome, double-signed with both Eisenberg Original and R for Reinad, 1941, 3-3/4", **$300-$500** because of double mark.

Scrub-bucket maid fur clip, enameled, gilded sterling with RS accents, articulated bucket, signed Eisenberg Original Sterling, 1944, 3", **$600-$1,200.**

Charwoman fur clip, enameled, gilded sterling with RS accents, signed Eisenberg Original Sterling, 1944, 3", **$600-$1,200.**

Jeweled Fruit fur clip, metallic green enameling, large, faceted jewel fruit, signed Eisenberg Original, 1941, 4", **$400-$500.**

Pave-Wing Angel brooch, gilded angel, number mark illegible, possibly Reinad for Eisenberg, 1940, 3-1/2", **$500-$750.**

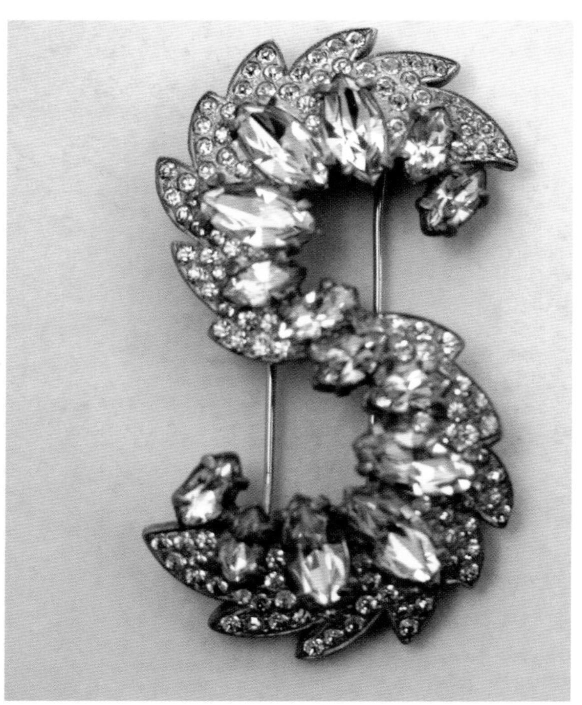

Jeweled Letter S fur clip, pot metal, multi-cut crystal stones, signed Eisenberg Original, 1939, 3", **$150-$200.**

Jeweled clock brooch, mirrored gold-plated metal and multi-cut crystal stones, jeweled rotating hands to set appointment time, signed E, 1949, 2-3/4", **$150-$250.**

Angel pendant, pewter base metal, 3-D, signed Eisenberg, age unknown, 2-1/2", **$25-$50.**

CHAPTER 4  HUMBLE HUMMEL PINS

How Childish

Two English brothers named Jack and Victor Silson (né Silberfeld) launched their Silson jewelry company in America in the mid- to late-1930s. In figurals, Silson is probably best known for eccentric pin clip designs such as the drunken tiger; its Early American series of pins featuring a Revolutionary theme; its jewelry that American ex-pat William Spratling produced in Mexico; and its British war-relief-related jewelry, which makes sense since the Silsons were Brits.

But Silson also created a series of child-like pins based on a licensing arrangement the company had with Hummel. Two factors leave the deal a little confusing. One is the fact Silson obtained design patents on the pins – strange, since the illustrations are in effect the drawings of the Bavarian nun, Sister Maria Innocentia "M.I." Hummel (née Berta Hummel). So evidently the renderings differ enough from Hummel's drawings to be patented for a different use (i.e., jewelry versus literary art or porcelain figurines). This also clears up the second bit of confusion: the figural brooches are based on the actual artwork by M.I. Hummel, rather than the famed Goebel figurines. The pins are true to the art, not the statuettes.

Briefly, Hummels, the most successful collectible ever made, were born out of a business partnership between Hummel, her Siessen convent, and the Goebel Porzellanfabrik in Rodenthal, Germany, owned by father Franz and son William Goebel. Berta's artwork was published in a book in 1933, when she was only 24, two years after she entered the convent. The Goebels gained permission to translate Sister's art, portraying charming children in bucolic settings, into porcelain figurines. First produced in 1935, the figurines are still made today, so it seems the talented religious woman who died at the young age of 37 lives on through the art she created.

Silson designer William Regelmann signed the 1941 design patents for pins of at least four Hummels: The Little Fiddler, The Merry Wanderer, The Little Hiker, and The Apple Thief (later called Culprits). The Little Fiddler was one of the first three figurines ever produced, and The Merry Wanderer is the most popular Hummel of all time, so the Silson company chose wisely.

Hummel brooch "The Apple Thief."

"Meditation."

"The Book Worm."

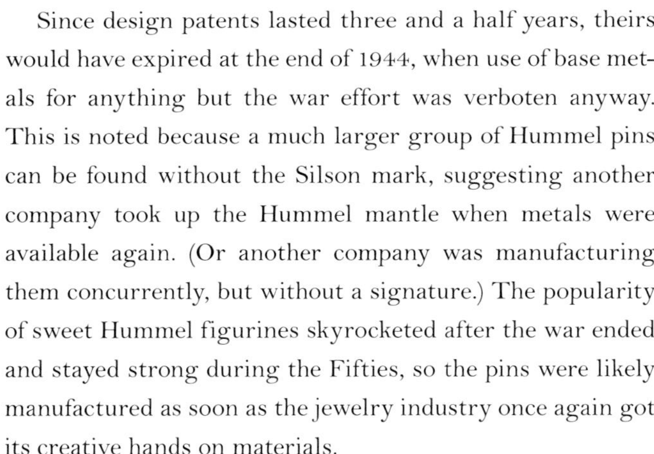

Since design patents lasted three and a half years, theirs would have expired at the end of 1944, when use of base metals for anything but the war effort was verboten anyway. This is noted because a much larger group of Hummel pins can be found without the Silson mark, suggesting another company took up the Hummel mantle when metals were available again. (Or another company was manufacturing them concurrently, but without a signature.) The popularity of sweet Hummel figurines skyrocketed after the war ended and stayed strong during the Fifties, so the pins were likely manufactured as soon as the jewelry industry once again got its creative hands on materials.

Each Hummel brooch is approximately 3 inches tall. Some are enameled, some are gilded, none are jeweled, most are made of pot metal. The pins marked Silson are the most refined castings, but some unmarked pieces clearly have solder over the old plaques, which may be Silson's. Brooches shown here are unsigned except where noted.

Known Hummel brooches include:

The Little Fiddler, signed Silson
Goose Girl, signed Silson
The Merry Wanderer, signed Silson
The Little Hiker
The Apple Thief
Eventide
Meditation
Goose Girl
Letter to Santa Claus
Knit One, Purl One
The Book Worm
The Shepherd Boy (variation)
Have the Sun in Your Heart
Retreat to Safety

Each Hummel brooch here and on Pages 40 and 42 is approximately 3 inches high. Some are enameled, some are gilded, none are jeweled, most are made of pot metal. The pins marked Silson are the most refined castings, but some unmarked pieces have solder over plaques, which may originally have been Silson's. Brooches shown are unsigned except where noted. Other pins found but not pictured here include "Have the Sun in Your Heart," "Knit One, Purl One" and "Retreat to Safety." Values are $25-$150 each.

"The Little Fiddler," signed Silson.

"Goose Girl," signed Silson.

"The Merry Wanderer," signed Silson.

"Eventide."

"Letter to Santa Claus."

"The Shepherd Boy" (variation).

Other figural categories that seem young across the board include the cartoonish Har characters, as well as a host of 1935-42 figural fur clips with juvenile themes.

They in fact seem so childish, it is hard to imagine sophisticated women wearing them.

Recalling old movies with little prisses wearing white ermine capelets tied with satin ribbon, we guessed they were perhaps designed for well-heeled children of the era.

But a pink Teddy bear pin clip that seemed meant for a young miss turned up in a *Glamour* magazine ad in 1940, along with other circus-themed pieces including the spectacular Boucher movable clown, evidence the pink Teddy was destined for grown women after all.

That same year, a little-girl hat-look was all the rage in fashion styles, sitting on the side of a woman's head as if she were an organ grinder's monkey, so maybe women were embracing their inner child in 1940-41, something they'd be unable to do much longer.

Pink Teddy Bear fur clip, enameled base metal, RS flower, unmarked, 1940, 2-1/8", **$100.**

Pooh-like Bear with Landed Butterfly fur clip, painted metal, 1940, unsigned, 2-1/8", **$50-$100.**

Big-Top Bunny Ringmaster pin, enameled metal, RS accent, signed CFW (Chas. F. Worth), 1955-65, 1-3/4", **$50-$100.**

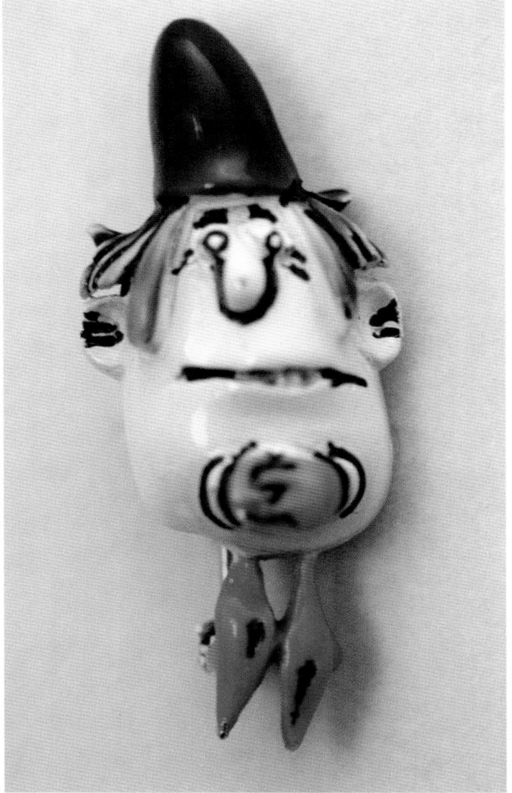

Worrywart Guy pin, freaky little people series, enameled metal, 1-1/2", signed HAR (possibly for Harrods' Way-In youth shop), 1955-65, **$25-$50.**

Chain-Haired Girl with polka-dot bow, RS eyes, enameled gold-plated metal, signed Mamselle, 1960s, 1-3/4", **$25-$50.**

Nervous cat with bird pin, enameled metal, pave-set faux pearls, signed CFW (Chas. F. Worth), 1955-65, 1-3/4", **$50.**

Duck in Bonnet pin, enameled metal, signed Puccini, 1960s, 2-1/2", **$25.**

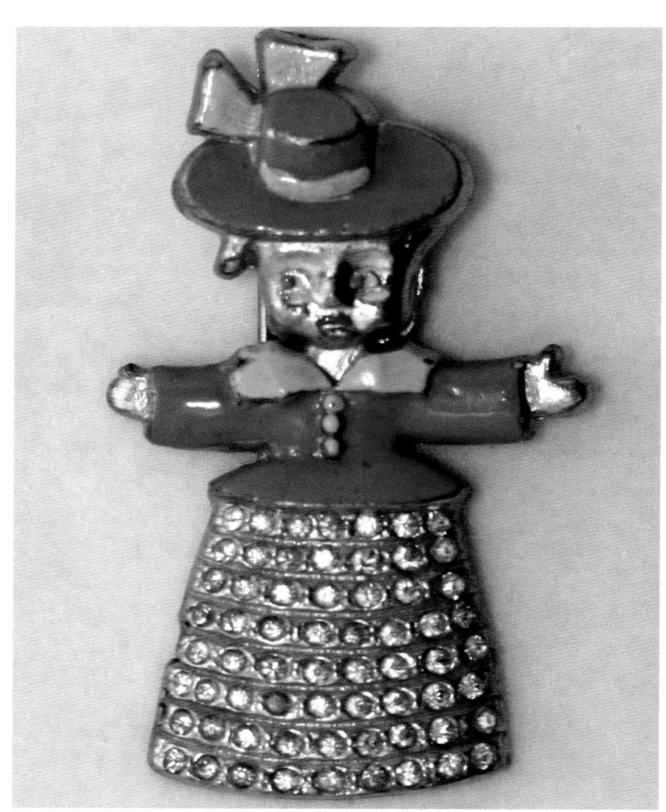

Shepherdess fur clip, enameled metal, RS accents, 1940s, 2", **$50-$100.**

Mary Had a Little Lamb fur clip, enameled pot metal, 1940s, unsigned, 2-7/8", **$150.**

Chain-haired girl pin, pave-set RS collar, satinoir cabochon hat and painted face, signed Weiss, 1950s, 2", **$150.**

3-D Carousel pin, gilded sterling, mixed cuts and colors in crystal RS, stylish horse, great detail, marked Sterling Pat.Pend., 1940s, 2-1/4", **$250.**

Girl on Carousel pin, heavy gilded sterling, RS accents, 1940s, 2-5/8", **$50.**

Hobby Horse pin, enameled silver- and rhodium-plated metal, lavish chain mane, flat woven reins, 1940s, unsigned, 3-1/2", **$100.**

Golliwog fur clip, enameled metal, articulated arms and legs, unsigned, 1940s, 1-3/4", **$25-$50.**

Dutch Girl pin, stamped gilded sterling, blue faux moonstone face, 1940s, 2", **$25.**

Elzac Story

One of the most colorful and exotic jewelry categories experiencing an upsurge in values and sales is the vast figurals line known as Elzac. So many Elzac pieces appear on the market for show-or-sell, it's clear many women purchased Elzac pieces in the Forties.

The Elzac story is worth exploring because the pins were popular (again) in the 1980s and 1990s even before anyone knew who made them decades earlier. Carla Ginelli and Roberto Brunialti first pointed to Elzac as maker in their 1997 Italian-language book, *American costume jewelry.* When they showed design patents for pins credited to Elliot Handler, I recognized the name and began efforts to interview him, the founder of Mattel.

"Josephine Baker" pin, ceramic face, cherry Lucite swirled headdress, silver woven metallic cord headband, unsigned Elzac, 1942, 3-3/4", **$150-$200.**

A closer look at Elzac shows that in 1941, a Russian immigrant named Zachary Zemby approached a designer named Elliot Handler and proposed a partnership. Zemby, a savvy businessman who owned Zemby Watch Crystal, had taken note of an unusual figural brooch in stores that enjoyed great sales success. Zemby tracked down its maker, who happened to be the founder of Elliot Handler Plastics. Handler felt he could use a partner and said yes immediately. The two men put their identities together to form a firm with the fresh new name of Elzac.

Love actually shoved Handler off on the road toward Elzac. Ruth Mosko set both their fates in motion when she vacationed on the coast and was so smitten with California, she decided to stay. Back in Colorado, Handler, her sweetheart, wanted to join her, both to be with her and to enroll in art school. Like many young couples, the two adventurous Denver prospectors set out in search of a golden future together in 1930s California.

Elliot enrolled in the fall of '38 in what is now the California Institute of the Arts. There, he had the opportunity to experiment with a revolutionary material called Lucite, an important wartime plastic stirring excitement as a medium with new possibilities. Elliot used Lucite for his first projects, designing items such as trays, lamps and picture frames for the couple's apartment. Ruth urged her husband to build a business on Lucite products she would sell.

He cobbled together the necessary tools and machinery. Working out of their apartment garage space and the kitchen, he cooked up Lucite products in the oven. Ruth made sales appointments on days off from Paramount Studios.

Carmen Miranda pin, estate of Joan Crawford (this brooch also owned by Lana Turner per old photos), carved walnut, felt neck wrap, plastic fruit, unsigned Elzac, 1942, 4", **$200-$300.**

Polka-dotty pair: Shakespearean Gentleman pin, painted, carved walnut with Lucite swirl, unsigned Elzac, 1941, 3", **$150.** Giant giraffe head pin, painted, carved walnut with Lucite horns, unsigned Elzac, 1941, 4", **$100-$150.**

By 1939 he could afford to quit his day job and officially call Elliot Handler Plastics home. The first novelty to bring him success – and the attention of Zach Zemby – was the brooch he designed in 1940: a small glass vial around which he wrapped a sinuous plastic hand with red fingernails. The item was a brooch into which a woman could add tiny flowers, pinning the whole affair to her wide lapel.

When Zemby approached Handler to form Elzac in '41, Handler had tons of Lucite and scrap wood because Handler's company was originally founded to make larger furnishings, trays, decorative frames and home accessories of plastic, metal and wood. Handler would not have bet the hand brooch for posies would be his first big thing. It just turned out that way after Uncle Sam eliminated the availability of metals for the war effort. Without metal, clever man he was, Handler figured women wanted whimsy more than ever during wartime and believed he could make jewelry out of just plastic and scrap wood.

So, before the Lucited pottery ladies with crazing faces for which Elzac is best known, Handler first raised a menagerie of flora and fauna at his design farm.

The earliest Elzac pins are made of either carved wood alone or wood with Lucite (some with sparse silver-metal accents)—first flowers, then animals and faces. They did not begin using ceramics (at last, a mercifully plentiful medium!) until 1942, when the partners made a move to bring an old friend of the Handlers on board, fashion designer Beatrice Weld. One of the first ideas Weld had was creating decorated pins in the likeness of women's faces. Her initial inspiration was one of the hottest stars of the day, Carmen Miranda. Many more ladies came along even later in 1942, Latin lovelies, Polynesian islanders and glamorous fashion-setters with elaborate hats and headpieces. Cleverly decorated with whatever materials worked, they enjoyed leather, feathers, fur, beads, ribbon, felt, soutache braid, wood, flowers, metallic cord. No wonder the Elzac dames would be nicknamed, in the vernacular, "Victims of Fashion" by avid collectors still unaware of their provenance even in the late 20th Century.

Lucite and *ceramic* animals predate the classic ladies too, but are also contemporaries of them (meaning they continued to be made during the ceramic-lady years.) Materials used were all first rate, the ceramics voluptuous. The company took pride in the pottery's luster and light weight despite the large size of the figurals. The company's staff artisans and trades people expertly carved and manipulated the wood and Lucite.

Recognizing Elzac

Elzac jewelry is usually easily recognizable, but some pins cause confusion. Here are some specifics to clarify what is and isn't Elzac.

The wood, almost always either walnut or ebony, is heavily carved. Any wood that is uncarved or poorly carved signals a non-Elzac piece.

Pins may be all wood, all ceramic, even all Lucite, or any combination of those materials. But they used no Bakelite, nor any metal beyond accent studs or wire accents.

Turquoise-ceramic pieces with collars and backings of patterned copper are not Elzac. In general, the most desirable Elzac brooches are ceramic with colorful Lucite, and the ladies (along with some men) continue to bring the highest prices, up to $250 each.

Patent records indicate designs could be identified by name, such as the girl with braids dubbed "Daisy." Handler says he's sure the faces had names for identification, but is unfamiliar with them because that was the marketing department's domain.

During Elzac's peak years of 1942-44, some 15 ceramic sculptors and eight wood carvers were employed among a workforce of 300 people.

Zemby brought in more partners in order to expand the company, but they proved difficult to get along with. Tensions mounted. Concurrently, Handler went to the partners to urge expansion into different areas, such as toys. They believed the status quo was satisfactory, so Handler asked them to buy him out.

They did, that year, 1944. By 1945, Elzac, Inc. was in decline and Zemby left to form his own jewelry company. By 1947, Elzac, now producing metal and rhinestone jewelry and already in bankruptcy, went out of business.

Handler went on to co-found Mattel with his partner in life and labor, Ruth, and with another former Elzac employee, Harold "Matt" Mattson.

Zemby died at a young age and would no doubt shake his head incredulously if he knew his name is still famed in the jewelry world 60 years after the company closed. An interview with his grandson, also Zachary Zemby, provided more information that would cause Zemby to shake his head in a different way: When the Zembys moved to a new house years after Elzac closed, hundreds of boxes stored in the garage were thrown out. Those boxes were filled with Elzac jewelry.

As for Handler, who still makes his home in Los Angeles, he was shopping with his daughter, Barbara, namesake of the Barbie doll, in an antiques store when they came upon two Elzac pins locked in a jewelry case. No doubt both father and daughter realized that no matter how popular those lovely ladies were and still are, they were no match for the unparalleled power of the Barbie doll.

Fabulous Flapper pin, ceramic face with scrap wire and lemon Lucite curls, ribbon and leather head band, wire-wrap accent necklace, unsigned Elzac, 1942, 3-1/4", **$150-$200.**

Femme Chinoise pin (this particular face paint resembles actress Julianna Margulies), painted ceramic head, Mandarin collar, elaborate cherry Lucite headdress, unsigned Elzac, 1942, 3-3/4", **$150-$200.**

Victim of Fashion lady pin, ceramic face on wooden base, jet-black hair, pipe-cleaner feathers, furry collar with golden rickrack, unsigned Elzac, 1942, 4-1/8", **$50-$100**.

Genghis Khan pin, ceramic face, multicolor fabric braiding headdress, plastic shiv, unsigned Elzac, 1943, 3", **$50-$100.**

Siamese Prince pin, ceramic head on wooden base, black bristle beard, pipe-cleaner and gold-cord collar, bronze metallic silk thread coiffure, decorative metal hair accent, unsigned Elzac, 1943, 4-5/8", **$100-$150**.

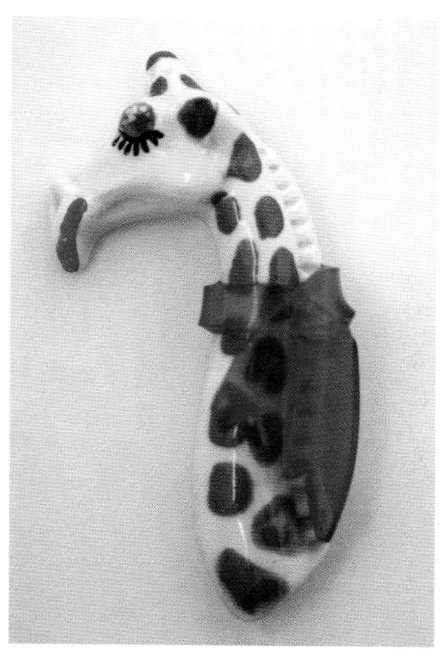

Flirtacious Giraffe, butter ceramic with sienna spots, cherry Lucite bow, unsigned Elzac, 1942, 4-1/8", **$200-$250**.

Roman Centurion pin, ceramic face, chain-mail mesh helmet with chain chinstrap, red feather, unsigned Elzac, 1943, 3-1/2", **$150**.

CHAPTER 6  THE SHAPE OF BLINGS TO COME

Romance of the Stones

The thrill for many costume jewelry collectors is the stone that makes a pin flamboyant.

Some of the most spectacular glass and crystal cuts affiliated with jewelry companies, however, do not appear in their figural brooches. For instance, the flashiest of all rhinestone colors and art-glass Easter egg specialty stones DeLizza & Elster (aka Juliana) used – the ones that drive collectors mad and willing to part with serious rupees – do not show up in the company's vintage flora and fauna. Nor do Schreiner's bubbly art glass and the keystones that make its most famous creations appear ruffled.

But glass lovers have no reason to be disheartened. Costume jewelry boasts many stones to shout about.

It's amusing to think maybe Reinad, the great old metal house, suffered a glitz complex that led it to include the most sensational stones in its designs of homely base metal. One trademark stone to watch for is the baguette so long it's called a baton. The most-wanted figural pin employing batons is the huge feathered swan Reinad made for its own line. But batons are also a good clue to identify pieces Reinad made for Eisenberg. Both signed pieces marked Eisenberg Original, and unsigned because so early (the ones decorating Eisenberg dresses), turn up with batons.

Collectors partial to enormous, colorful glass stones have a lot to choose from. CoroCraft designed one sought-after line featuring sterling enameled animals balancing on large, tilted square cuts in deep jewel tones.

Another famous figural grouping is composed of bunnies and bees with ears and wings of oversized, kite-shaped or faceted lozenge stones. The only signed example of these ever to turn up was marked H Pomerantz. Interestingly, Elzac produced virtual twins of the metal rabbits, but done in the firm's signature ceramic-and-Lucite combination. In an interview, Elliot Handler, the company's co-founder, said they never copied or reproduced other companies' designs, so we are left to assume that metal and rhinestone houses later helped themselves to Elzac's popular figural repertoire. After World War II ended, freeing up base metals for decorative purposes once again, Elzac had closed. So it's possible other companies used Elzac's figural menu for fancy fur clips and brooches with spectacular strass.

Faceted glass that becomes figural itself is especially inventive in costume jewelry. Rectangular radiant cuts cast as suitcases, packages or even torsos add eye-catching flash to figural pins and have an advantage over precious gems that would prove far too extravagant to use

Swan brooch, gold-plated metals, pave-set RS tail feathers and wing tips, six large cherry-red faceted baton stones, signed Reinad, 1940s, 3-1/2", **$500-$750.**

Ballerina brooch, rose-pink pentagons, probably inspired by Walt Disney's "Fantasia," unsigned, marked 23694 EXX, 1940-42 or 1946-48, 3-1/4", **$250-$500.** Possibly made by John Rubel's company La Danse des Fleurs or Le Ballet des Fleurs if a later-1940s piece.

Huge pale-violet stones make this necklace fabulous on actress Vivien Leigh. (So does she.)

in the same manner. (Exceptions to that general rule exist, though. Think of Verdura's mermaid Naiad, which eventually morphed into an Eisenberg Original gem. In the Verdura version, the jeweler used precious gems.) And who knows, perhaps the showman Liberace used his 51-carat rhinestone as a handy paperweight.

One unusual and effective figural motif in the costume jewelry world includes faceted glass ovals serving as entire faces or bodies in large fur clips and dress clips. One fur-clip penguin's whole 2-inch body is faceted amethyst crystal; a Lidz Bros. exotic dress-clip princess has a 2-inch face that's all aquamarine glass with honeycomb facets; and another brooch has the stone in topaz acting as a huge hand mirror. (In the princess and mirror, the flat table is set to the back, while in the penguin the smooth table is turned to the front.)

Intriguing stone shapes beyond baguettes and navettes that turn up in figural jewelry include such standouts as:

Cheetoh-like curlicue stones (think Nike swoosh) mimicking horns on a Viking's helmet, plain metal that also boasts bell-shaped strass (the stones so showy and unusual, Reinad would be suspected as manufacturer).

A shield-shaped cut that serves as bird body in a Van S Authentics eagle pin.

Rose-colored pentagons prong-set into a ballerina's elaborate tutu.

Kites and trapezoidal keystones set in different directions to form a king's tunic and tights.Pointed rivoli stones, whether the square watermelon tourmaline coloration Schiaparelli favored, or fluted round marguerites in sea blues so beloved by Albert Weiss.

Bee brooch and Bunny fur clip, large kite-shaped ginger-ale stones, enameled gold-plated metal; sometimes signed H. Pomerantz, 1940s, 2-1/8" unsigned bee, 3" unsigned bunny, **$50-$150.**

Filigree Fan dress clip, sapphire multi-cut paste stones, unsigned, 1930s, 2", **$50.**

When it comes to desirable rhinestones (whether you call them that, or strass, or diamante), most roads lead to Swarovski. Mechanical genius Daniel Swarovski founded his eponymous enterprise more than a century ago in the Austrian Tyrol. The company was built on his invention of the first electric machine to precision cut high-quality crystal stones in large quantities. Manufactured, not mined, the main Swarovski jewelry product is the "stone" of glass that becomes refined crystal when lead content and other ingredients are added to the mix.

Stork pin, huge emerald-cut royal-blue crystals, gold-plated metal, RS accents, unsigned, 1940s, 3", **$75-$100.**

Historically speaking, the key stone events of greatest interest to costume jewelry aficionados at Swarovski include: invention of the precision cutting machine that made mass production of crystals possible in the first place; vacuum plating capability to apply gold or silver to crystal's base for added brilliance; invention in 1955 for Christian Dior of a metallic iridescent coating known as Aurora Borealis (typically abbreviated AB); and of course the heralding of any specialty stone that comes to mesmerize collectors, such as the dimensional rivoli, with its signature point and equal facets above and below.

A personal note: Long before rhinestones ever caught my eye, I moved to Strasbourg to attend graduate school in journalism. I frequently walked back and forth across the border between France and Germany, along the Rhine. Little did I consider then that the river's beds had been full of the rock crystal quartz that made up what were the original rhinestones. Nor did I know that George Frederic Strass, the man who made gem quartz stones more diamond-like by coating them with metal powders, was from that area of Alsace-Lorraine. If only we all knew earlier what would eventually capture our imaginations ... later.

Hand-held mirror brooch, 2" topaz faceted glass stone, Reinad for signed B. Blumenthal, 1940s, 4", **$250-$500.**
Ann Mitchell Pitman photo

Penguin clown fur clip, enameled, gilded metal, large amethyst glass oval, unsigned Reinad, 1935-42, 3", **$250-$500;** Oriental Queen dress clip, pot metal and large aquamarine glass oval, 1935-42, Reinad for signed Lidz Bros., 3-1/2", **$250-$500.** From a series of figurals starring 2-inch faceted glass stones made by Reinad for button companies such as Lidz Bros. and B. Blumenthal.

Viking pin, pot metal, multi-cut pastes including bell-shape and specialty curlicues, unsigned (probably Reinad for Blumenthal), 1935-42, 3", **$75-$150.**

Donkey pin with art glass beads, unsigned DeLizza & Elster (Juliana), 1960s, 2", **$150.**

Christmas gift pin, antiqued golden metal ribbon-bow surrounding large simulated topaz stone, unsigned, 2000s, 1-3/4", **$25.**

Traveling saleslady or bellhop pin clip, enameled and pave-set RS pot metal, emerald-cut pastes serving as suitcases, signed BM (Bauman-Massa), 1938-42, 2", **$100-$150.**

Eagle pin-pendant, gold-plated metal, shield-shaped pale yellow faceted crystal, signed Van S Authentics, 1940s, 2-1/4", **$50-$100.**

CHAPTER 7  EVEN COWGIRLS GET THE JEWELS

Westward Faux

In 1975, two decades after it debuted, "Gunsmoke" was the last TV western standing. America's thirst for the cowboy life had taken 20 years to be even half-slaked, and almost three dozen dust dramas came and went before Kitty, Chester and the Marshall rode off into the sunset. On the big screen, though, the minimalist Spaghetti Western was still simmering, and 30 years after that, the world's fascination with wide-open spaces and masculine-looking men of few words was rekindled by the movie "Brokeback Mountain." Is it any wonder there's lots of western-themed figural jewelry in ranch houses across the country?

Wild West Saloon Scene, drunken cowboy shoots pistol, dancer covers face with fan during Can-Can, sterling silver, marked Sterling, 1960s, 2-1/2", **$100.**

After cowboy actors Bronco Billy, William S. Hart, William Boyd and John Wayne made the range look grittily glamorous on the silver screen, trains and cars, Route 66 and transcontinental highways let Americans taste the west for themselves, just as the Orgeon Trail and wagon trains did the century before. Icons of the West settled into every corner of U.S. homes, from the fabrics used on curtains to cacti in the windows. Every boy and girl had a holster, cap gun, 10-gallon hat and never missed "Hopalong Cassidy" and "The Lone Ranger." But how funny that fashionable women were piercing their mink coats with rhinestone and enamel cowgirls twirling lassos, clad in leather boots.

Elzac's heavily carved wood pins in western motifs sold like hotcakes off a griddle even before metals were totally rationed for the war. They are big and brawny, some using accents of Lucite for oversized hats, leather for reins, and brush for horses' manes.

One famous series that looks like Elzac but isn't uses wooden hat, hair and scarves as frames for riveted-in translucent Bakelite faces with hand-painted features. An Indian, a cowgirl and cowboy are part of the set.

The vision of a cowpoke resting on the fences with his ropes and a smoke was such a familiar image, it showed up everywhere, including jewelry, in unadorned copper metal of large scale. Indians and horses were made in such profusion it's impossible to scout them all, from tin to sterling silver, plastic to jeweled masterpieces.

Bakelite totem poles, bucking broncos, Native Americans smoking peace pipes, it's all there on the vast figurals horizon.

Fancy Cowgirl pin, plastic blue chaps, celluloid, wood-bead face, unsigned, 1920s, 3", **$150.**

Cowgirl fur clip, enameled, jeweled pot metal, unsigned, 1940s, 1-1/2", **$50.**

Out Ridin' Fences pin, cowboy lights up after a long day's work, popular motif seen in many categories, copper metal, unsigned, 1940s, 2-3/4", **$50-$100.**

Cowboy & Indian pins, wood-Lucite Hopalong Cassidy-like pin, 3-1/2", wood-Bakelite (hand-painted apple-juice face) Indian pin, 3", unsigned, 1940s, **$150-$200** each.

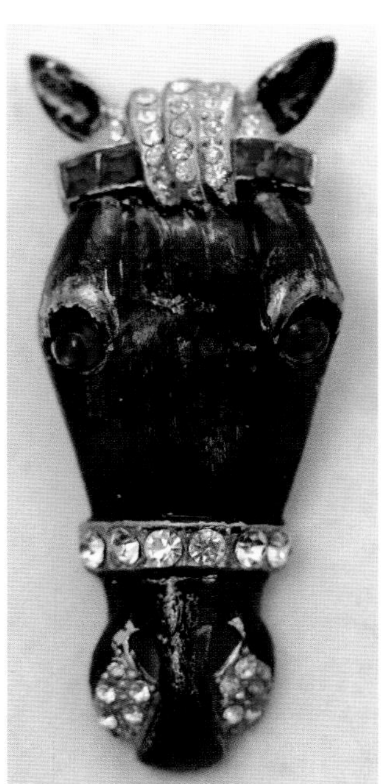

Horse heads, two versions of Coro design; enameled and jeweled pot metal fur clip plus tin pin with cabochon eyes, unsigned, 1940s, each 2-1/4", **$150** and **$25.**

Inlaid Indian pin, construction and materials frequently used on jewelry marked Philippines, unsigned, 1970s, 2-1/4", **$10-$25.**

Warpath Indian, copper, Rebajes-style design, 3-D (sculptural Indian extends out from plaque), unsigned, 1950s, **$25-$50.**

Baby Brave fur clip, silver-plated metal painted with turquoise and red enamels, signed Monet, 1930s, 2-7/8", **$50.**

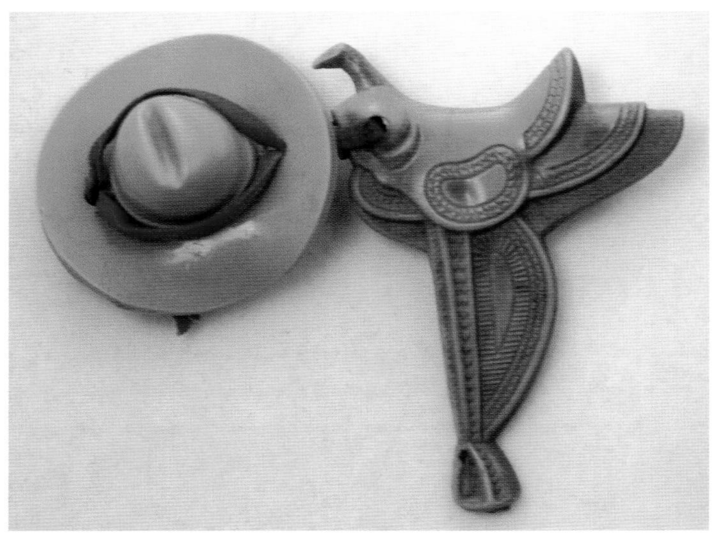

Cowboy Accoutrements pin, ten-gallon hat and saddle, tan celluloid and red leather, unsigned, 1920s, 2-1/4", **$25-$50.**

Wagon Wheels and log pin, charms suspended from celluloid chain links dangling from log bar, unsigned, 1920s, 3", **$25-$50.**

CHAPTER 8 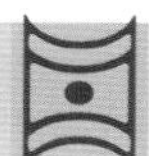 The Growth in Christmas Tree Pins

A Jeweled Forest

The reason so much mystery still shrouds this motif's history is because neither jewelry houses nor department stores advertised Christmas tree pins. Holiday arbors were impulse purchases, so jewelry makers simply set out to make them as festive and fetching as possible. Editorially, Christmas tree pins did receive annual ink in magazines, which is how collectors have learned, to their dismay, that the most famous Weiss Christmas tree was a pin of the Sixties, not the Forties, as is so often suggested.

Retail catalogues are a great source for dating trees too. Exploring the archives containing the annual extravaganza known as *The Neiman-Marcus Christmas Book* proved a wealth of information on Christmas tree pins, where a researcher can see the tree lineup from year to year, almost all of them by Cadoro (beginning in the Sixties), then DeNicola, then R.J. Graziano.

Because Christmas tree pins have become so collectible, it's hard to believe jewelry makers and retailers don't rethink the no-advertising strategy. When Lord & Taylor took a chance on a large newspaper ad for Christmas tree pins in November 2002, featuring creations by Swarovski, Judith Jack, and Christopher Radko, the L&T jewelry counters went quickly bare; saleswomen said for the record that purchases after the ad appeared were brisk.

Redbook published a short item about the popularity of the Billie Beads Christmas tree pin in 2002 and the boutiques mentioned as carrying inventory quickly sold out.

But catalogues remain the best way to nail down dates on holiday jewelry, for memories fade fast. Legendary costume jewelry designer Kenneth J. Lane is miscredited with making hundreds of Christmas tree pins he had no hand in producing and wants no part of, period, largely because their design and construction are so sub-par. Counterfeiters (if they can be called that when they steal not a design but a name only, in this case, Lane's) simply attach signature cartouches to whatever they make. The point is, the only Christmas tree pin KJL ever designed may be found on the front cover of the 1997 Franklin Mint holiday catalogue.

Con artists have become emboldened, once content to copy jewelry from defunct manufacturers and designers only, now willing to risk using names of companies still in business. In 1994, Eisenberg created a line of jewelry called Eisenberg Ice Classics, replays of some of their most beautiful old designs. The lavish

Catalin Creations by Lains, **$250-$350.**

Christmas tree brooch of that year, produced in very few pieces, has a provenance that remains unclear (had it in fact ever been produced before 1994?), but its desirability is clear as crystal. No wonder a reproduction of it, complete with the Eisenberg name, is regularly traded in eBay auctions. The fake version usually includes emerald- and fuchsia-colored navettes. A call to the company to inquire about its authenticity yielded the response that these trees are not products of Eisenberg.

As most collectors are aware, dealers purchase important pins and have them copied, new castings made whether in China or closer to home. This had been done for years with Weiss and Hollycraft trees, but not on any large scale with products of firms still doing business. Authentic Swarovski Christmas tree pins are being copied in China as well, but without the Swan-mark signature.

Another conundrum that needles collectors is the actual age of vintage Christmas trees. Most theories sound like sheer speculation and prove impossible to verify, usually because incorrect. Collectors have probably queried thousands of people who were average jewelry purchasers during WWII and during the Korean War, attempting to ascertain if Christmas tree pins actually were ever made and worn to show support of soldiers fighting in the Asian and European arenas during WWII or sent to soldiers in Korea as cheerful, morale-boosting souvenirs of holidays at home. Neither of these theories holds eggnog.

While some scattered Christmas tree pins sprouted up on lapels from the 1920s through '40s, the mid- to late '50s and all of the '60s marked the first heyday of the holiday arbor, with Gem-Craft and clever Cadoro and Mylu major early players in that realm. But what trees do we know for sure came before that?

The only certifiable pre-1950s Christmas tree pins are these:

1. Depression-era jewelry. Felt brooches (flat or stuffed) might have been the only decorative note someone flat broke or out of work could in good conscience buy in the 1930s, and the Christmas tree was definitely one motif made in pins then. Decorated with sequins and beads, the Depression-era felt tree is sometimes confused with its

"Celluloid Holly," **$10-$50.**

"Sequined Felt," **$10-$25.**

near-twin from the '50s, so look at pin findings for clues, and also the jewels: Sequins with an Aurora Borealis film, making them iridescent, are definitely '50s firs. Gold metallic sequins that look ancient, plus lots of bugle beads, suggest the 1920s.

2. Celluloid jewelry. The Christmas tree pin form was absolutely molded in celluloid plastic (and celluloid acetate) as early as the 1920s.

3. The earliest Christmas tree brooch with a firm affiliated date is the high Art Deco design by Cartier in 1928. Because it is a rare platinum-and-diamonds masterpiece few people in the world will ever own, collectors look for costume-jewelry-version knockoffs.

4. The great French designer Suzanne Belperron, whose clients, to mention only the tiniest fraction of celebrity names, included Fred Astaire and Clark Gable, also designed a precious-gems Christmas tree brooch in the 1930s, with a deeply Oriental effect. Lucky collectors have its costume copy.

5. Brush trees. The bristly brush Christmas tree that decorated households in the 1950s became brooches in that era too, sold on cardboard backings at emporia such as Woolworth's. One maker featured on cards still attached to the brush brooches was Vogue.

Corsage concoctions not unrelated to these brush trees first inspired two sisters who were looking for a business to launch together. Marge Borofsky and Lynne Gordon had an instant success with holiday corsages and then moved fairly quickly to metal pins at their company, Mylu. Like Dan Steneskieu and Steve Brody at Cadoro, all four worked with Gem-Craft for the production of their metal brooches, where great talents such as founder Alfeo Verrecchia and designer Robert Mandle huddled closely with clients on the designs. The Cadoro partnership began in 1945 and the first Neiman-Marcus exclusive holiday brooch, a partridge in a pear tree, is credited to them in 1965. It's possible Cadoro created a Christmas tree pin with Gem-Craft before 1960 (since Alfeo Verrecchia founded his company in 1945, the same year Cadoro was opened), but both Cadoro and Mylu trees have only been verified beginning in 1961.

Another area of vintage curiosity to collectors is Christmas at Eisenberg. While sellers regularly offer tree pins sworn to date from the Forties and Fifties, Karl Eisenberg, grandson of the founder, in fact launched the Christmas program at Eisenberg in 1972. The classic tree, a gold-plated pine with molded-ball overlay, striated trunk and multicolor rhinestones scattered like tiny ornaments, is the tree that launched a million sales there and is still a bestseller today. Eisenberg says it takes ales in the millions before a pin turns up with such frequency all over the world, on the lapels of women in Chicago, New York, Paris, Rome and London, where it has been sold at Harrods. The '72 classic cost $13.50 at retail as a direct-mail piece through Marshall Field (selling 4,800 pieces) and is only $15 today. When Neiman-Marcus featured the

Eisenberg Classic 1972 tree.

Actress Margaret O'Brien seems to have gotten cozier with Christmas since her days as a child thespian and her memorable beheading of snowmen in "Meet Me in St. Louis," the Vincent Minelli film in which she co-starred with Judy Garland. Here, O'Brien sports a selection of seven Swoboda Christmas tree pins. Other actresses known to own or collect Swoboda jewelry include Elizabeth Taylor, Demi Moore, Debbie Reynolds, June Haver, Jane Russell and Jane Withers. *Photo courtesy Nate Waxman.*

tree in 1988 and 1989, sales totaled roughly $100,000. It is one of the most recognized Christmas tree pins in the world.

Dating and counterfeiting hardly captures the spirit of the stoned saplings Christmas collectors pine for, though. Many collectors come to this category from a love of the Yuletide season and then focus their collecting on firs, which have the added appeal of small size, especially when compared with figurines, wreaths or even candles.

The cheerful news that ensues is discovering the breadth of Christmas trees. No collector is ever prepared for how many different pines there are. It's impossible to imagine that a tree, even decorated, could be done in 5,000 different ways. Even the basic categories of composition materials are broad: base metal, sterling silver, gold, wood, celluloid, Bakelite, Lucite, glass, textiles, crystal stones or beads glued or wired to filigree. Green and red hues still please modern collectors, but designers have incorporated every color into their creations, from pink or blue to black and purple.

It's much harder to come up with big names in jewelry that did not have trees to their credit than ones that did. Pat Ciner herself said Ciner never made one. Interestingly, while Eisenberg is strongly associated with Christmas tree pins, famed designer Ruth Kamke never created one during all her years at Fallon & Kappel doing work for Eisenberg. A company known for figurals, Lea Stein Paris seemed to have every motif imaginable under its belt but a tree. It turned out Stein had designed one in the Sixties but did not produce it until decades later, when a collector requested it. Other names not known for pines include Pennino, Mazer, Reja, Reinad, DeRosa, DuJay, Joseff, Silson and Staret. Renowned companies with Christmas trees include Boucher, Hattie Carnegie, Trifari, Coro, Sandor, Hobe, Castlecliff, Schiaparelli, Accessocraft, Lisner, Swoboda, Kramer and many others known widely for trees – Jonette and Lianna – plus many 21st-Century jewelry companies.

Why the tree is so much more desirable than Santa Claus, reindeer or snowmen is anyone's guess. It remains a puzzle, because any brooch with a face has more potential personality. People who find no fascination with trees say trees are too boring to be enthused about. Legions of tree saps disagree, however. About their pines they happily opine...there's just something about merry.

Tree Key

Christmas tree pins are 2 inches to 4 inches tall and made between the years 1965-2005. If the name under the tree is left plain, the tree is marked as indicated. If the name under tree is in quotes, it is the name given the tree for reference, but the tree itself is unmarked. If the name under the tree has brackets around it, the tree is unmarked but still in its original box or on its original card. An asterisk next to the name means the brooch may not have originally been designed as a Christmas tree.

"Electric Blue Ice*," **$25-$50.**

"Matisse Blue," **$50-$100.**

K.C., **$25-$50.**

Judy Clarke (Lucite), **$200-$300.**

"Bella Verrecchia," **$125-$150.**

Anderson Originals, **$100-$125.**

Lea Stein Paris, **$75-$150.**

Eisenberg Ice, **$175.**

Carolee, **$75-$125.**

F.M. Begay Navajo, **$250-$500.**

"Juliana," **$250.**

Austria, **$250.**

Sandor, **$250.**

Weiss, **$150-$250.**

Craft, **$50-$75.**

Nicky Butler, **$250.**

Hobé, **$100-$200.**

Sardi, **$75-$100.**

Tara, **$50-$100.**

Cristobal London, **$100-$150.**

Blumenthal*, **$150-$250.**

J.L. Foltz (Bakelite), **$150-$250.**

Brad Elfrink (Bakelite), **$100-$150.**

Shultz (Bakelite), **$350.**

[Venoire], **$50.**

"Bakelite Bits," **$50-$100.**

Albert, **$75-$150.**

"Savvy" (Swarovksi Swan), **$50-$100.**

LC (Liz Claiborne), **$50-$75.**

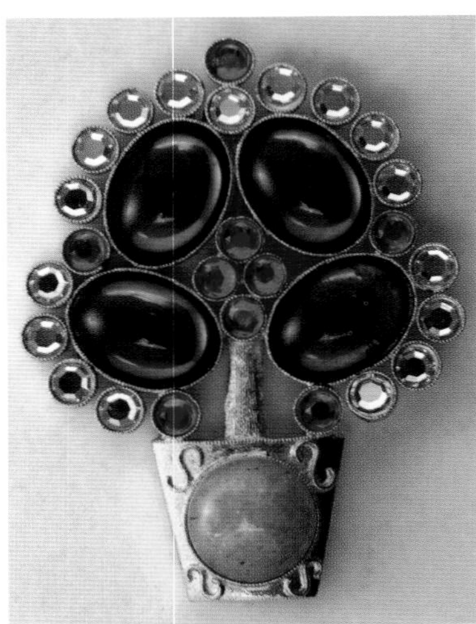

C "Art Deco," **$150.**

Ian St. Gielar for Stanley Hagler NYC, **$150.**

The Show Must Go On, **$300.**

Miriam Haskell, **$150.**

Dominique, **$150.**

Bettina von Walhof, **$140.**

Castlecliff, **$100-$150.**

LG, **$25-$50.**

Roma, **$25-$50.**

Dodds, **$50.**

St. Labre, **$150.**

Sarah Coventry, **$25-$50.**

New Pro, **$25-$50.**

Holland (ceramic), **$25-$50.**

Gerry's, **$75-$150.**

Hard Rock Café Guam, **$25.**

Stuart Freeman, **$250-$500.**

Coro, **$50-$100.**

Billie Beads, **$75-$150.**

[David Wright] (sheet metal), **$25-$50.**

Trifari "Mosaics," **$100-$200.**

Pell "Birthstone," **$150.**

Two Hands, **$25.**

Monet, **$25.**

Jez Sterling, **$25-$50.**

Givenchy, **$100-$150.**

[Longaberger], **$25.**

New View, **$25-$50.**

Florenza, **$150-$200.**

Krementz, **$75-$125.**

[Napier], **$50.**

Graziano, **$50-$75.**

Zentall, **$25-$50.**

Chr Dior, **$150-$250.**

Boucher, **$150.**

Danecraft Sterling, **$150-$250.**

GCI (Gold Crown), **$25-$50.**

[Blair Delmonico], **$150-$200.**

Bold Elegance, **$250.**

Lenox (porcelain), **$25.**

[Margot Townsend], **$50-$75.**

Beatrix, **$50-$75.**

[Agatha Paris], **$75-$150.**

DeMario, **$500.**

[Erwin Pearl], **$100.**

Original by Robert, **$150-$200.**

Claude Montana*, **$25.**

Dorothea, **$75.**

Gale & Friends Ltd. Ed, **$50-$100.**

Wendy Gell, **$100-$150.**

Lawrence Vrba, **$150-$250.**

Ann Hand, **$100-$150.**

Pakula, **$50-$100.**

Panetta, **$150.**

Bauer (Dorothy), **$150.**

Best, **$25.**

Swoboda, **$50-$100.**

Jeanne, **$75-$100.**

Oscar de la Renta*, **$50.**

Art, **$75-$100.**

LJM, **$50.**

Ultra-Craft, **$50.**

Vero, **$50-$75.**

Nina Ricci, **$250.**

Molyneux, **$150.**

Freirich, **$150-$250.**

Hallmark, **$25.**

MMA, **$75-$100.**

Jollé, **$75-$150.**

Stanley Hagler N.Y.C, **$125-$175.**

Judith Jack, **$150-$200.**

Mimi di N', **$50.**

[Nina Kodera], **$50.**

Marvella "Mosaics," **$150-$200.**

Lisner, **$50-$75.**

Stefanie Somers, **$50-$100.**

[Coldwater Creek], **$25-$50.**

BG, **$75-$100.**

Don-Lin, **$50-$75.**

FM (Franklin Mint), **$50-$100.**

Nordstrom, **$75-$100.**

Merksamer, **$50.**

Bellini by Formart, **$50-$100.**

Figment, **$50.**

"Elzac," **$150.**

SGH, **$150.**

Laguna, **$150.**

"Faux Cartier," **$100-$150.**

Emilia Castillo, **$50-$150.**

J.J., **$75-$100.**

Regency, **$150-$200.**

Avante, **$50.**

VanDell, **$50.**

CDN, **$50.**

Schiaparelli, **$300-$500.**

Warner, **$150-$175.**

Corel, **$50-$100.**

Sphinx, **$75-$125.**

Brooks, **$50.**

Keyes, **$50.**

Hattie Carnegie, **$150.**

MJ ENT, **$50.**

Patricia Locke, **$75-$125.**

Suzi Chauvet, **$50.**

Tancer-II, **$100-$150.**

Button Chic, **$50.**

Lia, **$125-$150.**

Vendôme, **$300.**

"Millennium," **$50-$100.**

Mylu, **$50.**

Sphinx, **$75-$125.**

LJM, **$50.**

Gerard Yosca, **$150-$250.**

Alice Caviness, **$100-$150.**

Capri, **$50-$100.**

CHAPTER 9  SHOWBIZ FIGURALS

Starring Roles

Artists often are shown shut off in garrets or studios with only their imaginations to keep them company. Usually the opposite is true, artists "out there" soaking up the culture and visual inspiration from magazines, art museums, and the street itself, with something potentially intriguing around every corner. And when it came to artistry in the jewelry field, even a company's salespeople and managers had to stay on top of trends and translate them quickly into jewelry, especially true when the jewelry was figural.

One of the most revered names in the costume jewelry world is designer Ruth Kamke, who created most of Eisenberg's famous figurals during her tenure at Fallon & Kappel. Young Ruth took in a movie one day that included a Bugs Bunny cartoon, and the pantaloon'd rabbit-in-drag morphed crazily (in her fertile imagination) into the famous Eisenberg Can-Can dancer. As Kamke says today, inspiration can come from anywhere: "A friend of mine, who's a little crazy like me, said she could see a fox in the nap of my bathroom carpet. I told her, 'I think I saw it, too.'" Kamke's knack for dreaming big is evident in the teensy line sketch (presented to her by *Harper's Bazaar* ad girls for a brooch they wanted on the cover) she turned into the enormous Eisenberg eagle that became one of the greatest costume-jewelry attention-getters of all time. Kamke saw a unicorn in an encyclopedia and made it a megawatt masterpiece as well.

"The Jungle Book" Drummer brooch, enameled gilded metal, signed Alexander Korda, 1942, 2-1/4", **$100-$150.**

But costume jewelry inspiration often harks from the entertainment world. When the connection is unclear and so old or passé it's no longer obvious, reading books provides clues. A Cary Grant bio that included details of one of Archie Leach's first Broadway productions said a song performed by men in black face was a hit showstopper, and their outrageous costumes included oversized bow ties. Did a jewelry house designer attend this musical, "Golden Dawn," and at work the next morning design a fur clip featuring a man in black face with a huge bow tie? (See photo P. 78.)

The most valuable *series* of movie-related costume jewelry is probably the panoply of designs affiliated with Alexander Korda and his 1940s productions of "The Thief of Bagdad" and "The Jungle Book." The figurals and elaborate necklaces are conveniently marked, often with both Korda's name and the movie title. (Manufactured by Rice-Weiner, the company seems to have continued producing them in unsigned versions when the movie connection was no longer key.) The marvelous myth that long-surrounded Korda pieces was that the director had jewelry made for cast and crew on his film sets. Instead, it seems Rice-Weiner contracted with the production studio to make jewelry related to his movies' themes. The fact remains that the designs, from ships, galloping equine and seated shiva to exotic characters of the Far East, hold high appeal for collectors because of their cinematic relationship, and the fact they are beautifully made. Harder to find than even the Korda pieces are figurals such as the Indian Chief based on Cecil B. DeMille's 1940 flick, "Northwest Mounted Police." Eugene Joseff's company created jewelry both for the movies and jewelry for the public based on movies, such as C.B. DeMille's 1950s remake of his "The Ten Commandments."

Disney jewelry is in a category of its own, with the rarest pieces being "Bambi"-related Bakelite figurals (Bambi, Thumper, Fleur) and "Dumbo" circus designs with the sought-after WDP (Walt Disney Productions) mark. Name a Disney deal and there is jewelry from it: a "Snow White and the Seven Dwarves" charm bracelet or the famous Mary Beth for Pell *Tinkerbell* brooch from "Peter Pan." Even narrowing Disney figurals to a niche leaves a lot of room for collecting. The Christmas pins alone are as deep as snow in Denver.

As for The Great White Way, it's BSK's series of enameled symbols celebrating Broadway's 1957 opening of "My Fair Lady"—an Ascot riding crop, the Rain-in-Spain Victrola, ruffled parasols, Higgins's slippers, Eliza's flower cart—that takes the Tony among collectors. The BSK collection is broad and charming, and just when collectors figure they've seen them all, up pops another shade of Miss Doolittle's elaborate Ascot bonnet. Collectors who love Eliza have their work cut out for them finding every version of the Cockney's chapeaux and every key prop employed by the professor as he slowly learns the language of love.

Television is not to be forgotten in the figurals sweepstakes. From radio-turned-TV superstar Charlie McCarthy to "Saturday Night Live's" Beldar Conehead, with Lassie, Mr. Bill and Bart Simpson in between, the small screen made major stars of characters captured in pins. Mickey Mouse must have been made in 1,000 permutations, and even a homely bloke like Popeye was frequently cast, as was the always glamorous Olive Oyl.

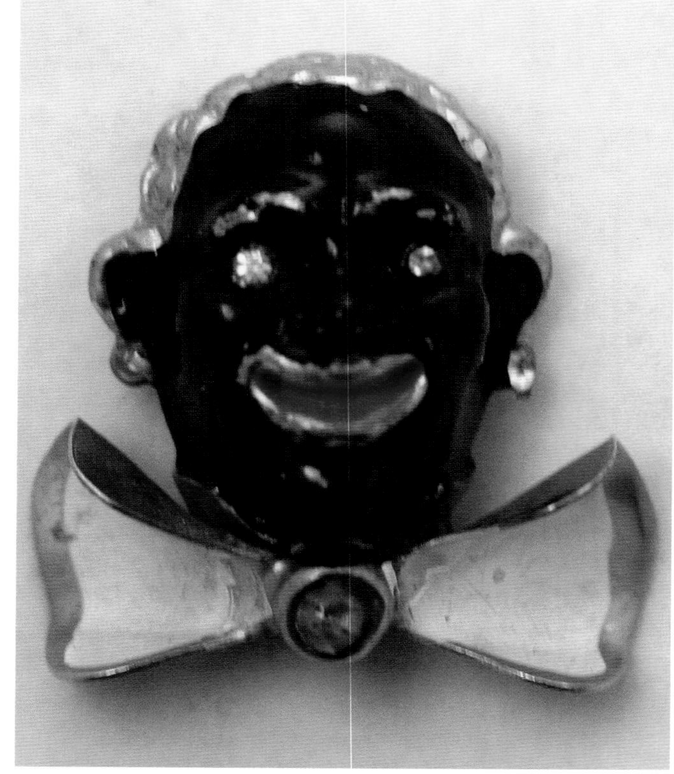

"Golden Dawn" Minstrel in Oversized Bow Tie fur clip, enameled metal with RS accents, 1930s, unsigned, 2-1/4", **$100-$150.**

One tough get from television land is the bejeweled map of the United States that Laura Petrie inherited from Rob Petrie's family. By the time that episode, "The Curse of the Petrie People," aired in 1966, during the last season of "The Dick Van Dyke Show," the sitcom had been a hit for years (after its rocky start in 1961 and subsequent cancellation), and some clever jewelry maker decided to take a chance and market the huge, jeweled USA figural pin to the public. In the show, Laura, who likes the brooch about as much as she liked the humongous heirloom necklace Rob gave her in a much-earlier episode, accidentally drops the cursed USA brooch down the garbage disposal. This pin is not easy to find.

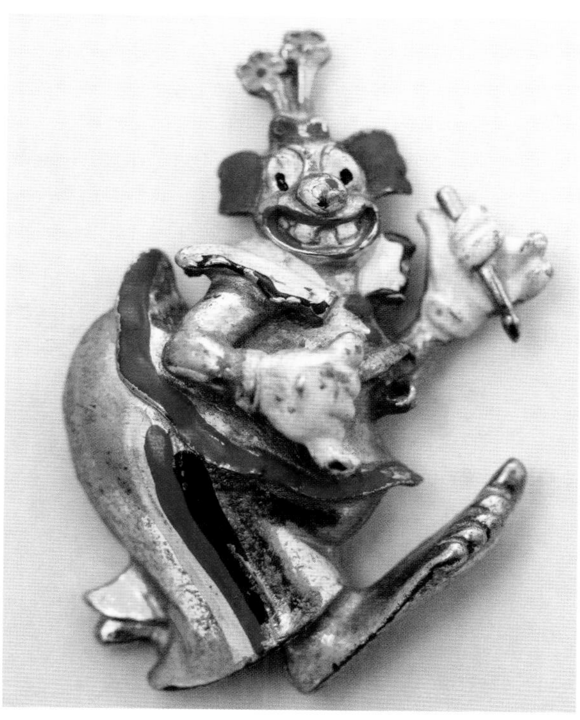

"Dumbo" Circus Clown fur clip, enameled, gilded metal, drum charm (missing here), signed C W. D.P., 1941, 2-3/8", **$75-$150.**

"101 Dalmatians" Sled Dog pin, enameled pewter-toned metal, signed Disney and H (in a heart) for Hedy, 1961, 2", **$25.**

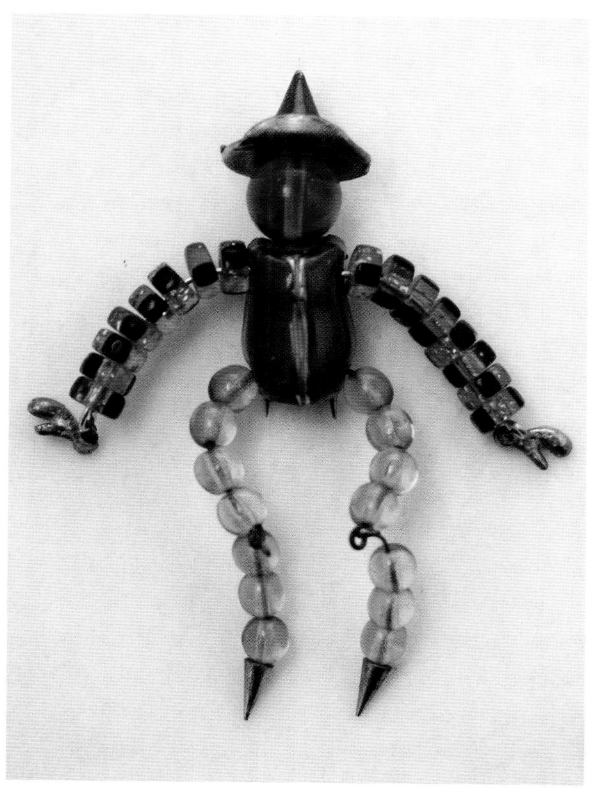

"The Wizard of Oz" Scarecrow fur clip, enameled metal torso and hat, beaded arms and legs, tiny metal hands and feet, 2-7/8", unsigned, 1939-40, **$100-$150.**

"Pinocchio" fur clip, enameled gilded metal with RS accents, 2", marked MB, 1940, **$100.**

"Rigoletto" Opera Scene pin, portrays Rigoletto, Gilda and Sparafucile during tragic climax of the production, 3-D, metallic paints on pot metal, 2-3/8", unsigned, 1947-55, **$50-$100.**

"Have Gun Will Travel" TV pin, featuring Palladin, metal and plastic, 1-1/8", unsigned, 1950s, **$25.**

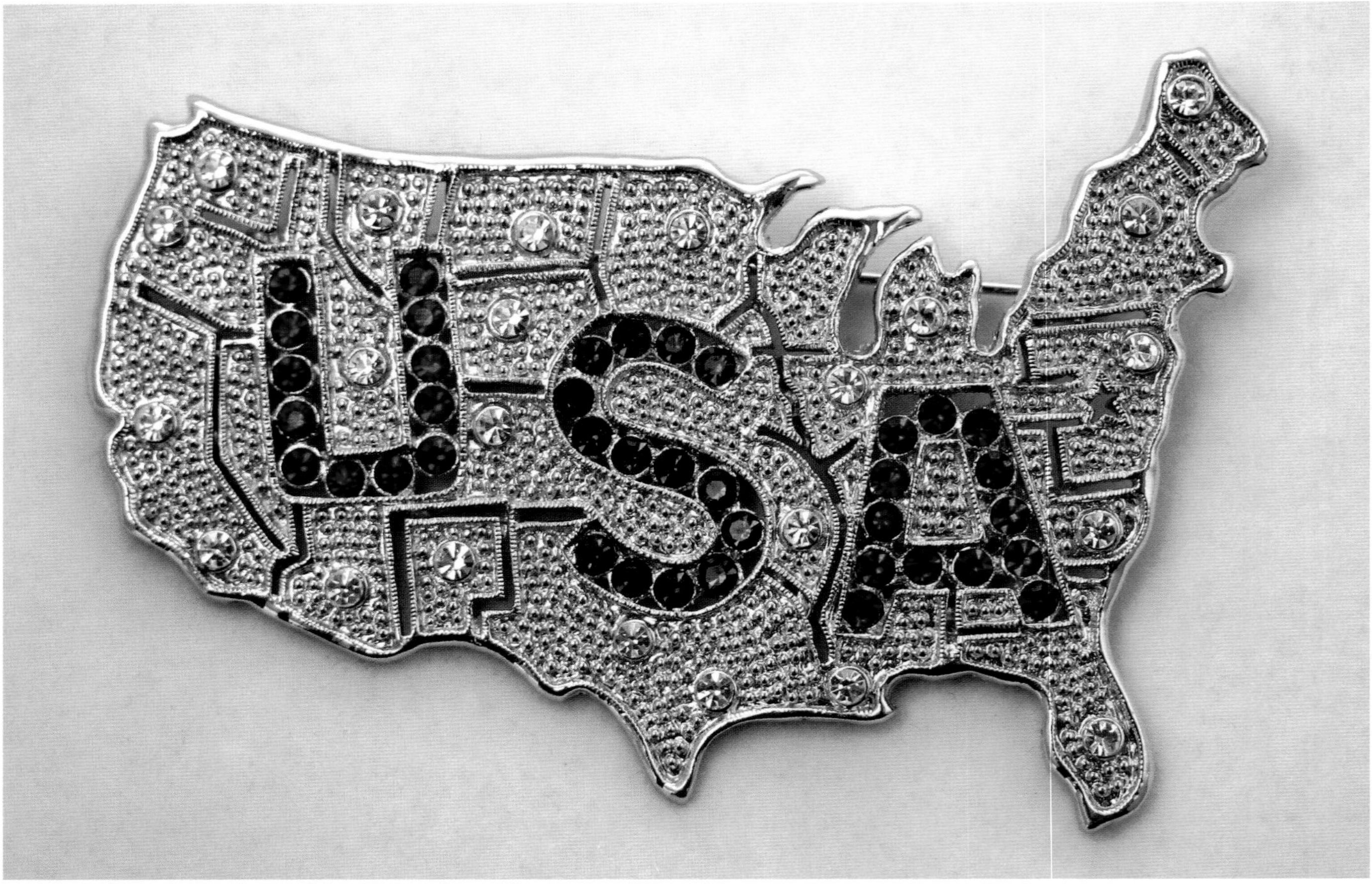

"The Dick VanDyke Show" USA Map brooch, jeweled, silver-plated metal, USA in red and blue RS, states delineated, Washington, D.C. indicated by star, 3-3/8", unsigned, 1960s, **$75-$150.**

My Fair Lady by BSK

The many figural designs in BSK's 1957 "My Fair Lady" series includes four themed groups: Covent Garden, Higgins' Home, The Ascot Races and Doolittle's Church Wedding. The pins shown here and on Pages 82-83 are 1-1/2 to 3 inches. Prices range from $25 to $150, depending on perceived scarcity. Pieces are signed BSK and *My Fair Lady*. Collectors interested in this broad Broadway line like to collect every piece, which includes many color variations. The series includes bracelets, brooches, earrings and cufflinks. One bracelet boasts charms representing every key scene.

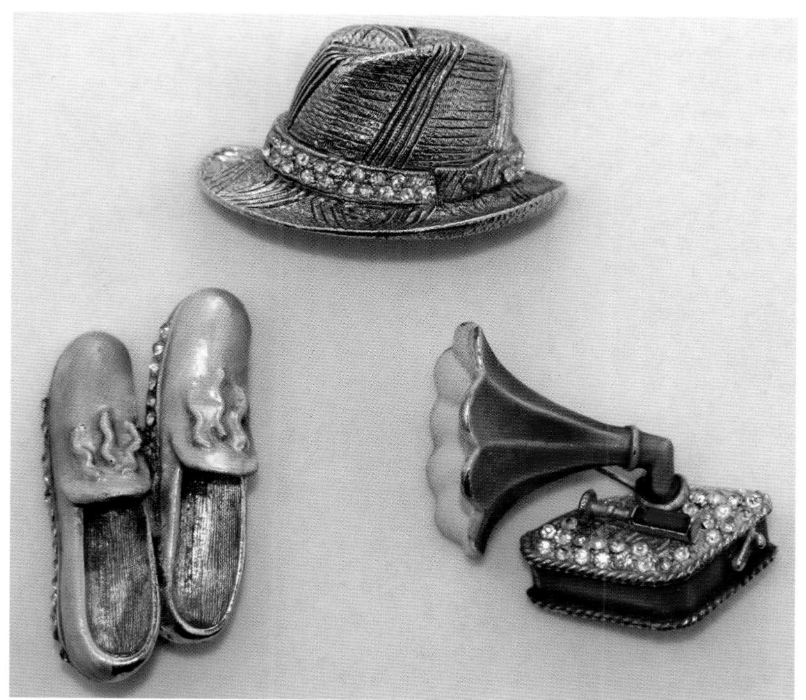

Henry Higgins' hat, Gramophone and slippers.

Ascot races binoculars and racehorses with jockeys.

Eliza's elaborate black-and-white Ascot bonnet with memorable bow.

Ruffled parasol, top hat with glove and stick, riding crop with cap.

Eliza's flower cart and a basket of flowers.

Trio of chapeaux.

Trio of bouquets.

Pair of vases with flowers.

Two floral hats.

Eliza's straw hat.

CHAPTER 10  PATRIOTIC, MILITARY & POLITICAL PINS

A Salute to Jewelry

World War II remains the richest source of commemorative costume jewelry because jewelry makers such as Trifari, Coro, Eisenberg, Silson (whose gas mask, after all the bombings in Britain, must be one of the most novel figurals ever, reading "Britain Can Take It," and on the reverse, "Bundles For Britain" with the Silson mark); Walter Lampl, McClelland Barclay and others went all out with ingenious designs or boldly bejeweled and enameled eagles, drapeaux, sailors—and even multiple versions of Winston Churchill, bulldog to man. Simple celluloid Sweetheart jewelry and the Sons-in-Service stars worn by proud mothers are other tender keepsakes of that war and how it affected the homefront. Bakelite figurals of soldiers and Uncle Sam sometimes sell for tremendous amounts of money.

The V for Victory sign, along with anything related to Old Glory or old Uncle Sam, are the most popular patriotic motifs of WWII, from humble bullet-casing Vs crafted by soldiers as trench art, to elaborate rhinestoned confections with eagle, flag and V combined. Eisenberg's gem-loaded vintage eagle brooch may be the fairest of all, designed by Ruth Kamke.

As for political jewelry, standard metal campaign buttons advertising Bush & Cheney pale when compared with true political jewelry like the GOP elephant by Coro, a pachyderm proclaiming fervent devotion with an "I Love Dick!" sign done in rhinestones. There is Polcini's big brooch of Churchill, gold-plated dogs and seahorses wearing Goldwater glasses, a carved plastic bust of Gen. Douglas MacArthur or a Tricky Dick Nixon himself, who seems to be Trick-or-Treating on Halloween, waving his V for Victory fingers and ready to pull down a paper-bag mask to hide his presidential mug at any minute.

Revolutionary War Fife & Drum Corps, polychrome enamels on pot metal, dimensional and complicated casting, rare, unsigned (probably Coro), 1936-46, 2-3/4", **$500.**

Military figurals portray soldiers of every stripe, from Revolutionary War fife-and-drum corps to WWI doughboys to WWII sailors, battleships and bombers. Such is the nature of the jewelry business—and wars themselves—that since that time, the major jewelry companies do not design elaborate celebrations of war symbols or the military.

After the explosion of patriotic military pins during WWII, there seemed to be less taste for Korea. The important jewelry figurals of the Vietnam War were the anti-war Peace Sign, and flora symbolizing Flower Power, often accompanied by the slogan suggestion, "Make Love, Not War." T-shirts replaced jewelry as the medium for the war or anti-war message, but that changed after Sept. 11, 2001, when rhinestone-chain pins in red, clear and blue jewels sold like mad in motifs from flags to Christmas tree pins. When the patriotic spirit of Americans is raised to fever pitch, demand for jewelry symbols skyrockets, and that was as true in 2001 as it was in 1941.

Betsy Ross sewing Flag pin, 13 RS stars, enameled stripes, unsigned, 1936-46, 1-7/8", **$150.**

Victory Sign Wooden Hand pin, carved wood with Lucite bracelet, red, clear and blue charms spell U-S-A, unsigned Elzac, 1942, 3-1/2", **$150.**

Large Eagle on V for Victory brooch, silvered pot metal, dimensional, unsigned, 1941, 2-3/4", **$50-$100.**

Declaration of Independence pin, enameled pot metal, feathered signing pen, signed Silson, 1940s, 2-5/8", **$75-$150.**

Liberty Tree pin, enameled gold-plated metal with Lady Liberty surrounded by Liberty Bell, eagle, flag, torch, star and Minuteman, all growing on branches, signed Rafaelian, 1976, 2-1/4", **$50.**

WWI Gun-Toting Doughboy double brooch with U.S.A. chatelaine attachment, khaki enameling, 3-D stick figure, 3-1/4" soldier, unsigned, 1930s, **$50-$100.**

U.S.A. Army barracks mechanical pin, celluloid, Victory sign behind door shows when closed door is unhinged, opens via beaded chain, unsigned, 1942, 2-1/8", **$50-$100.**

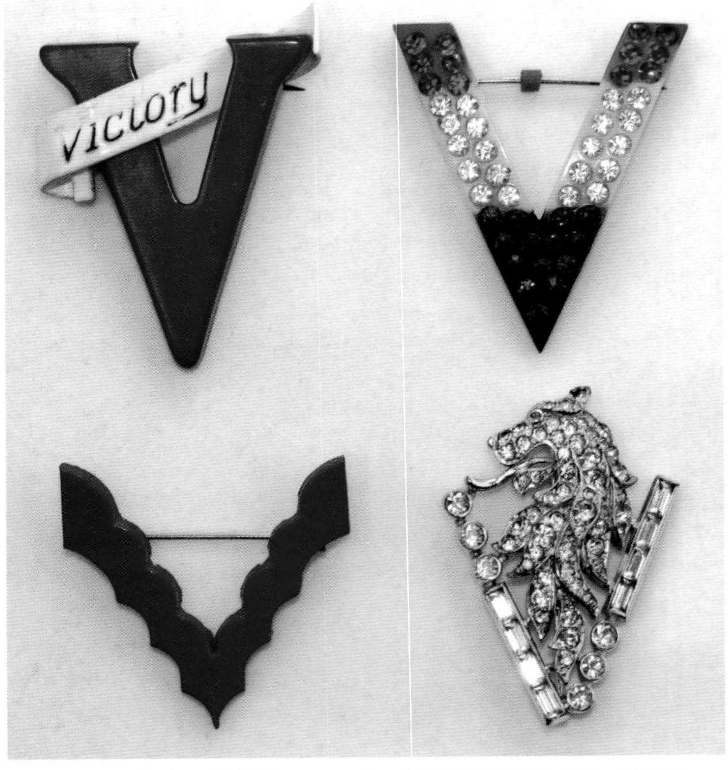

Bakelite Victory V pin, celluloid banner, unsigned, 1942, 2", **$200;** V pin, celluloid, unsigned, 1942, 1-3/4", **$50;** Red, white and blue celluloid RS V pin, 1942, 2", **$50;** Jeweled Lion for Victory brooch, signed Trifari, 1946, 2", **$250.**

B-17 Bomber pin, silver metal, spinning propellers, compasses dangle on sides reading "Japan," 1940s, 3", **$25-$50.**

Gen. Douglas MacArthur pin, pinkish sepia-effect celluloid, unsigned, 1944, 2-1/4", **$25-$50.**

Military Hat & Bugle pin, enameled metal, unsigned, 1940s, 2-1/4", **$25.**

Eagle pin, gold-plated metal, signed Van S Authentics, 1960, 2", **$25.**

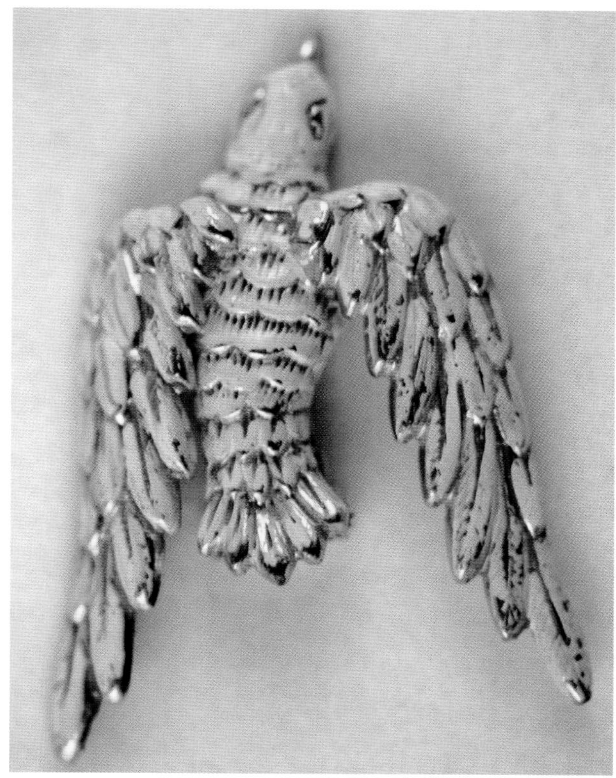

Dove of Peace fur clip, white enamel on gilded metal, matches enormous fur clip shown in Birds chapter, signed Authentics, 1947, 2", **$50+.** (Joanne Moonan's company made many different eagles and doves.)

"Amigos Siempre" brooch, "Friends Forever" booster pin for the Americas; American flag flanked by 20 other flags representing Union of American Republics, enameled, gold-plated metal, signed Coro, 1941, 2-1/2", **$50-$250.** (Information from the Brunialtis' *A Tribute to America.*)

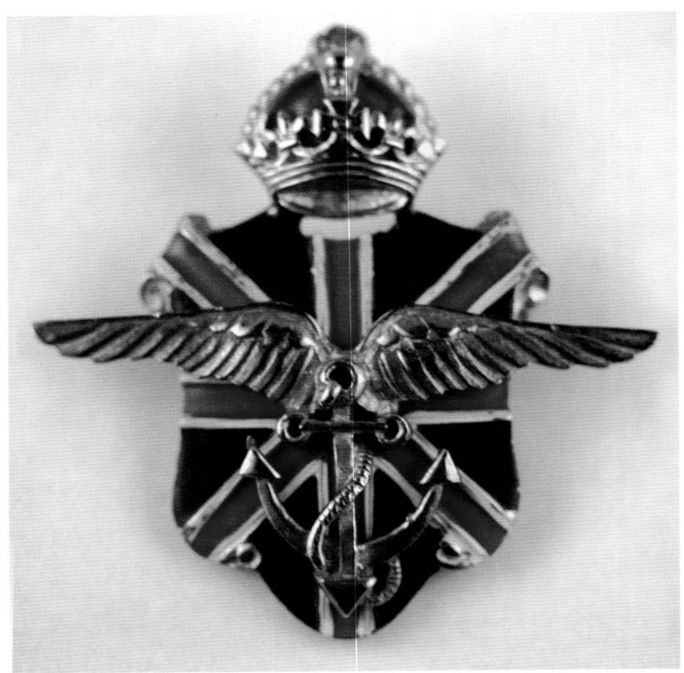

British & American Ambulance Services Badge, enameled, gold-plated metal, eagle, anchor, Union Jack, signed Silson, 1942, 2", **$50-$75.**

Jeweled Stars & Stripes brooch, blue chaton, large ruby and crystal diamante ovals, unsigned, 1941, 2-1/2", **$150-$200;** Old Glory pin, red and blue enamel on pot metal, crystals, unsigned, 1941, 2-1/4", **$100-$150;** Flourished flag pin, red, white, blue celluloid and matching stones, unsigned, 1940s, 2-1/4", **$50-$100;** Spread eagle brooch, pot metal, red, white and blue, unsigned, 1940s, 3", **$150;** Son-in-Service pin, celluloid, unsigned, 1942, 1", **$50.**

Uncle Sam Hat fur clip, red and blue jewels mixed with faux pearls, 1930s, unsigned, 1-7/8", **$150.**

"My Uncle's Hat" pin, red, white and blue 3-D celluloid hat dangles from red celluloid bar pin, unsigned, 1942-46, 2-1/4", **$50-$100.**

Honeycombed drapeau, gilded pot metal, red, white, blue chaton forming stripes, eagle-topped flag pole, unsigned, 1930s, 3", **$150-$200.**

Patriotic Christmas Tree pin, red, white and blue epoxy tiers with RS accents, first holiday post 9-11, unsigned, 2001, 2-1/4", **$25-$50.**

Uncle Elephant pin, GOP mascot dons classic Uncle Sam red-white-blue topper, gold-plated metal, enameled hat, unsigned, 1960s, 2-14", **$25.**

"Vote Democratic" patriot-girl pin, translucent epoxy on silver-plated metal with ribbon, sequins, RS accents, red feather, signed AJM, 2000s, 4-1/4", **$25-$50.** For 2000 Al Gore campaign against Bush and 2004 John Kerry campaign against Bush. "Be kind to dogs and vote Democratic." - the late Sen. Thomas Eagleton, D-Missouri.

Peace Symbol Christmas Tree pin, multicolor RS crystals in silver-plated cast metal, peace symbol star top, signed MV, 1970, 3", **$150.**

Sailor, Boat & Anchor pin, silver-plated metal with RS accents, chained anchor, unsigned, 1940s, 2-1/2", **$50-$100.**

Patriotic Ribbon, **$50;** Clinton-Gore Democratic donkey pin, gold-plate metal, enamel and red RS accent, signed D, 1996, 1-7/8", **$25-$50;** Red-white-blue RS chain mule with tail, unsigned, 1980, 1-1/2", **$25;** Single-star Clinton-Gore donkey pin, convention hat, red and blue enamel, signed Monet, 1992, 1-7/8", **$25;** Saddled donkey pin, celluloid, red-white-blue, unsigned, 1920s, 1-1/4", **$25-$50.**

Saluting Sailor on Warship pin, thickly enameled gilded metal, RS accents, unsigned, 1941, 2-1/8", **$50.**

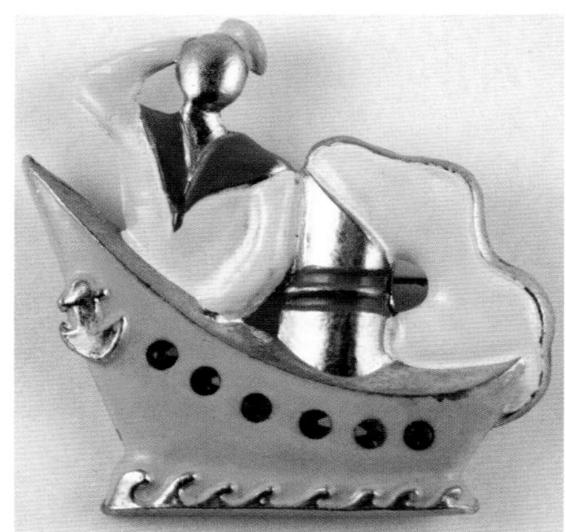

Sailor fur clip, basic enameling lost, base metal, signed, appears to be Marie e Dorette, 1938-42, 1-7/8", **$25-$50.**

Steering Sailor Helmsman pin, enameled pot metal, cabochon accent, movable wheel, unsigned, 1941, 2-1/4", **$50.**

CHAPTER 11  FAR-OUT FUR-CLIP FANTASIES

Imaginations Gone Wild

Two reasons to collect clip figurals are that reproductions rarely crop up in the category, and for some reason, designers unbridled their imaginations when dreaming them up.

In an interview, Neil Cuddy at jewelmuseum.com reminds everyone the common term "fur clip" is actually a misnomer. The specialty spring-loaded findings with pointed double-prong tines (sharp enough to permit piercing animal fur pelts of coats and wraps) should correctly be called "pin clips," since that is what they were called at the time and how they are referenced on original design patents. (Additionally, for instance, some Trifari and Eisenberg clips incorporate actual pin-finding closures to capture the tines' points, but most clips do not feature those.) Dress clips, with the single, wide flat metal flaps, were first made earlier, in the 1920s.

The most recognized category of clip pin is the Duette, introduced by Coro and based on a Frenchman's 1931 invention. The Duette is a pair of clips mounted in a single brooch frame from which they can be removed and worn separately or singly. The most valuable examples feature faces. Coro created the most well-known and popularly collected Duette, but other companies issued their own versions.

While fur clips aren't the most sought-after figural format, collectors who like them swear by them and are steadfast in their pursuit. For one thing, unusual designer-name marks turn up in these antique clips: Mary e Dorette, Charles Cooper, Sonia Lee ... Also, jewelry designers seemed to park their inhibitions at the door when it came to creating decorative accents for furs and coats. Neil Cuddy believes there's a rationale for that, since 1938-42 is simply the classic period for great costume-jewelry designs. "By the early '50s, the use of the pin clip was almost over, so the coincidence of the classic 1938-42 period with the widest use of the pin clip probably is the best way to explain why the best figurals are also pin clips."

Nevertheless, we observe that the strangest concepts of all were destined to front pointy prongs. A shortlist of maniacal masterpieces includes:

- Cocktail-celestial themed pitcher signed P.J. Co., designed by Stanley MacNeil, with fruit features on its semi-human face.
- Silson's drunken tiger by Samuel Rubin, with screw-off goblet top for perfumed cotton
- Cartoonish character set including Cyclops bug, vaguely political or military; creature with human face and scaled body with heart on head and clutching diamond engagement ring; chubby royal in vaguely Dutch shoes; genie holding envelope.

Moorish Prince, well-cast, heavy, gilded metal, elaborate construction, figural frame for large simulated emerald, refined chain drape under skirt holding three strands crystal beads, unsigned (probably Reinad for Hattie Carnegie or Eisenberg), 1940s, 4", **$250-$500.**

• Five-plus-inch articulated lizard – demonstrating size was never an issue when it came to fur clips. (The mammoth creations could be supported by heavy fur or wool – not delicate satin or cotton.)

• Eisenberg's charwomen with scrub brush, bucket, mop, cleaning ladies whose impetus designer Ruth Kamke no longer remembers.

Wolf on the Prowl, nightclub predator in formalwear, ready to steal anyone's girlfriend, enameled pot metal, unsigned 1938-42, 3-1/3", **$100-$150.**

Abstract Characters, part of series (two shown): "hammered" effect metal cabochon faces with indented features, both with hats, 2-1/2" gentleman with marbled emerald-glass body under jester-style collar; 1-3/4" lady decorated with tiny beads; unsigned, 1930s, **$150-$250** each.

Series Characters, enameled gold-plated metal with RS accents: 2-5/8" Cyclops Insect King, 2-3/8" Casablancan Alien, 2-3/4" Reptilian Lover with Diamond Ring (not shown: swami with letter; scaled creature holding star), possibly from a popular cartoon strip; marked Des. Pat. Pend.; unsigned, but at least one is a patented Mazer design); 1938-42, **$250-$750** each (actual sales prices), **$2,500+** for series of five (unknown if additional characters were made).

Framed Silhouettes on beaded gilded-metal ribbon, signed Mosell N.Y., 1950s, 4-1/4", **$250-$300.**

Toasting Tiger Perfumer, stripe-pattern enameled gold-plated metal, screw-off goblet top holds perfumed cotton, signed Silson, 1940, 2-7/8", **$500.**

Cocktail Shaker Pitcher, gold-plated enameled metal, fruit and astrological, mysterious theme due to mix of planetary and mixology motifs: stars, moon, planets, cherries, oranges, grapes, cocktail glass, swizzle sticks; bronze-finish metal, enamel, RS and pale violet cabochon grapes; signed P.J. Co., design patent assigned to Stanley MacNeil, 1940, 3-1/4", **$1,295.**

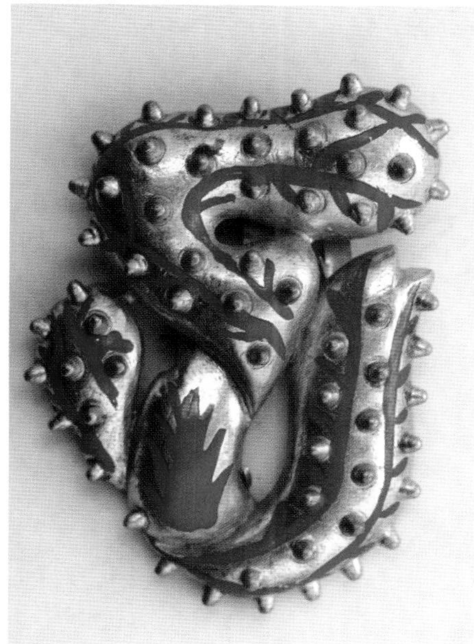

Cactus dress clip parure (clip-only shown, other pieces include ladies' cufflinks and button studs), enameled pot metal, unsigned (possibly Tortolani), 1938-42, 2-1/8", **$150-$200.**

Hands Holding Up Blackamoor Queen cameo, enameled metal, marked Made in France, 2-1/2", **$150-$200.**

Quick-Change Lipstick Dispenser, metal, mimics a conductors change dispenser but holds three lipstick tubes, attaches to coat as a fur clip, signed Lucien Lelong, 1930s, 1-3/4", **$125-$150.**

Articulated Lizard, brown-enameled legs, gold-plated metal encrusted with small emerald cabochons and faceted crystals down center, signed LB in bell, 1930s, 5-1/4", **$250.**

CHAPTER 12  REINVENTING DESIGNS

K.J. L. Alone

Kenneth Jay Lane is a self-confessed aficionado of the Royal Jewels in all their splendor, and self-professed student of the artistic achievements of artists in British museums and the palaces of Italy, Germany, India and much of the world. But the man known by a monogram (KJL) also adores flea-market stalls and tourist traps where pure junk is peddled. If it possesses a flight of fancy, an over-the-top aesthetic, he's there.

Stylized Seahorse brooch, black enamel on gold-plated metal, cast pearl resin head and tail, KJL, 1980s, 4-1/8", **$150.**

Some of the greatest jewels of antiquity drive KJL's figurals. In his highly coveted Sixties series, brooches with enhancers, such as Europa and the Bull, or mermaids and warriors, hark back to 16th-Century Renaissance masterpieces. Making the pins all the more dramatic is Lane's use of what looks like baroque pearls for faces and bellies on the exotic cast of characters – pearl that is actually cast-plastic resin. The face and snout of a seahorse looks like a baroque pearl in the familiar shape of an aquatic equine's head. Lane achieves equally striking results with richly colored resins acting as carved jade, coral and lapis lazuli, whether a turtle's gem-studded shell, a seahorse's branched hideaway or a moth's elaborate wings.

In 2007, Lane marked 45 years in the jewelry business. His biggest hits have included such disparate decorative *objets* as intricately embroidered oversized earrings and Chanel-esque cuffs with Maltese crosses, but since the focus here is on figural pins, we can hang out in that universe and explore without fear of a shortage. Renaissance fantasy animals are important in Lane's mythic bestiary.

Is his wildlife a little more exciting because creatures exude a hint of menace in eerie jeweled eyes, a curve of the neck or the slightly open mouths? One animal is reminiscent of Picasso's savage faun.

Lane's plastic cabochons pretend to be molten glass; carved glass is sculpted rubies. Lane likes pearls, so besides the baroque-pearled cast forms, he makes generous use of dangling pearl beads. He has his own unique deity lineup in a primitive pantheon of ancient-looking people and "pets."

While many collectors covet the jewelry that came out of the Hattie Carnegie firm in the Thirties and Forties, when houses such as Reinad made it under Carnegie's supervision, Ken Lane also did a stint at Hattie's after the legendary fashion maven had died. KJL was head designer for less than a year during 1962-63 at Carnegie, but the original animal and clown brooches he created there, some of which he used in his own line, are compelling—and desirable on the secondary market. A series of energetic clowns, made in varying metal finishes, plastics and beads, are still being copied today by other companies and reproduced in China. Lane's authentic vintage series of funny men includes a clown head, a clown balancing on a ball, and clown tipping his hat. In some, Lane used ivorine for the head, while others have faux jade or coral faces. Hattie Carnegie's array of primitive pups and fantastic fauna were clearly conceived by someone with a wicked imagination.

Lane is known as a mastermind of creative mimicry, whether emulating Verdura, Webb or JAR. His feat has always been to make the result his own, and absolutely original. His lavish warrior and Neptune brooches are, taken together, almost a twin of the Renaissiance masterpiece Canning Jewel. That 16th-Century Tuscan pendant is all rubies, diamonds, enamels and gold, with a jaw-dropping baroque pearl torso and pearl drops balancing the pendant.

Lane's attraction to the Renaissance makes sense, considering the spirited exuberance of that era's uninhibited creative expression. The baroque pearl reigned supreme in many designs in the late 1500s.

Smiling Clown Head pin, cast coral resin face, blue-enameled metal frame of hat and collar, RS accents, unsigned, 1960s-70s, 2-1/2", **$100-$200.**

It's to Lane's credit he developed a way to achieve a similar, pleasing result—using plastics, no less.

Before that, though, as noted in Lane's autobiography, *Faking It*, with Harrice Simons Miller, KJL achieved the same effect by painting metal with pearly white nail polish!

First, Last and Never

1) For his fitted figural bracelets, Lane was first to use a spring hinge, which he invented.

2) Lane's spotted enamel leopards with diamante-bow collars may be the last figurals with retro fur-clip mechanisms to be designed, in 1985. (Note: Stuart Freeman did create a small collection of Christmas tree fur clips in 2005.)

3) We interviewed Lane in his New York City showroom, where the world's most beautiful women, from Audrey Hepburn to Julie Christie, had shopped. We presented him with a dozen Christmas tree pins, all marked with his famous initials or monicker, in order to learn if they were his, or fakes. Each and every one was a fake. (See also Chapter 8.) Lane only designed one Christmas tree, but it was for the Franklin Mint and does not bear his mark.

Balancing Clown pins, gold-plated and striped-enamel costumes with RS accents, pearl resin face signed KJL; coral resin face unsigned; cast green resin face signed Hattie Carnegie; 1960s-70s, each 2-1/2", **$50-$150** each.

Balancing Clown, Smiling Clown Head and Hat-Tipping Clown pins, related series, antiqued Russian gold-plated metal, cast ivorine resin, tiny coral and turquoise beads, unsigned, 1960s-70s, each 2-1/2", **$100-$200** each.

Ferocious Fish pin, navy and jade cast resin body in gold-plated metal, RS accents, emerald-bead ball fins, signed Hattie Carnegie, 1960s-70s, 2-1/4", **$150-$250.**

Chinese Sea Serpent Fish pin, pale sea-green enamels, mouth holds faux pearl, signed K.J.L., 1960s, 2-1/2", **$100-$150.** *Courtesy Lisa Corcoran, Jazzle Dazzle, jazbot.com.*

Pegasus pin, turquoise enamel, well-cast metal with curling tail and mane, 3-D wings, pave-set RS on wings, face, saddle, signed K.J.L., 1960s, 2-1/2", **$185-$250.** *Courtesy Lisa Corcoran, Jazzle Dazzle, jazbot.com*

Primitive Rooster, navy blue and ivory cast resin, lustrous blue and white balls, gold-plated metal, RS pave accents, signed Hattie Carnegie, 1960s-70s, 2-1/4", **$150-$350.**

Horse & Hound brooch, two-tone metals, faux pearls and turquoise beads, bezel-set cabochons and faceted square-cuts, signed Kenneth Lane, 1980-90s, 2-1/8", **$50-$100.**

Renaissance Fantasy Animal pin, gold-plated metal, pistachio enameling, mixed jewels, signed K.J.L., 1960s, 2-1/2", **$250-$500.**

Primitives on Parade pins, frosted cast acrylic with silver-plated metal and jewel accents, unsigned Hattie Carnegie, 1970s, 1-3/4" pink elephant, 2" yellow anteater and 1-1/2" white dog, **$50-$100** each.

Gembuck head brooch, coral resin face, black plastic horns with faux pearl and metal accents, unsigned, 1970-80s, 3-1/2", **$150-$300.**

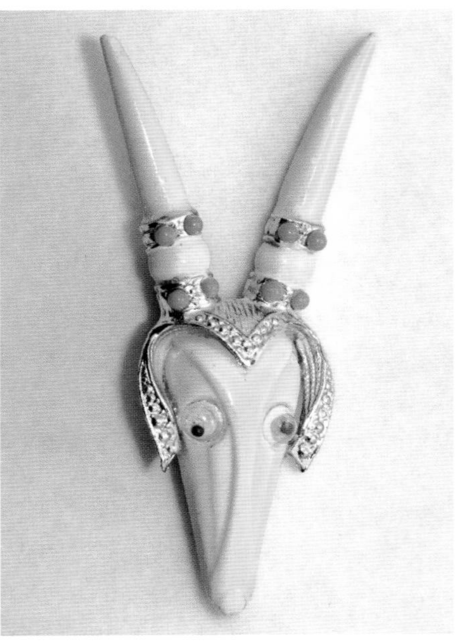

Gembuck head brooch, ivory enameled gold-tone metal, plastic turquoise beading, google eyes, probably a copy of an original design, unsigned, 1970s, 3", **$50-$100.**

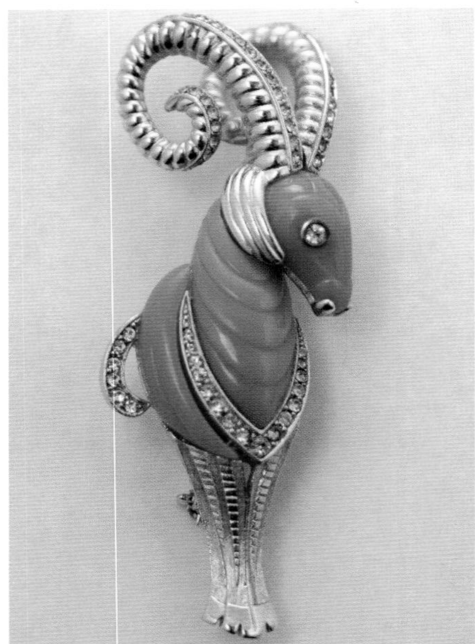

Ram pin, cast coral and jade resin head and body, gold-plated frame, RS accents, unsigned (same design as DeNicola Zodiac-series ram), 1970s, 2-3/4", **$50-$100.**

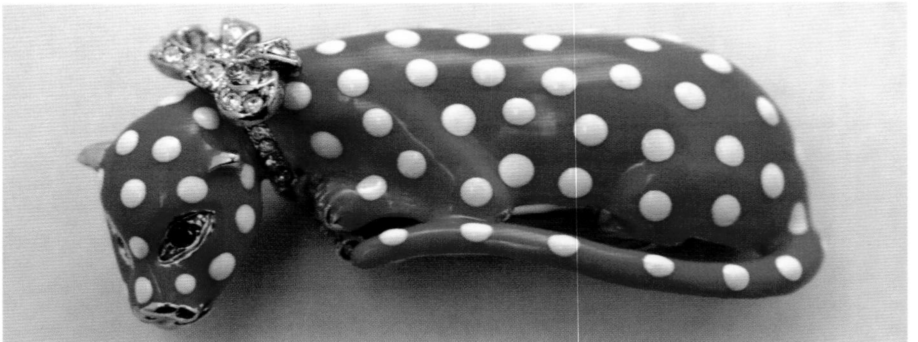

Spotted leopard fur clip, white polka-dots on red enamel, jeweled-beribboned collar, signed Kenneth Lane, 1980s, 2-1/2", **$50-$100.**

Macaw pin, cast ivorine resin beak, plastic turquoise wing, coral resin head, pave-set RS back, accents, swirling-enamels tail, unsigned, 1990s, 3-1/4", **$50.**

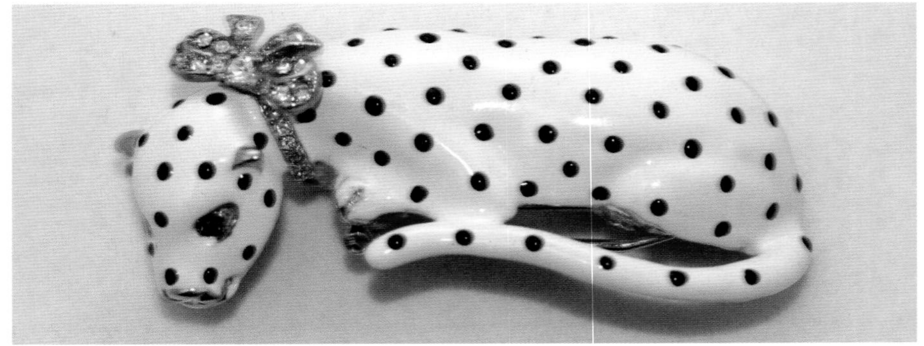

Spotted leopard fur clip, black polka dots on white enamel, jeweled-beribboned collar, signed Kenneth Lane, 1980, 2-1/2", **$50-$100.**

CHAPTER 13  WOOD'S ARRIVAL NOT UNWELCOME

Knock, Knock

If humankind's love of jewelry came from a desire to glorify oneself with gleaming light and glamorous colors, no wonder wood was rarely the go-to medium for decoration. And no doubt women during the Great War, the Great Depression and WWII felt deprived of their metals and glittering stones, but the shortages did at least give wood its due and cast a bright light on what artists could concoct with tree products.

Woods are wonderful on their own or mixed with Lucite, Bakelite, metal and even rhinestones. Real works of art in this humble medium – the seeming province of whittlers, carvers, Ozarks crafts people, grandpaps rocking on the porch – were made by first-rate jewelry houses. In her book *Wooden Jewelry and Novelties*, Jo Izard says companies including Coro, Castlecliff and Authentics were known for their use of wood in jewelry, and that Chanel, Schiaparelli and LeLong carved a niche in it as well. Izard's interview with Alta Novelty's Rod Moure cleared up one shadowy area, that Alta made wood with galalith or Catalin pins from 1935-40. This is of particular interest because Elzac never incorporated Bakelite, Catalin or galalith in its wood and Lucite figurals, so it becomes clear who did.

Miriam Haskell's early, unsigned creations of wood, beads, glass, plastic and seeds, spilling in asymmetrical profusion from pins and clips, are startling for their aesthetic splash. Another excellent use of wood was in the tiny, colorful beads composing layered brooches made in Czecho-Slovakia. Many Elzac products include elaborate, exotic human heads and animals or fruit of wood and clear or colored plastics. (Before paying a lot for a pin hoped to be Elzac, check to see the wood is heavily carved.) One of the most successful brooches Elliot Handler made at Elzac is the large-scale wood snake charmer playing a Lucite horn for an acrylic cobra.

Jewelry woods included walnut, rosewood and ebony. In *Wooden Jewelry*, Izard adds teak, snakewood and African onyx to that list. Current artists such as Breeze Verdant may employ every exotic wood there is on earth in jewelry design figurals because they can be used so sparingly.

One of the most exciting finds in vintage wood and composition jewelry is the carved version of famous cast-metal creations. The costly Boucher Mexican man in jeweled som-

Lord Nelson pin, carved, painted hardwood, red feathers, unmarked, 1944, 4-3/4", **$50-$100.**

brero turns up in affordable wood, and so does the showgirl in profile, manufactured by numerous companies that include Fred Block, Sandor and Eisenberg. The wagon train stagecoach fur clip of metal was also made in painted wood, but sometimes wood or compo versions of pins are found first.

For instance, a specific wood composition-with-rhinestones figural head of Rumpelstiltskin suggests it is likely modeled on a metal original. In all instances, metal clearly preceded wood versions, surely during the metal-rationed war years. But who made them? Did Boucher carve wood versions of its own famed brooches? Or did another company co-opt successful designs for its own woodworks?

African Native bust brooch, painted, carved wood, undecorated (also found with elaborate Lucite accents), unsigned Elzac, 1940s, 3-3/4", **$50-$100.**

African Native pin, carved wood with wire accents, red-bead earrings, unsigned Elzac, 1940s, 3-1/2", **$50.**

Clown head pin, plastic-beaded red nose, black eyes, large green felt ruffled collar, 1950s, unsigned, 4", **$25-$50.**

Rare pair of Penguin fur clips, painted, carved wood, unsigned Elzac, 1940s, 2-3/4" graduate and 2-1/4" sailor, **$250** each. These are symbolic of wartime life, when boys graduated from high school, often early, to enter military service, participate in WWII, and later graduate from college on the G.I. Bill.

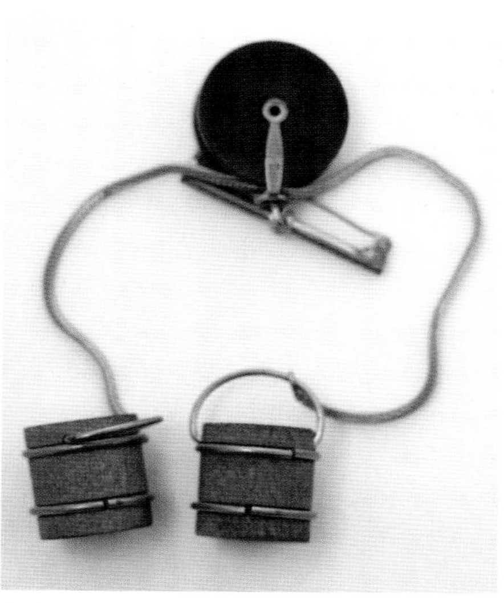

Buckets brooch, wood and metal, move up and down, higher-lower, via chain pulley, unsigned, 1945-55, 5", **$25-$50.**

Collie dog brooch, carved Lucite and wood combination, 1940s, unsigned, 3-1/4", **$100-$150.**

"Tribute to Elzac" Christmas Tree pin, carved mahogany with Lucite jelly belly ornaments, plastic star, Elzac sticker, 2000, 4", **$150.**

Sailboat pin, painted, carved wood, unsigned, possibly Elzac, 1940s, 3-1/2", **$50.**

Facial Features

One of the most popular categories in figural costume jewelry is the face pin. Expressive visages go on and on, so a vast array may people a collection with no end in sight.

Ken Lane recast ancient Mayan mask faces in jade-like plastic. Mazer made an impassive, eyeless, pave mask in countless recreations. Eisenberg has its name on enormous, exotic faces everyone wants in their jewel boxes. One of the early, common faces is a genuine Art Nouveau sterling woman's visage with flowing tresses. But why start such a list when it will never come to an end?

Exotic 'Cambodian Prince' brooch, bronze-copper finish over pot metal, large rhinestones set into gunmetal headpiece setting, huge ruby-colored rose-montee centerpiece stone, unsigned, 1940s, 3-1/4", **$250-$500**. Possibly a Reinad piece intended for Carnegie or Eisenberg.

Coro created striking faces in pairs with its Duettes, especially the relatively rare Indian maiden and brave, king and queen, and the French deux called Apache and Putain.

In fact, couples are an amusing sub-category in human forms, whether they fall into the faces or full-figure category. Find one-half of a pair when they have somehow been separated and many collectors cannot rest until they find the missing partner. The Coro Empress and Emperor, for example, must rule together. The elf with sledgehammer must hit the nail on the head held by his partner. Peter loves Helen, etc.

When Elzac's occasionally freaky Forties faces were still anonymous and identified only in the vernacular as "Victims of Fashion," collectors of novelties had already succumbed to their weird charm. But when the Brunialtis pronounced them Elzac issues, they took on new momentum. Naturally, the next step was broadening the identity of these lovelies to *all* large faces in wood, ceramic or even resin—in order to sell them for a higher price or at all. But most of the common *resin* figural faces actually came out of the 1980s. One of the most ubiquitous pins is a porcelain-finished resin design dressed in every get-up imaginable, including gold lame, metallic blue chapeaux, beads, and other garish fabrications. The first one a collector sees is slightly charming, but by the time 1,000 have passed by in the eternal pin parade, they grow difficult to look at at all. A slightly more interesting version of them includes the addition of a watch by Digits. Digits watches were attached to a variety of figural pins in the 1980s and 1990s, from faces to Christmas tree pins. Another related group of newer faces is from the Adagio collection, like small porcelain doll faces. Decorated as Flappers, Mardi Gras girls and Broadway babies, some winking, others with rhinestone eyes, they are colorful Eighties specimens of pouty-lipped girlishness.

A true Mardi Gras line includes a vast assemblage of face pins likely made for Fat Tuesday because they are signed "The Pinman of New Orleans." In guises from pirate to *roi*, the colorful plastic pieces are strangely captivating despite plainness and modest size.

Most face pins have pleasant expressions, so some of the Chinese men, such as Coro's Fujiman and Chinaman, are startling in their anger. Few women appear angry, but one Monet royal looks extremely displeased.

Some of the most desirable faces are in profile, including the Coro Josephine Baker, the famed Fred Block and a version of a Reinad profile for Eisenberg.

Vivid colors and heightened expressions in "Negro" and African caricature faces are politically incorrect and out of sync with the correct tenor of the times, making these pins at once odious and odd to own. They are worthwhile as historical artifacts of an unenlightened era; in terms of design, they are over the top.

Face figurals, in all their variations, make it obvious why some collectors find flowers and fish a bore compared with the infinitesimal variations of expression in the faces of women and men.

"Apache and Putain" fur clips, dimensional, enameled pot metal, hollow eyes, RS-accented neckerchiefs, 3-D cigarette in gigolo's mouth, signed Coro, 1942, 2-1/4" and 2-1/2", **$75-250** each.

"La Dame aux Camellias" (Camille) brooch, enameled, gilded rhodium, mask-like face surrounded by flowers, unsigned but still tagged Coro, 1940s, 3", **$200-$250.**

White Lady fur clip, pave-set RS curls, enameled face and accent flowers, hollow eyes, signed Coro, 1938-42, 2-1/8", **$150.**

Jeweled Face brooch, hollow eyes, pave-set RS face, enameled eyebrows, lips, multicolor mix of square cuts, teardrops and baguettes, unsigned Reinad or Mazer design, 1938-42, 2-1/4", **$150.**

Glitz Face pin, large pave-set RS, two-tone metal turban wrap, powder-blue bindi jewel, glittering earrings, 1980s-90s, 2-1/4", **$25-$50.**

Turban'd head fur clip, large prong-set ruby jewel bindi, exotic hollow eyes, gilded base metal, signed Mazer, 1938-42, 3", **$250-$300.**

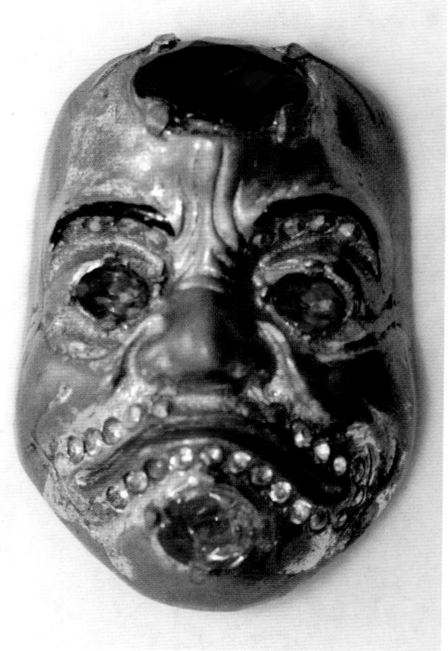

Buddha Face pin, pot metal, imbedded prong-set jewels, same visage also seen gold-plated, with 'Chanel beard' (strands of Chanel-style necklace) and signed Eisenberg Original, unsigned, 1930s, 1-3/4", **$75-$150.**

Brunette Beauty fur clip, gold-plated enameled lady with headdress (strongly resembles the huge Eisenberg Original so-called 'Mayan Mask'), unsigned, 1938-42, 2-1/4", **$150+.**

Alien Geisha face brooch, faceted navettes give an eerie or other-worldly look, highly unusual, coppery finish on deeply cast metal, 1935-42, unsigned but likely Reinad, rare, 3"+, **$500.**

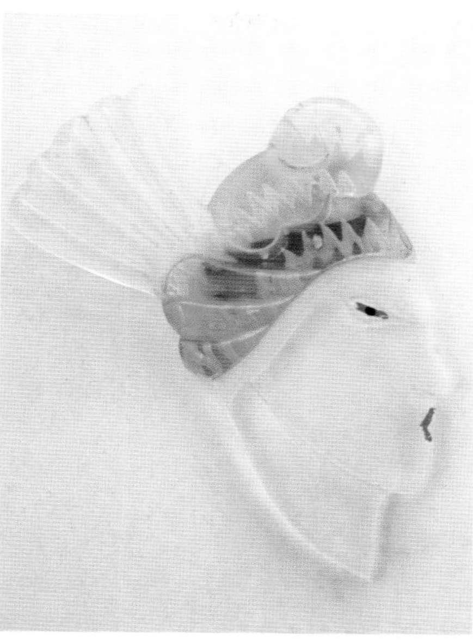

Feathered Flapper pin, carved and reverse-carved painted and dyed Lucite, unsigned, 1940s, 3-5/8", **$150+.**

Joan of Arc brooch, helmeted, painted porcelain face/head on gilded fleur-de-lys, signed Freirich, 1960s, 2-1/4", **$100.** The Maid of Orleans and the fleur-de-lys are pertinent symbol of the company's heritage and its origins as Maison David in France.

Flapper in profile, RS chain, ivory resin, illegible signature, date unknown, 2-1/4", **$50.**

Jeweled headdress mask brooch, hollow, heavy, double-sided gilded face mask with two rows of inset twisted wires topped with 12 polychrome baguettes, each accented with crystal chatons; unsigned Fashioncraft Robert, 1940, 3", **$250.**

Masterpiece Mask brooch, gilded metal, heavily jeweled with multi-cut, multicolor stones, elaborate array of chain strands as hair (remain partially erect and springy when brought forward), signed Fashioncraft Robert, 6", **$300-$500.**

Exotic mask brooch, antiqued silver-plated metal, face with flourish or beard of 50 silver bell charms, five ruby cabochons inset into graduated raised bezels, 1970s, unsigned, 4", **$150-$200.**

Riot of Colors mask pin, enamels and brightly colored multicolor flat-back rhinestones, 1980s, French, signed Louis Feraud, 4", **$75-$150.**

French Artist pin (matching earrings not shown), heavily enameled (navy and powder blue) gold-plated metal, hollow-eyed painter in beret and tied smock collar, unsigned, 1950s, 2-1/4", **$150-$250+.** (A dealer tagged set 'Schiaparelli,' and in fact the artist does resemble Schiap pal Salvador Dali. More importantly, this artist is an exact match to a large charm on bracelet signed Har, so these enameled pins and related pieces were probably made by Chas. F. Worth for Har, possibly Elsa Schiaparelli and others.)

Tyrolean gentleman in hat, fur clip, painted resin face prong-set into gilded rhodium frame including necktie and hat, unsigned, 1938-42, 1-1/2", **$100.** (Possibly Hobe or Napier; each company used this cast resin face, painted in different ways for greatly varying effects.)

Decoriental Dames pins, gilded sterling silver, larger size (3-1/2") with confetti fruit-salad cabochons (gold-flecked navy blue) hair ornaments, smaller size (1-7/8") plain; 1942, unsigned but identified as products of Evans Case Co. (see Brunialti, *Tribute to America*), marked sterling. One other piece in this series is a large, stylized, botanical-effect seahorse of gilded sterling with same navy-blue fruit-salad cabs. **$50-$250.**

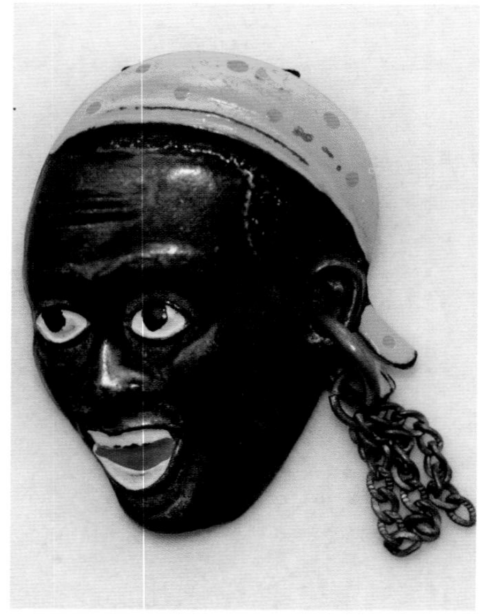

Moorish Pirate fur clip, enameled, bronzed pot metal, look of determination or shock on face, real earring through lobe, unsigned, 1935-42, 2", **$50-$100.**

Lady in Babushka pin, balsa head, RS-studded scarf, painted, real eyelashes, unsigned, 1940s, 3-1/4", **$50-$100;** Lady in Kerchief pin, suede wrap, unsigned Elzac, 1943, 2-1/2", **$75-$150.** Lady in Bandana pin, enameled metal, marked Made In France, 1950s, 2-1/2", **$50.**

Goatee Gent brooch, gilded, exotically enameled face, beaded drop earrings, ruby RS mouth, RS eyebrows, colorful headpiece, unsigned, 1940s-50s, 2-3/4", **$150.**

Cartoonish Black Faces pins, one plastic, one tin (lever makes eyes roll), unsigned, age unknown, 2" to 2-1/2", **$25** each.

Male Character pins from top: Bald Strongman, Fortune Teller, Pirate, painted, molded plastic, signed The Pinman of New Orleans, 1950s, 1-1/2", **$25-$50** each. Probably related to Carnival in New Orleans, the original set contained eight different characters.

Sleepy Flapper pin, painted, fired ceramic face pin of chic brunette, unsigned (possibly a later take-off on Elzac 'Victims of Fashion'), 1960s, 2-1/2", **$25.**

Diamond-Eyed Lady pin, multicolor plastic, RS accent, unsigned, 2-1/2", **$5.**

Lady in Blue pin, resin face in profile, stiffened metallic royal-blue lame, unsigned, 1980s, 3", **$15.**

Madame Beads pin, resin face with beads and stiffened lame, resembles Sailor Moon or Susan St. James, unsigned, 1980s, 3", **$10.**

CHAPTER 15 Solving Mistaken Identities

Mysterious

CFW and HAR

Lucky coincidence comes in handy in costume jewelry research.

An unusual figural brooch in the form of an African witch doctor sitting on a Bakelite log while holding a medicine stick topped with a skull, for instance, seemed like a good purchase. The workmanship was top of the line in casting, enamels, versatile use of Bakelite; the subject matter was intriguing and amusing. The coincidence came into the equation when the pin arrived and was marked—with the initials CFW.

How fortunate just to have finished reading a biography of Charles F. Worth, the Englishman considered the father of haute couture—French haute couture at that. It was immediately apparent CFW stood for Worth, yet how could that be? How could someone so long deceased, whose top client was the Empress Eugenie, wind up with a kooky metal figural to his credit?

It turned out Worth's sons and then grandsons continued the business and, in the 1950s, although the House of Worth closed in Paris, it remained open in London, and was still in business during the 1960s, possibly into the '70s. It created jewelry too, and one mention was made that it capitalized on the Carnaby Street rage. Serendipitously, a helpful website based in France, devoted to Worth, soon appeared on the Internet, but it rather quickly vanished, so other pressing questions could not be answered.

The mysterious CFW is the Charles F. Worth monogram, which is good to know because jewelry lovers have been so desperate to crack the mystery of these initials that they decided it stood for Cultured Fresh Water because some CFW pieces feature tiny faux pearls.

Many of the motifs in CFW pins suggest its actual French heritage, especially the Fleur de Lys and crown categories. But the plot thickens when it is observed that duplicates of CFW figural pins—flowers, fruit, veggies, even cartoonish characters—overlap with another famous mark, HAR. The figurals are literally identical, and CFW and HAR clearly had a relationship. But what was it? My own theory, still not proven or disproven, is that the English branch of Worth made jewelry for HAR, which may be the luxury department store, Harrods.

Speculation among costume jewelry cognescenti has long been that HAR was a European company, not American. While some people believe HAR stands for an American company called Hargo, any editorial references to Hargo in old magazines never show the HAR-style jewelry seen today on the secondary market, and there are more glove and handbag references to Hargo than jewelry credits.

Efforts were made to prove the HAR-Harrods connection during correspondence with an archivist at the firm. He could turn up nothing there; however, the archives on site in

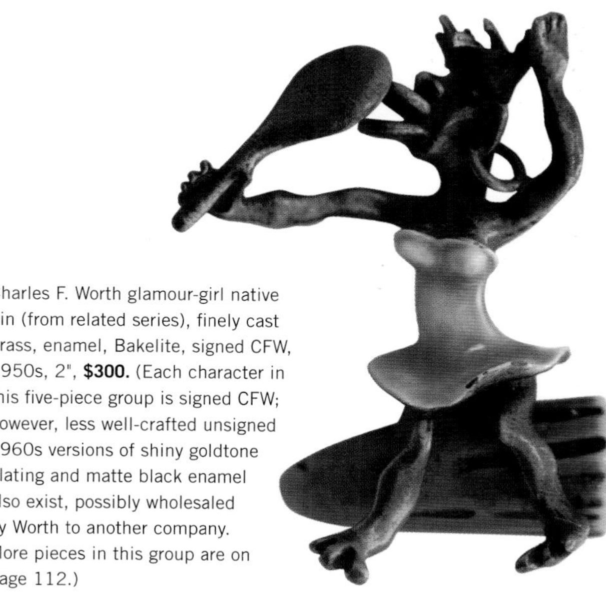

Charles F. Worth glamour-girl native pin (from related series), finely cast brass, enamel, Bakelite, signed CFW, 1950s, 2", **$300.** (Each character in this five-piece group is signed CFW; however, less well-crafted unsigned 1960s versions of shiny goldtone plating and matte black enamel also exist, possibly wholesaled by Worth to another company. More pieces in this group are on Page 112.)

London are thin. Evidently the meat of the archives were unavailable and located in Scotland.

A fact that bolsters the theory is that Harrods opened a hip youth store called The Way-In Shop in the '60s, perfect location for the enameled novelties signed HAR, such as the beetle brooch representing The Beatles, a bug swathed in a bright Union Jack flag. The same goes for the numerous juvenile cartoon characters marked HAR, from a rabbit ringmaster to insane-looking troll. These would fall into the purview of kids and teens, not adults, and surely must be from some television or theatrical show at the time.

How the more sophisticated and fantastical HAR jewelry made its way to America may have happened in one of three ways—or all three ways: Some shops at Harrods catered to American tourists, of which there were many. What American woman visiting London did not stop in for a shop at Harrods? The lavish genie and dragon jewelry surely could have traveled across the Atlantic to the United States in the return suitcases of many delighted tourists. Or, Americans could have ordered such jewelry through the Harrods catalogue. Finally, and this is quite feasible, Worth-London may have developed a relationship with an American importer or wholesaler for its jewelry, either unmarked categories or marked pieces for Harrods that buyers for the department store did not order. The signed jewelry designs also may have come to America once their lifetime in the London store was over for the season and became last year's merchandise. Another tag line that stood out in jewelry descriptions in old Harrods catalogues was, "Made exclusively for Harrods." Wouldn't it make sense to mark such jewelry "HAR"?

While costume jewelry originating in America 40 and 50 years ago did cover the full gamut of subjects, HAR and CFW jewelry taken together has an accent that seems much more British-French-African. A relationship may have existed between Worth and Schiaparelli as well, and possibly Worth with Carnegie for a period of time. An enameled Frenchman artist brooch with matching earrings, purchased in an antiques mall, was tagged by the dealer as being "unsigned Schiaparelli" according to its owner. The very same French artist, resembling Dali, is a large charm on a HAR bracelet. As for Carnegie, one wonders if her series of French figural vignettes—an artist painting a canvas in Montmartre, a Gendarme, two Apache dancers—might have been conceived by the House of Worth.

Reinad and B. Blumenthal

Luck was again involved at the turn of this century with a first purchase of B.Blumenthal jewelry. The antiques mall dealer suggested on the tag it might be French. That directed research to Europe again, this time for a fact-finding mission that was something of a wild-goose chase.

The Cubist-like Blumenthal rooster pin was so striking, it seemed worth collecting, even not knowing if another piece of Blumenthal would turn up again. Only one BB pin in a world-wide search via the Internet could be located: three graduated-size penguins connected by chains. Next step: researching the name B. Blumenthal, happily an old button manufacturer still in business after 125 years (in 2002). The bad news was, no one at the company knew much about its history. A spokeswoman said each time the company moved around New York and New Jersey after its 1877 founding, they thinned the archives and dumped old records. As for BB jewelry, they'd never heard of it. (A month later, she called back to say they had briefly produced an inexpensive line in the 1970s. But the signed rooster and penguin pins were older than that by 30 years.)

Things looked up the day a second triple-penguins pin, exactly like the first one, popped up on the Internet, this time enameled—and marked Chanel. Suddenly France seemed like the right place to settle in on the Blumenthal front after all. Tracking down two past presidents of Blumenthal helped fill in some blanks: Blumenthal, with an office in Paris many decades earlier, made buttons for both Chanel and Schiaparelli. Didn't it therefore seem reasonable Chanel and Schiap may have made jewelry for Blumenthal? The former execs sent historical literature on the company, and during more interviews one of them mentioned the company was represented in Paris, by the House of Winter.

Consulting Ginger Moro's *European Designer Jewelry* book harvested two references to Francis Winter. Moro noted that along with Gripoix and Rousselet, the Maison Winter was in an elite class of supplier manufacturers who executed or conceived fabulous *bijoux de couture*, the most exceptional fashion jewelry to show with a season's collections. Second, Moro said the great jewelry designer Roger Jean-Pierre was director of the Maison Winter from 1947-58 and produced work with and for Dior, Balmain, Lelong and others. An investigation tracing Jean-Pierre finally yielded his home address and telephone number on the Boulevard Raspail in Paris. Because I had majored in French as an undergrad and lived in France, I was prepared to conduct what would surely be an enlightening interview. The dismal news was pronounced in short order: The great designer had just died.

Research came to a screeching halt until the Brunialtis' *A Tribute to America* was published. The Italian couple learned through archival research in *WWD* that Chanel in script on metal jewelry in 1941 was actually an American company, Chanel Novelty, the retail name an old New York metal house, Reinad, took for its own first retail collection.

It was Reinad, in fact, that made all of Blumenthal's jewelry, probably because Reinad made metal findings and buttons for the garment trade. Broadening into jewelry was only natural. A seminal piece in research was a floral Bakelite and metal dress clip with both the Blumenthal mark and a large stylized R for Reinad. (Reinad sometimes uses the R on designs also signed Mazer, Eisenberg, Hattie Carnegie and Blumenthal.) The company also made jewelry for Lidz Bros., another notions firm, so clearly Reinad must have sewn up a range of jewelry deals with button makers.

Reinad for Eisenberg Original Floral dress clip, pot metal, RS accents, large molded ruby glass dome, double-signed with both Reinad's R and Eisenberg Original, 1941, 3-3/4", **$300-$500** because of double mark.

Floral dress clip by Reinad for Blumenthal, brass with molded red plastic petals, signed B. Blumenthal & Co., 2-1/4", **$50.**

Charles F. Worth crown pin, brass with marbled faux jade cabochons and pearls, signed CFW, 1955-65, 2", **$50.**

Rooster pin, enameled metal with tiny faux pearls, signed CFW, 1960s, 1-3/4", **$25.**

Thistle pin, matching clip earrings, emerald pave-set RS in antiqued brass setting, signed HAR, 1955-65, 2-1/4", **$50.**

Charles F. Worth Witch Doctor pin (from related series), finely cast brass, enamel, Bakelite, signed CFW, 1950s, 2", **$300.** (Each character in this five-piece group is signed CFW, but less well-crafted, unsigned 1960s versions of shiny goldtone plating and matte black enamel also exist, possibly wholesaled by Worth to another company.)

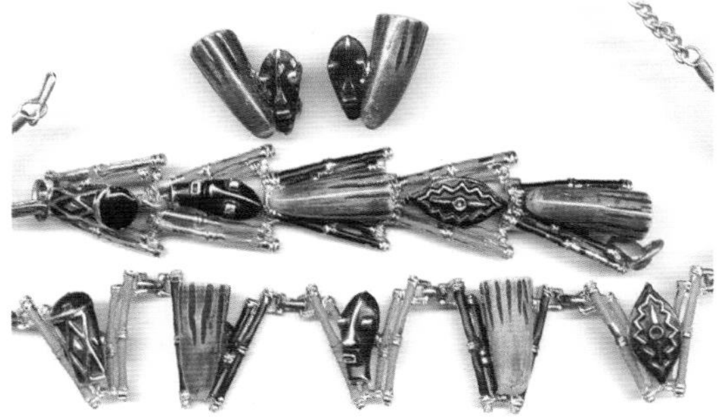

African tribal natives parure (bracelet, necklace, earrings), enameled metal and Bakelite, unsigned Chas. F. Worth, 1950s, 1-1/2" deep, **$750-$1,000.**

Bracelet with African native pendant charm, gold-plated metal and Bakelite chunks plus Medicine Man or Witch Doctor charm, unsigned (probably Chas. F. Worth), 1950s, 2" charm, **$100.**

Egyptian Cleopatra-Caesar figural bracelet, enameled metal and Bakelite, unsigned Charles F. Worth,1-1/4" deep, 1950s, **$500.** Varied matching earrings not shown. Possibly inspired by production of "Cleopatra."

Cuban Drummers-Dancers figural bracelet, enameled metal and Bakelite, unsigned Charles F. Worth, 1950s, 1-1/4" deep, **$500.** Varied matching earrings not shown. Possibly inspired by the Havana scene in "Guys & Dolls."

Cambodian queen brooch, gilded metal, large faceted stone accent, signed Eisenberg, date uncertain, 2-1/2", **$250**. Use of large accent stone in this design suggests Reinad for Eisenberg piece, especially in light of their established relationship. *Photo by Brenda Duff.*

Crown pin by Reinad for Blumenthal, gunmetal setting with multi-cut pastes, signed B. Blumenthal Inc., 1938-42, 2", **$75-$150.**

Floral fur clip of pot metal with chains and marbled poured-glass rocks, unsigned, early Reinad, probably for Eisenberg garments, 1938-42, 6-1/2", **$500.**

Flower pin by Reinad for the Benjamin Blumenthal button company, brass metal with emerald and peridot RS, signed B. Blumenthal Inc., 1938-42, 3-1/4", **$50.**

"Josephine Baker" pin, reversed profile of well-known clip by Reinard, pot metal, chain and marbeled blue cabochons, signed Edw. Stempa, 1938-42, 5", **$500.** *Photo by Ann Mitchell Pitman.*

CHAPTER 16  Figurals Speak for Self Expression

Identity Jewelry

If tackling *The NY Times* Crossword Puzzle is a favorite way to spend precious leisure time, figural pins are available as souvenirs of the hours solvers have given to pondering the answer for "Proustian passion."

That's true for every hobby imaginable: knitting, gardening, wine tasting, stamp collecting, bowling or restoring vintage cars. Hobby figurals have their deepest roots in the Middle Ages, with club or guild membership pins, badges that announced to the world that someone was part of a group devoted to this activity or that specialization.

Mailman delivering letters fur clip, enameled, gilded metal with RS pave mailbag, unsigned, 1938-42, 2", **$100.**

Personal expression or identity jewelry isn't limited to pastime pins, which evolved into career or vocation pins in the 1980s, and at the same time into increasingly popular name-symbol figurals as well: women named Rose choosing rose pins, or the Byrd family buying bird brooches.

The variety of career pins burgeoned in the '90s, especially in real-estate sales motifs. Myriad house brooches serve as conversation pieces; agents could boldly proclaim themselves "No. 1 in Sales" with dollar signs pouring out of a house's chimney – right on their lapels. The number of career-related figural pins flourished to the point it seemed every jewelry company manufactured them.

But vintage pins could be discovered in every career permutation too, from old-fashioned typewriter fur clips for writers to mailmen pins delivering love letters, perfect for postal workers.

Some trends had a major impact on personal-expression jewelry, none more so than the Red Hat Society, a club with a philosophy of life suggesting women over 50 should embrace the eccentric facets of their personalities, live every day to the fullest, and just have fun. The concept is symbolized by the red hats women in the society sport, so it wasn't long before those colorful chapeaux found their way to jewelry. Different themes surrounding the trademark red hat abound.

While the 1970s was dubbed the Me Decade, the popularity of personal-expression jewelry in the 1990s into the 21st Century suggests these years be called the See Me Decade. Women (and men, mostly via cufflinks and tie pins) seem to want to proclaim their affiliations even more colorfully and proudly.

Personal expression jewelry occasionally causes controversy, never more than with the American flag icon. After Sept. 11, when sales of flag pins skyrocketed, some name-calling ensued when skeptics said just wearing a flag pin was no proof of anyone's patriotism. While a country's iconic symbols usually remain in the realm of political and patriotic jewelry, they become motifs of personal expression too, as with the 21st-Century wartime revival of the Peace sign.

Record album dress clip brooch, copper-plated metal, signed Ernest Steiner, 1940s, 1-1/2", **$50.**

Lady gardener carrying parasol and watering can, 3-D stick figure, unsigned, painted brass, 1930s, 2-1/2", **$50.**

Stamp brooch, vintage 1966 French stamp with Daumier illustration in metal frame, glass encasement, wired bead trim, illegible mark, 1980s, 2-7/8", **$50.**

Writer's typewriter fur clip, enameled metal, RS accents, mechanical roller, highly detailed, 1938-42, unmarked, 1-1/2", **$150.**

Red Hat Society brooch, RS accents and red epoxy on bright gold-plated metal, unsigned, 2006, 2", **$10.**

"Knit One, Purl One" pin, pot metal, replicated from Hummel art of that name, unmarked (sometimes signed Silson), 1940, 2-1/2", **$50.**

'57 Chevy with cat couple under crescent moon, novel figural for cat lovers and classic-car enthusiasts; black enamel on silver-plated metal, signed AJC (Alan Jewelry Mfg.), 1980s, 2-1/4", **$25.**

Crossword puzzle pin, enameled and incised gold-plated metal with RS accents, unsigned, 1980s, 1-1/2", **$25.**

CHAPTER 17  One Collection Reigns Supreme

Crowning Glory

Crowns are one of the oldest figural motifs in history. Modern collectors appreciate the classic diadem as much as their distant ancestors did, and interest has never flagged in creating them, whether for têtes, fêtes, even pets. A bejeweled crown brooch on a lapel has always been classy—maybe slightly less so now that factories in China manufacture thousands of them daily for export, some 6 inches wide and totally over the top in terms of glitzy "glam." That creates a different aesthetic from the heavy old gilded sterling crowns loaded with liquidy cabochons. But who's judging?

Hanna Bernhard, 4", **$1,000.**

Passionate crown-pin collectors are legion. Men may be bedazzled as well. For one such smitten fellow, it all began when he accompanied a pageant-loving pal to a Miss Texas competition. Before the show began, they noticed a vendor in the lobby selling event souvenirs. Dennis' friend purchased a small crown, which was the seed of a collection that blossomed profusely.

Like many people, Dennis had sampled the joy of collecting as a child, after his grandfather gave him a small group of stamps. But he couldn't guess where his love of hunting and gathering would lead. "My friend passed away, and knowing my interest in collecting, he willed his collection to me," says the Texas educator who has enlarged the royal jewels to 1,000-plus pieces.

The crown affair hasn't grown dull at all. "It's a lot of fun," Dennis says. "There's a sense of accomplishment that's hard to explain after you look for, locate and acquire a key item. It helps to be something of a bulldog, refusing to give up until you get it. And in the process I've learned a lot about jewelry, the manufacturers, designers, and where to shop."

Asked to name his favorite crowns, he responds good-naturedly, "Choosing favorites isn't a fair question; every parent knows you're not supposed to pick favorites among your children." Dennis did say, "My favorites don't necessarily include the most famous designers, the most expensive or the rarest, although my Hanna Bernhard crowns are an exception to that. I look for crowns that are elegant, stylish, and well-designed." Those may not sound like the words of a high-school computer-science teacher who now works with computer teachers in the school district's curriculum division, but jewelry has always gotten people to wax poetic.

Corralling crowns isn't all fun and games, though. "Managing a collection this size is challenging. It becomes impossible to rely upon memory to know exactly what you have, so," he advises, "consider creating a data base that includes pictures, dates, locations of acquisition, the purchase price and other useful information.

It also helps to divide a collection into categories, such as "signed" versus "unsigned" pieces; motifs, such as plain crowns, crowns with hearts or shields, people wearing crowns, animals wearing crowns; and type, whether brooches, pendants, earrings, cufflinks, rings or sets.

"Crown prices vary greatly, depending on factors from manufacturer to size, materials to rarity and where you purchase the item. Great bargains abound, but sometimes you have to reach deep in your pocket to get that piece you just must have. For instance," Dennis recalls, "a beautiful Coro crown at an antiques show cost $5; a rare Eisenberg king and queen fur-clip chatelaine cost $1,500.

"I've found collecting crowns an exciting hobby. The field is open to anyone, including those like me who knew nothing about jewelry in the beginning. I've also been able to meet some very wonderful people in the process."

Something to Crown About

His most unusual crown is a brooch and cuff link set. "It was sold to me as HAR, although it is unsigned. The brooch is a little man in a brown robe, wearing a crown, sitting in front of a golden tree with dangling pearls. His arms are in an unusual position, as if playing an invisible flute. One cuff link shows the same man, and the other portrays the man standing."

Royal Rarities

Called "rare, rare, rare" is Dennis' Eisenberg Original matching king and queen fur clips with the original chatelaine. "Most people have never seen another one," Dennis notes.

Royal Oddities

A recent acquisition is Dennis' Coro crown chatelaine. "The crown pin is fairly standard, but linked to it by two chains is a rooster holding a dagger. I've never seen these symbols used together, but evidently some monarchies used the rooster to represent watchfulness or vigilance because it rises early in the morning."

Royal Names

These aren't what you'd dub commoners, but we asked Dennis for his list of marks most frequently found on his crowns. They are:

Art, Barclay, B. David, Boucher, Butler & Wilson, Carnegie, Castlecliff, Coro, Corocraft, Eisenberg, Florenza, Haskell, JJ, Jolie, Jomaz, Kramer, KJL, Lisner, Napier, Ora, Rosenstein, Sporrong, Swarovski, Swoboda, Trifari, Weiss.

Off With Their Heads!

Asked about his most disappointing purchase, Dennis declared, "I purchased a piece by Florenza on the Internet, described as a topaz stone topped by a crown. When it arrived, the stone was jet black, and the top looked like a sugar bowl lid. Moral of the story: always get pictures first."

Where's That Crown?

Some unexpected crowns are elusive. "I own the classic Trifari sterling crown in the small size in amber, but the larger one eludes me. This is probably because the other colors were more popular than amber, so fewer were made."

Rave Review: 'Fessing Up to His Faves

"Okay, my all-time favorite is the classic Trifari [see main story] in all of its various flavors. The classic Trifari is the one exception to my 'no duplicates' rule: I have tried to collect the small crown, 1-1/4", and the large crown, 1-7/8", in sterling, plus the 1-1/2" medium-size non-sterling crown, with each of the stone colors ever available: red, white, blue, green, purple, violet and amber. I believe it is simply the nicest crown of all."

Dennis says the rest of his favorites list changes depending on what day it is, but today it includes this even dozen (pictured left to right, top to bottom):

1) unmarked crown with red and clear baguettes

2) unmarked crown with red and green enamel

3) Weiss crown

4) Trifari crown

5) LCL sterling crown

6) unmarked crown with red enamel and faux pearls

7) unmarked crown with pink and clear rhinestones

8) Boucher crown

9) Butler and Wilson crown

10) unmarked crown with blue baguettes

11) Trifari crown

12) Sardi crown

(Soon after making the list, he found a Dior crown that trumped all.)

Blumenthal, 2", **$150.**

Bogoff Miss America-style, 2", **$185.**

Boucher, 1-3/4", **$210.**

Butler-Wilson Sterling, 2-3/4", **$195.**

Coro Golden Jubilee set, 2", **$200.**

Castlecliff set, 2", **$200.**

Corocraft, 1-3/4", **$195.**

Eisenberg, 1-1/3", **$275.**

Eisenberg, 1-3/4", **$185.**

Jeanne, 2", **$185.**

Margot, 1", **$200.**

Mazer, 1-1/4", **$200.**

Mazer, 2-1/4", **$250.**

Regency, 2", **$195.**

Robert, 1-3/4", **$200.**

Swoboda, 1-3/4", **$175.**

Trifari Sterling set, 2-3/4", **$150.**

Trifari Sterling, 2", **$200.**

Hanna Bernhard, 3-3/4", **$900.**

Vendôme, 2", **$175.**

Vogue, 2-1/2", **$200.**

Weiss, 2", **$195.**

Weiss, 2-1/3", **$250.**

Wendy Gell, 3-1/2", **$200.**

CHAPTER 18 Too Charming to Call Creepy-Crawly

Love Bugs

Women as freaked out by spiders as Diane Keaton was in the movie "Annie Hall" wouldn't hesitate to pin on a jewel-encrusted specimen. Insects and bugs are one of the most popular figural motifs, which is strange when you come to think about it. There are limits, of course, and spider pins with furry legs hit too close to reality to be popular, while Stuart Freeman's *La Cucaraca Christmas* tree pin, despite being almost regally Egyptian, gave some ardent collectors the willies: They couldn't wear cockroaches even if they *were* silver and as sparkly as silver bells.

Butterflies are at the opposite end of the insect spectrum, considered so pretty they are designed, sold and worn in swarms.

At some point every collector owns a bug brooch and decides if she or he will build a collection around it. It may be an old Damascene fly, French plastic katydid or patriotic ladybug that charms and disarms, then tempts the wearer to more (or not). One dealer most new collectors met as they considered collecting centipedes was a woman who gave bugs a good name (and home), the late Joan Vogel Elias.

In some ways her sign-off "Buzzz" word was a gimmick, and in fact she bought and sold every kind of costume jewelry in existence, but she did have a felicitous fondness for this variety of flying thing. JVE, as she was also known, made jewelry her profession long before the Internet was born, but ran with it even wider once she tagged a "www" onto her Absolutely Vintage costume jewelry web business.

There weren't many people who loved the costume-jewelry field more than JVE did, as both dealer and collector, and her relish for rock crystal in a jeweled beetle, or beautiful antique stones in a spider, was deep—and sometimes audible. Liza Amidon got to hear it all during her term as Vogel Elias's assistant, and then took over the business as queen bee at absolutelyvintage.net. "Joan involved me in every aspect of her business, from the smallest detail to the most important decisions, and what started as a two-days-a-week job on the side blossomed into a full-time collaboration," Amidon says. "I had a good foundation in antiques and collectibles, but knew little about vintage jewelry when I began. Joan was an incredible teacher, and I wound up counting her among the very best friends I've ever had."

Alluring insect brooch, faux moonstones, and pave-set rhinestones, 1940s, unsigned, **$50-$100.**

JVE's bugs tell as much about Joan Buzz as any human being can, whether collectors want to remember her or meet her for the first time. Liza Amidon served as tour guide and translator during a walk among the insect population.

Hovering Cartoon Bee, 1940s, unsigned (occasionally turns up marked H. Pomerantz), purple glass lozenge wings, clear pave-set rhinestones, big googly eye, 2-1/2", **$85-$95.** "This was one of Joan's favorite bugs to wear in the summertime. She wore this one a *lot*, probably one of the most-worn of all."

Art Glass Beetle Buckle-Pin, Victorian, 2-1/8", stamped metal and art glass, converted to brooch from buckle, priceless. "It didn't matter what an object was, if it was beautiful, Joan found a way to make it into a pin or earrings. No matter how big or outrageous, she was not afraid to wear it—and wear it well."

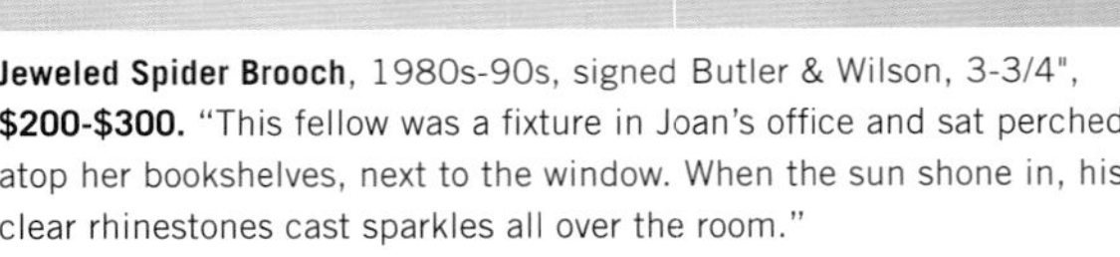

Jeweled Spider Brooch, 1980s-90s, signed Butler & Wilson, 3-3/4", **$200-$300.** "This fellow was a fixture in Joan's office and sat perched atop her bookshelves, next to the window. When the sun shone in, his clear rhinestones cast sparkles all over the room."

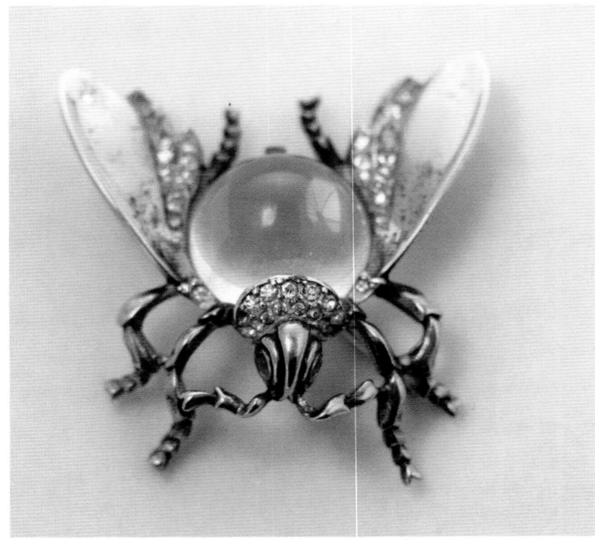

Jelly Belly Fly Pin, signed Trifari, gilded metal and Lucite, 1940s, 1-7/8", **$300-$400.** "Part of Joan's cherished personal collection. What vintage jewelry collection is complete without a jelly belly or two? Joan didn't often wear her jelly bellies, but she treasured them."

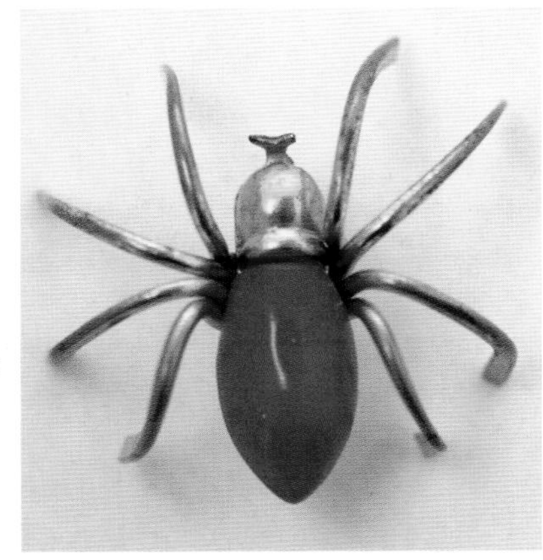

Lipstick-Red Spider Pin, 1930s, Bakelite and brass, 2", **$75-$95.** "Joan had a horde of these in various colors and displayed them grouped together in her studio. She also wore them around Halloween. Joan was an important part of the local haunted house, though she didn't 'dress up,' per se. After the youngsters were scared silly, they would meet Joan outside, where they delighted in seeing what creepy critters she was wearing that year."

Giant Mothra, wood with carved root-beer Lucite wings, 1940, 4-1/8", **$95-$125.** "Joan adored vintage Lucite-wood figurals, and this big, bold guy was right up her alley. It was freed for sale when Joan went through one of her 'I have too many things and need to sell some of my personal stuff' phases, which was usually followed by an 'I shouldn't have sold that, where will I ever find another?' phase. I think the only reason she finally decided to part with him was that she couldn't find earrings to match."

Contemporary Trembler Dragonfly Pin, Heidi Daus for Jim Walters, black diamante in japanned setting, 3-3/4", **$50-$75.** "Here are three of Joan's favorite things all in one: japanned metal, a figural, and a trembler. This dragonfly was a staple of her darker winter outfits. When he wasn't being worn, like so many of the others, he lived in her bedroom with other beautiful jewelry, displayed on one of her mannequins.

Praying Mantis, unsigned, 1940, enameled pot metal, "homage" version of Marcel Boucher's mantis, 3", **$95-$110.** "The praying mantis was very special to Joan because it reminded her so much of her late father, Milton Vogel. Joan was very close to him, and his failing health was a major reason she brought her business to the Internet, so she could be available to take care of him."

The Meaning of Moths and More

Like many living things, insects and bugs are symbols of values we assigned to them long ago. No need to heed.

Butterfly: Transformation, rejuvenation, beauty, joy, love.

Moth: Ugliness, plainness, insanity.

Ladybug: Good luck.

Bee: Chastity, industriousness, charity, selflessness.

Spider: Treachery, death.

Ant: Hard work, teamwork.

Grasshopper: Frivolity, irresponsibility.

Big in Bugdom

The five most desirable bugs in the insect world include:

1. Boucher praying mantis
2. Eisenberg Original Fly
3. Iradj Moini grasshopper
4. Trifari jelly belly spider
5. Schreiner large Lucite butterfly

A Controversial Grasshopper

Jewelry designs had to be altered so little before they could be legally copied by another company that vintage lawsuits stick out like sore thumbs in costume-jewelry history. This fiddling grasshopper from Aesop's Fable of "The Ant & The Grasshopper" is one such exception. The 1940 original, as documented in the Brunialtis' English-language book *A Tribute to America*, was a gold-plated trembler by Castlecliff. Evidently Brier Manufacturing made a version for Woolworth's that was close enough to the Willard Markle design, Castlecliff founder Clifford Furst was able to sue Brier, Woolworth and Crystal Novelty successfully for design patent infringement. The Woolworth version is shown here.

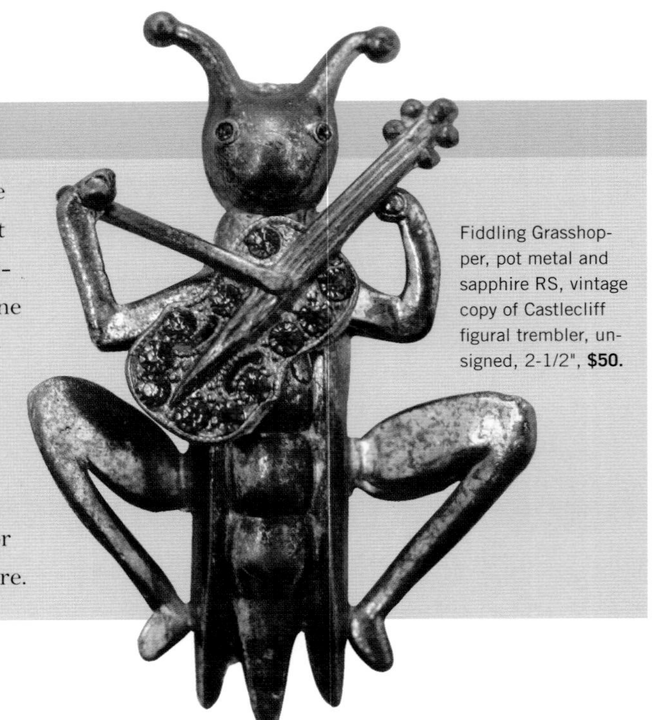

Fiddling Grasshopper, pot metal and sapphire RS, vintage copy of Castlecliff figural trembler, unsigned, 2-1/2", **$50.**

Ladybug tapestry brooch, seed-bead florals, signed Ian St. Gielar and Stanley Hagler N.Y.C., 2006, 4", **$150.**

Gilded Sterling bug fur clip, large faceted glass stone body, unsigned, 1942-46, 2-1/2", **$100.**

Frosted Butterfly pin, pave-set RS thorax, frosted plastic leaves, signed Kenneth Lane, 1999, **$50-$100.**

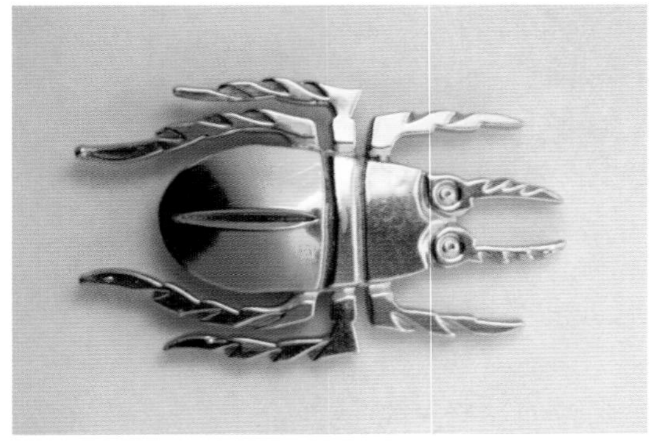

Large Golden Beetle brooch, dimensional, possibly by a studio artist, 1950-60s, 3", **$100-$150.**

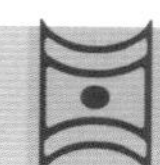

CHAPTER 19 It's Hard to Figure Some Pins

Body Beautiful

It's easy to understand why the Victorians, as well as their modern-day counterparts, were smitten with brooches in the form of graceful hands delicately holding flowers, mirrors, hearts and any other feminine object.

It's less obvious why jewelry companies ever started making bare feet. But they did. Perhaps the *pieds* were related to the romance and popularity of Robinson Crusoe. Bare feet must have a *raison d'être* in something more than portraying shoeless appendages.

When it comes to body parts, just about every one was covered by jewelry makers: lips for sure, eyes like crazy, but even legs, the torso, tootsies and an endless variety of hands. Eisenberg made what everyone thought might be the only vintage 3-D bust, in the form of a dress clip dubbed the Marilyn Monroe, but designer Ruth Kamke told Eisenberg historian Bobye Syverson it was simply an abstract form and not MM's shapely figure. (In a way it is stranger as an abstract form than as Norma Jean's bosom.)

Naturally, Surrealist jewelry designer Salvador Dali featured an eye in the repertoire, his *Eye of Time,* a large jeweled watch clip with blue iris shedding a tear. The house of Chanel created an especially glitzy window to the soul as well, and it too is dripping with jeweled tears. (My motto: Life is cruel; buy jewels.) Artist Stuart Freeman, who quit making jewelry more than five years ago, much to the consternation of collectors, cast an eye brooch that is unmistakably the peeper of Barbie. Freeman in fact issued an entire line of Barbie doll jewelry for adults and well-heeled kids, including a full, dimensional sterling face ring of Malibu Barbie, high-heel pump necklace stored in a tiny metal mesh shoebox, and even a Barbie torso pendant.

The most common motif is likely the human hand, mentioned earlier, from delicate Victorian renditions to more aggressive expressions of Thumbs Up! or Thumbs Down! One Silson pair of two gilded fur clips actually portrays the fingers of a man and a woman, close to intertwining. (This is determined by the fact one hand has polished fingernails while the other doesn't, and the way the clip mechanisms are configured, with one hand turned up and the other pinned down in a different direction. In the past they have mistakenly been described as scary freak hands belonging to an unseen ghoul because the fingers are slightly splayed and usually pictured next to each other, as if playing an organ.)

Female Torso brooch, very Venus de Milo, gold-plated metal, unsigned, 1970s, 3-3/8", **$50-$100.**

Finally, sensual, red-painted lips prove another popular feature in face jewelry and are still being made today. Dali likely designed the most famous *levres* ever, encrusted with ruby stones and baring, quite literally, "pearly whites." The original brooch, *Ruby Lips*, made in 1949, is shown on the cover of the book *Jewelry Talk*.

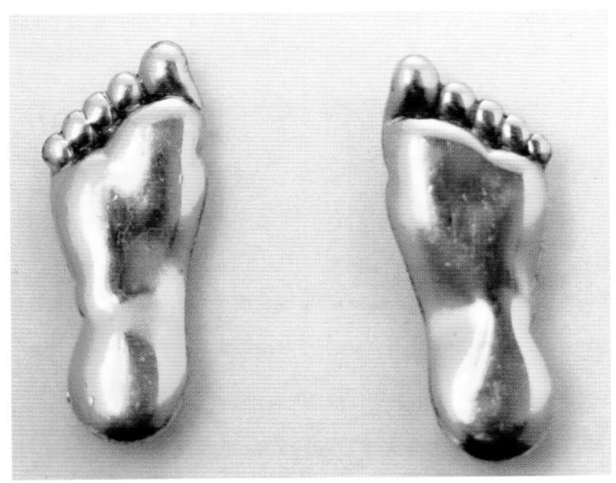

Footsie fur clips, bare feet in finely plated, well-cast metal, signed Deja, 1940s, 1-1/2", **$250** pair.

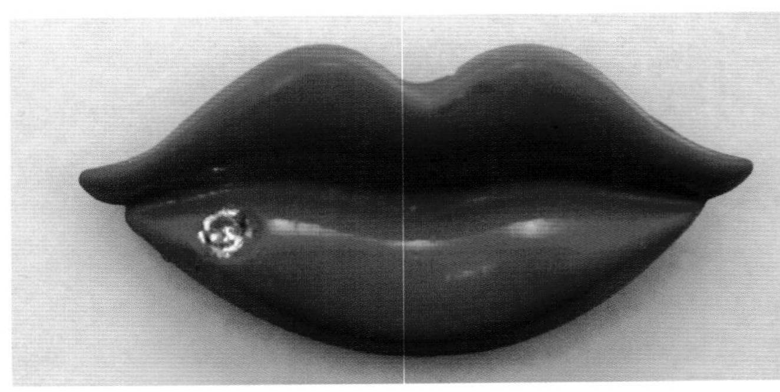

Jeweled Lips, red-enameled gold-plated metal, beauty mark-like RS-accent, unsigned, 1970s, 2", **$50.**

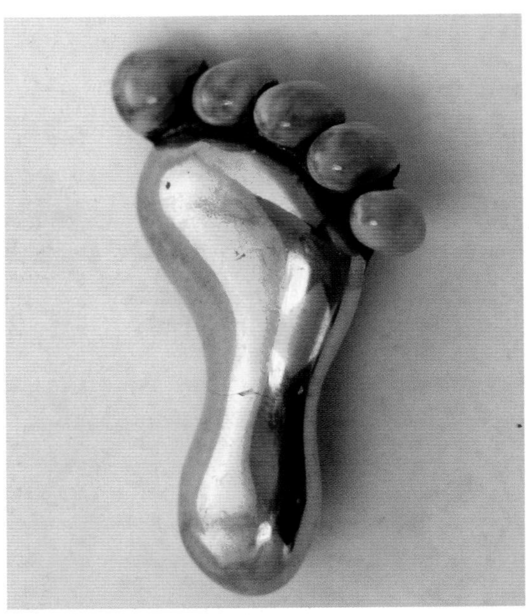

Cartoonish Foot pin, gilded and enameled ceramic, unsigned, 1960s, 2", **$10.**

Teardrops Eye pin, jeweled, gold-plated metal, bezel-set pastes, RS pave-set retina with entwined CC logo, faux pearls and RS teardrop attached to delicate chains, signed Chanel and marked Made In France, 2000s, 2-1/2", **$400.**

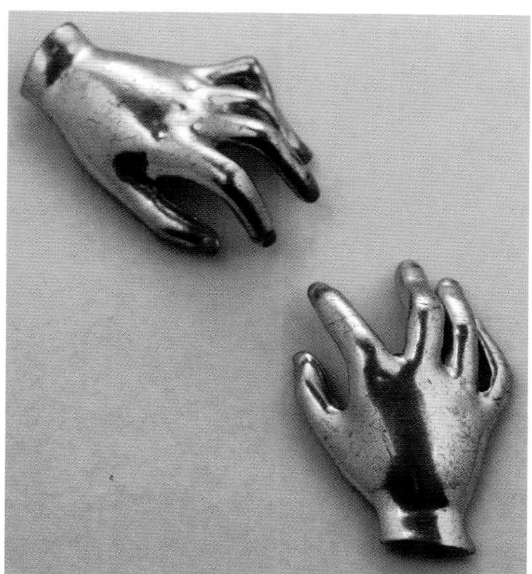

Almost-Touching Hands fur clips, gilded metal, enameled fingernails define woman's hand, direction of clip mechanisms dictates placement, may be worn with fingers entwined (often mistaken for "creepy man's hands"), 1940s, signed Silson, 1-5/8" each, **$250 pair.**

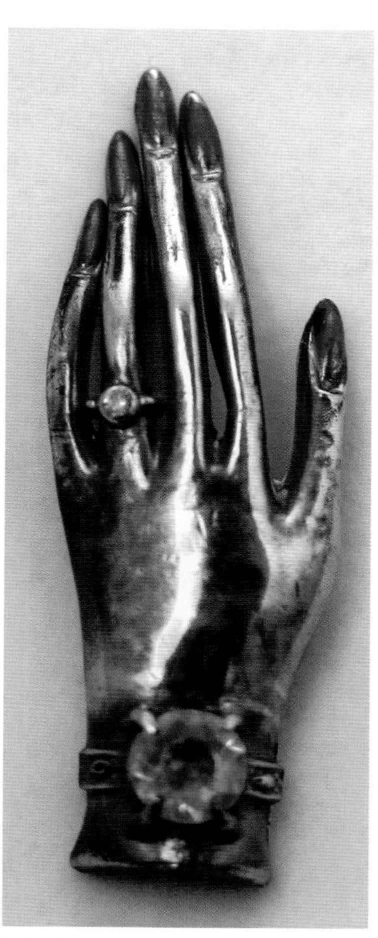

Lady's Hand brooch, gold-plated metal, jewel and enamel accents, unsigned Coro design, 1940s, 2-1/2", **$25.**

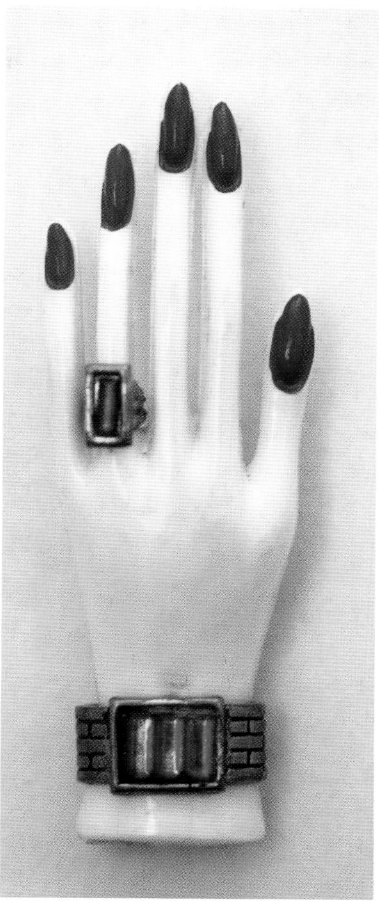

Elegant Hand pin, ivory celluloid, blood-red painted fingernails, wire bracelet and ring, plastic ruby jewels, unsigned, 1930-40s, 2-5/8", **$25-$50.**

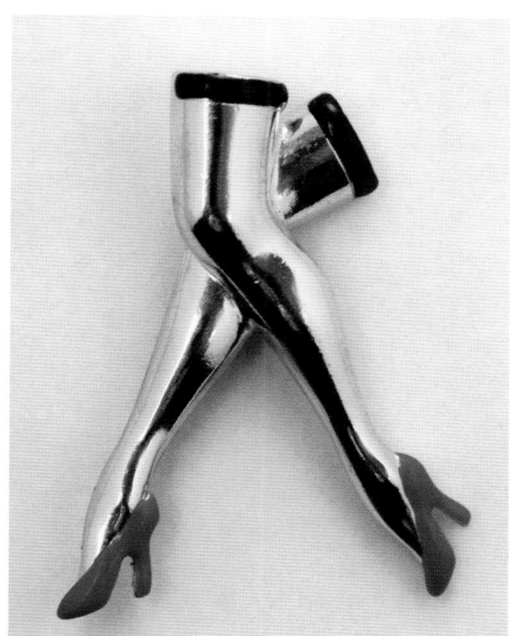

Pair of Shapely Legs pin, enameled pumps, black stockings defined, gold-plated metal, unsigned, 1960s, 2-1/2", **$50-$100.**

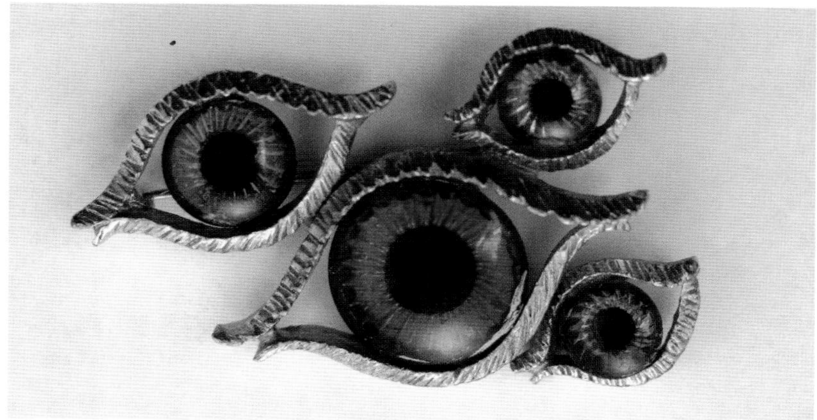

Four Eyes pin, glass in gold-plated metal frame, signed Kramer, 1970s, 2-3/8", **$150.**

CHAPTER 20  Pins as Promotional Pitches

Selling It

In the 1940s, '50s and '60s, no company would have dreamed of the nerve to ask the public to pay for products with the companies' names on them, so naturally, promotional pieces were basically free (and often kitschy) premiums. Back then, any business enterprise would have been ecstatic to get consumers to wear things plastered with the designer, retailer or manufacturer name on them, but why would anyone wear such commercial hype?

Skelley Carburetor Tiger brooch ("Put a Tiger in Your Tank"), rubber and plastic, marked Multiple Toymakers N.Y. and Skelley Performance Carburetion, 1950s, 3-3/4", **$150.**

It was tacky, almost vulgar, until Calvin Klein got the glitterati to swear nothing came between them and their Calvins. Almost overnight people seemed to become walking billboards—and we were paying for the billboards ourselves.

Perfume companies probably offer the bulk of advertising jewelry premiums, those familiar "gifts with purchase." An Eiffel Tower figural pin accompanied one Yves St. Laurent scent (probably Paris), cologne makers from Oscar de la Renta to Gaultier issued eponymous mini-perfume bottle brooches, and so on. The list is endless, with "free" figurals in the form of everything from lips and eyes to Christmas trees and flowers.

Cosmetics makers were always in on the same act, especially in lipsticks. Revlon issued many plastic promo pins. One of the most desirable ad-related pins in the jewelry world is a metal 1930s Lucien Lelong triple lipstick fur clip, with three mini tubes of lip color designed as a conductor's coin changer. Called Quick Change, it is a brilliant cosmetics-jewelry novelty that typically sells for more than $100 when it appears.

Certainly Dior seems to have the biggest ego in the fashion world, with its name pasted over everything, umbrellas to undies. The French fashion house's relentless marketing of its name in jewelry is something to behold, with Dior ID bracelets, necklaces, and countless versions of every figural letter in its monicker. Many of them are beautiful; at least one is a work of art.

Kids love free stuff and advertisers know it. One of the most sought-after promo pins is a cheap, large plastic Christmas tree pin that announces Woolworth's as the Ideal Toys mecca. Children themselves might not care about this Fifties fright of a brooch, but oh how adult collectors get into the spirit of finding one. When they do, it might take $250 to make it their own.

Two of the oddest promo pins to stumble across could be the official Christmas Tree pin badge announcing the wearer is with the "Secret Service," and a huge orange tiger brooch for Skelley Carbueration, a big cat with plastic head and rubber body. Gas station premiums were the greatest, especially when families traveled the roads seeing the USA together. That was a different time, when filling stations made presents of jewelry, dolls, and at Citgo, such exotica as rare model cars made in France. Lucky is the lass who still has her 1926 Isotta Fraschini.

Examples of other products promo'd via jewelry include Longaberger Baskets, Campbell's Soup, Lowenbrau beer, Mack Trucks, The Olympic Games, Beanie Babies, the Baseball Hall of Fame, Mattel Barbie Dolls, cities from Las Vegas to Paris and thousands of other products and places.

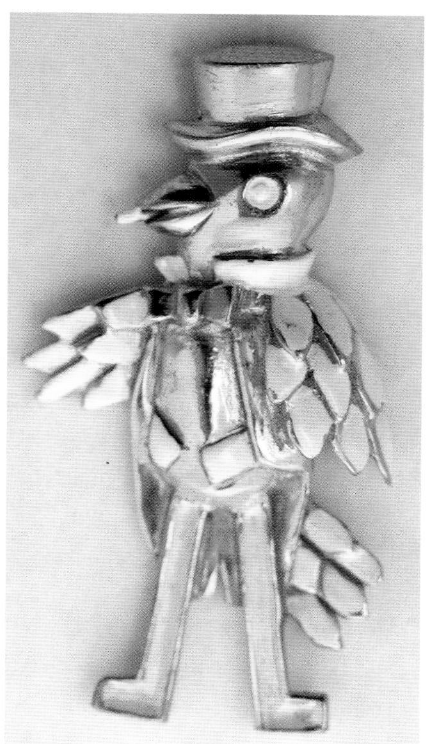

Willie the KOOL Penguin fur clip, cigarette mascot in formalwear, ready for nightclubbing; enameled, gold-plated metal, 1930s, 2-1/4", **$250.**

Woolworth and Ideal Toy Christmas Headquarters tree pin, plastic, signed Stoffel Seals, Tuckahoe, N.Y., 1950s, 3-1/4", **$250.**

Revlon Cosmetics pin promoting lipstick and nail lacquer, celluloid, 1940s, 2-1/8", **$50.**

Coca-Cola Christmas tree pin, enameled metal tac-pin, signed CR, The Coca-Cola Co., 1996, 1-1/4", **$10-$30.**

CHAPTER 21  JEWELRY COMMEMORATES EVENTS

Remember It Always

A fascinating category to collect, especially for history buffs, commemorative jewelry recalls centuries of important events and people, whether Lord Nelson's victory at Trafalgar, the fight against AIDS or America's last morning of 21st-Century "innocence," Sept. 11, 2001. One motif portrayed in brooches since then is the Manhattan skyline with the World Trade Center towers still upright and invincible. Judith Jack and other companies issued WTC pins showing pre-disaster cityscapes, as well as jeweled flags and flag-colored hearts as icons of renewed patriotism. (The all-purpose AIDS ribbon also went red, white and blue.) As soon as historians began comparing the devastating attack on New York with Pearl Harbor as an event in U.S. history with equal impact, collectors started searching in earnest for jewelry commemorating the 1941 fiasco, with Coro's pearl-studded vintage pin at the top of the list.

If any person, place or date has meaning, someone made jewelry to celebrate it: Coronation confections (especially for England's Elizabeth II); Charles Lindbergh's gem-studded Spirit of St. Louis airplane to mark the first non-stop transatlantic flight; sparkling Man in the Moon brooch looking pleased to have an American flag planted on his pate (the reverse reads "July 20, 1969"); or sparkling champagne flutes bubbling over with pearls to toast the new Millennium.

Twin Towers Christmas tree pin, metal and enamel, unsigned, 2002, 2-1/2", **$25-$50.**

My Fair Lady figural cufflinks, opening-night ticket stubs, fit together (as if torn), signed 1957 CBS (by jewelry maker BSK; these are the only pieces from the series not signed BSK). Text print on "tickets" says "March 21, 1957, Orchestra, $8.05, 1st Row, Seat 1." Original retail price, $2; **$75-$125.**

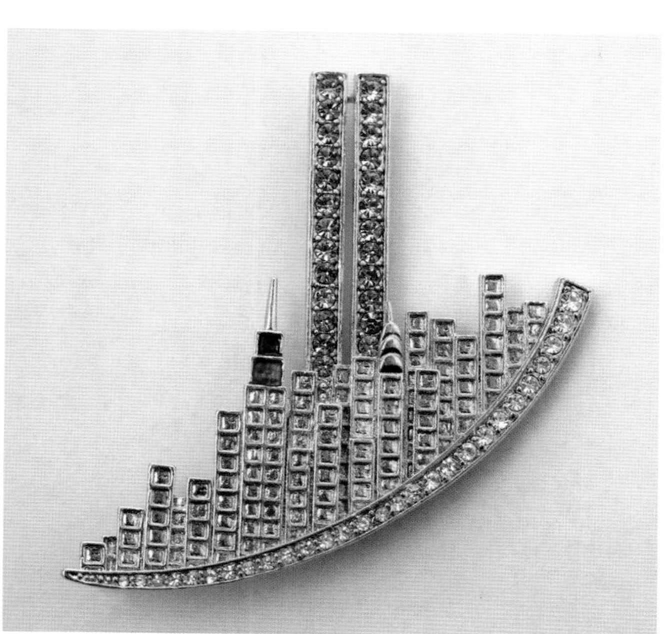

Twin Towers pin, silver-plated metal, sky-blue rhinestones, unsigned, 2002, 2-1/2", **$10-$25.**

Beatles memorabilia, Paul McCartney guitar pin, black plastic with photo, unmarked (no longer attached to original card), 1964-65, 4-1/4", **$25.**

Beatle Beetle pin with Union Jack colors, enameled metal, signed HAR, probably destined for Harrods' Way-In Shop, 1964-67, 1-1/8", **$25-$50.**

Man in the Moon pin, winking in approval at American flag being planted on his pate; goldtone metal, enamel, with rhinestone flag; marked "July 20, 1969," commemorating the Moon Landing; signed, 1969, 1-3/8", **$25-$50.**

CHAPTER 22

Clockwise from Top

Timing is Everything

Overall, men are wiser to watches than women. That's why a familiar sound inside antiques malls is the male of the species asking over and over, up and down the aisles, "Got any old watches?" The workmanship and history are alluring, but so is the tick-tock of big bucks. One ardent suitor of vintage timepieces tells of the day, at a dusty flea market, he uncovered an old Patek-Philippe. He trembled all the way home after paying $10 for it because he didn't know if he had the model worth $30,000 or $60,000.

Jelly Belly Crow fur clip watch, rare, colored Lucite belly (apple-juice) and beak (red-orange), polychrome cabochon navette tail feathers, faceted baguette jeweled feet and top feathers, watch face head, movement marked Chase Watch Corp., jewelry marked D.O. Pat Pend., 1938-42, 2-1/2", **$1,000-$1,500.**

If only *one* kind of crystal and jewel sounds exciting (and they have nothing to do with the hour), if dials and movement bring on no *frisson* of anticipation, ordinary figural watches may prove, minute by minute, much more fun, if not quite as lucrative. Serious watch collectors diss this jewelry category, since typically, they say, Providence jewelry manufacturers bought Swiss movements by the truckloads just to pop into their watch jewelry with not even a second thought to quality. Because? Jewelry design was the thing; movements were an afterthought. The movements were cheap and plentiful then, just as today watches made in China with quartz movements are popped into pendants. The movements in old brooches and fur clips were often the cheaper 7-jewel types. Better 15- and 17-jewel movements went into more expensive jewelry, such as the jeweled sterling Pennino pieces.

In vintage pin-on figural watches, dials always dangle upside down so women wearing them could see the hour correctly when held up from the lapel. One watch specialist says watch brooches were most popular in the 1940s and 1950s, during most of the heyday of American costume jewelry. Some are from the 1930s into the early war years, but evidently the Depression didn't do much for sales of watch pins because Thirties models are less commonly found.

What *is* crystal clear, though, is the attitude of jewelry designers when it came to watch figurals. Perhaps the serious matter of time made them feel especially frivolous, most of all in the Forties. A scarecrow fur clip calling to mind 1939's screen hit "The Wizard of Oz" got the gift of a timepiece for his face and a large round crystal for a head (a "ball watch"). Everything from down Mexico Way seemed exotic and mysterious, so a large, colorful Mexican musician strummed a guitar with an Art Deco watch face. A Hekyll-or-Jekyll crow of colored Lucite jelly belly wings, beak and belly is a fur clip with attitude—and a watch in his head. Like the women of the 1950s, who became more suburban and shorter-coiffed than their former cosmopolitan city-girl selves, the figural watches of the next decade appear tamer, in simple bells and less inspired objects. The Har genie watch is one exception.

Ticking timepieces weren't the only incorporation of passing hours into jewelry. All kinds of cute movable-hands motifs turned up. One especially clever idea was the changing placement of hands on a clock-faced brooch to the hour of an appointment to prevent a late arrival. So many decorative, nonworking watch faces appeared in brooches, it's clear the passage of time was on everyone's mind.

While watches still have cachet today, whether to suggest wealth, power or style, most people we see simply look to their cell phones or iPods whenever they really want to know what time it is.

Scarecrow Ball Watch fur clip, enameled, gilded metal frame serving as hat and torso, Wizard of Oz, watch marked Harman in ball crystal (workings exposed on reverse), unsigned, 1939-41, 2-1/2", **$200+.**

"Sunburst Watch" pin, heavy sterling silver with glittering multi-cut jewels, 17-jewel Swiss movement, Art Deco face, watch and brooch signed Pennino, 1947, 2-1/4", **$250-$450.**

Bell Lapel pin with watch, 2-1/4", unsigned, 1950s, **$25.**

Dapper Mexican Musician fur clip watch, festively enameled gilded metal, Swiss movement, watch (marked Fontain) incorporated into banjo, one of a series of musicians, unsigned fur clip, 1940s, 2-1/2", **$200+.**

Scottie Dog faux watch pin, enameled metal and plastic, signed DuBarry, 1940s, 2-1/8", **$25-$50.** (All the DuBarry Cosmetics faux watch faces are set to 8:20.)

Rococo Clock pin, with Art Nouveau-Deco flourishes, nudes flanking-supporting clock face of carved faux onyx with golden accents imitating marcasites; cupids frolic below, woman's bust sits on top, charm tic-toc dangle; stands upright, signed Dalsheim, 1960s, 3", **$50-$100.**

"Be On Time" Appointment Watch pin, white-enameled gilded metal, movable rotating hands, large simulated emerald cabochon accent, openwork clock face suspended from bow, marked with patent number assigned to Willard Markle for Castlecliff, 2-3/4", **$50-$150.**

Oversized Clock pin, garish gold-tone metal, large chatons, black enameled hands set to rendezvous time, unsigned, 1955-65, 2-1/2", **$25.**

Cuckoo Clock fur clip, pot metal, floral motif with bird, fixed clock face, pinecone weights, signed Coro, 1938-40, 3-1/8", **$25-$50.**

Weathervane Clock Tower fur clip, gilded pot metal, enameled clock face, unsigned, 1935-42, 3-1/8", **$50.**

Cuckoo Clock watch pin, gold-tone metal, battery-operated timepiece, marked China, 2-1/4", **$10.**

Date Keeper Clock Face pin, simple gold-plated version of Eisenberg's jeweled faux watch pin, hands revolve and may be set for appointments, signed Eisenberg, date unknown, 2-1/2", **$25-$50.**

Fabulous Fifties Compass pin, black and white enamel on gold-plated metal, unsigned, 1950s, 2-1/2", **$10-$25.**

CHAPTER 23 The Styles of Stein & Pavone

Plastic's Wit

Judy Smith will tell any interested party, when it comes to figural jewelry, plastics are addictive. The longtime collector still enjoys the thrill of the hunt for the perfect piece of plastic jewelry. She opened Baubles-and-Bibelots.com in 2001 to showcase her favorite French designers, Lea Stein and Marie-Christine Pavone, as well as Italian artist Angela Caputi. Smith also collects vintage and new unsigned plastic jewelry, both European and American.

She appreciates the collectibility factor, but also says, "What I love about these plastics is, they add a chic note of pizzazz to any wardrobe. And since they're comfortable and so light to wear, I like them for travel."

The fabrication of figural French plastic pins is a long process. Lea Stein, a French, trained artist, produces jewelry that has been collected for decades under the name Lea Stein Paris. She began making her whimsical, signature pieces of jewelry in 1969, when her husband, Fernand Steinberger, invented a process of laminating layers of rhodoid (cellulose acetate sheets) with interesting textures and colors. The layers, baked overnight with a secret component or ingredient he developed, are cut into shapes for the various designs of jewelry and decorative objects. Look at the side of a pin and as many as 20 layers of cellulose may be seen, bonded together to create the end result.

Fox, 1975-present, 3-3/4", **$75.**

The most recognizable Lea Stein pin of all, Smith says, is the 3-D fox, which has been produced in myriad colors and designs. Lace or metal layers may be incorporated into the celluloid, producing an astounding number of unique textures. The dimensional fox tail is looped from one piece of celluloid. Collector note: Clasps on Stein's pins may be v-shaped and signed Lea Stein Paris or feature tiny, straight clasps signed Lea Stein.

Marie-Christine Pavone's jewelry, on the other hand, is made of galalith, and she too has a menagerie of whimsical cats and quirky animals that acquired a devout following of collectors.

Creating objects from galalith is a complex, time-consuming process. Galalith cannot be molded, which sets it apart from other plastics. Each piece of galalith receives a preliminary sanding, then is hand cut. Those pieces are polished for days in a rotating drum, dyed, polished by hand, and lacquered. Pavone embellishes and hand paints each product in a unique style that creates figural pins in the forms of bears, mice and other motifs recognized for their bold colors and sense of whimsy. Each pin is made by hand and signed, one at a time, so Pavone's jewelry is priced to reflect the amount of time required to make each piece. Smith has photos of Pavone working in her studio at baubles-and-bibelots.com/mcp.html.

In many collecting categories, finding out something is made of plastic is a major disappointment, but that isn't true in costume jewelry, where Bakelite, cellulose acetate, galalith and others have established a level of sex appeal that shows no sign of getting old.

Note: In each photo caption description, date is the approximate date pin was first released. Most of Lea Stein's pins have been re-released and are still in production. All Lea Stein pieces are signed on the clasp and are made of cellulose acetate. All Pavone pieces are made of galalith and signed with a painted signature—important because Pavone knock-offs have cropped up on eBay.

Fox, 1975-present, 3-3/4", **$75.**

Ric the Dog, 1990-present, 3-5/8", **$75.**

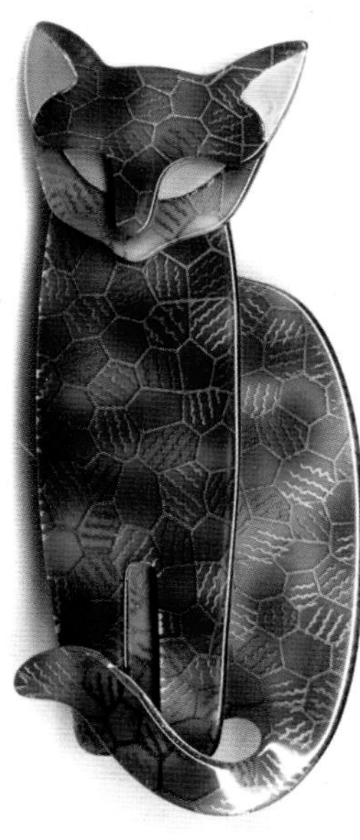

Quarrelsome, 2003, 4", **$90.**

Kokokah the Parrot, 2005, 4-1/2", **$100.**

Kokokah the Parrot, 2005, 4-1/2", **$100.**

Tortoise, 1990-present, 3-3/8", **$75.**

Lea Stein Paris

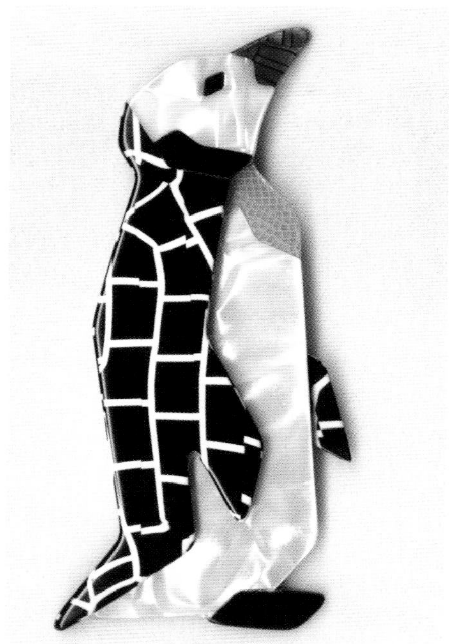

Penguin, 2000, 3-3/8", **$90.**

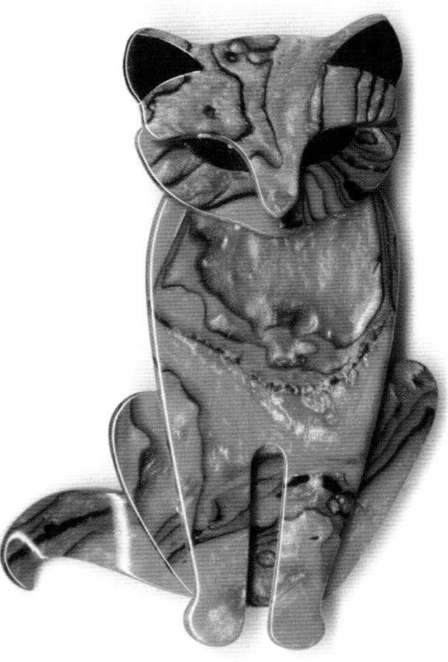

Sacha, 2003, 3-1/4", **$85.**

Flying Geese Pair, 1968-1981 to present, 2-3/4", **$70** each.

Double Eidelweiss, 1968-1981 to present, 3-3/8", **$130.**

Kimdoo the Scottie Dog, 2005, 3-1/8", **$75.**

Rhinestone Sailor Pair, 1968-1981 to present, 1-3/4", **$65** each.

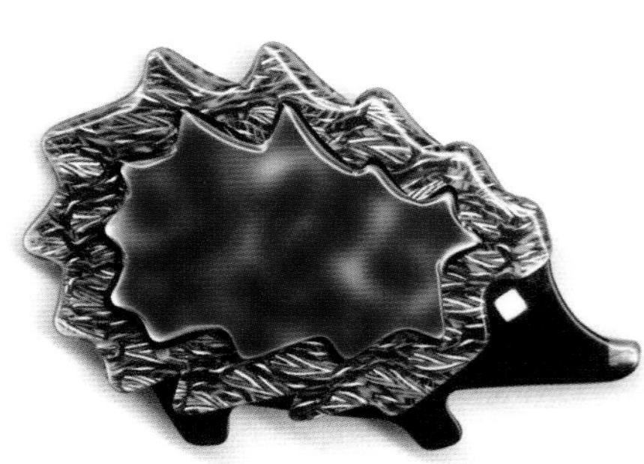

Hedgehog, 2000, 3", **$75.**

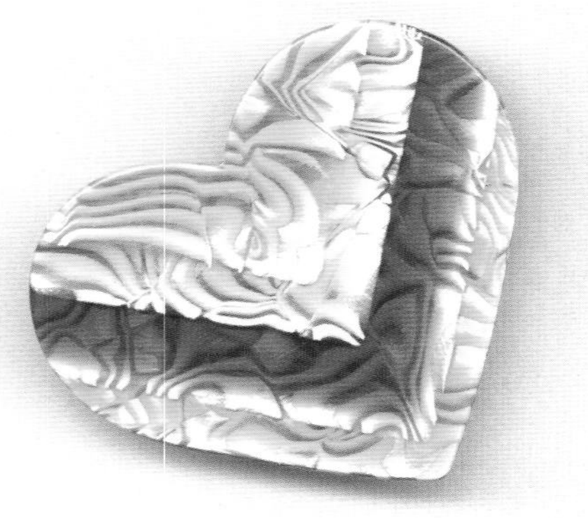

Layered Heart, 1968-1981 to present, **$70.**

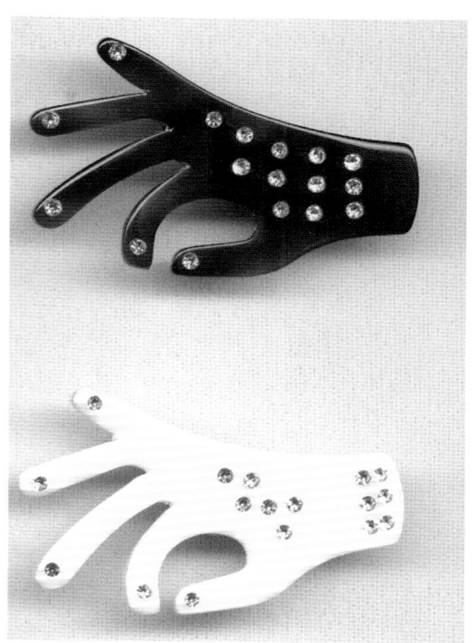

Rhinestone Hand Pair, 1968-1981 to present, 1-7/8", **$80** each.

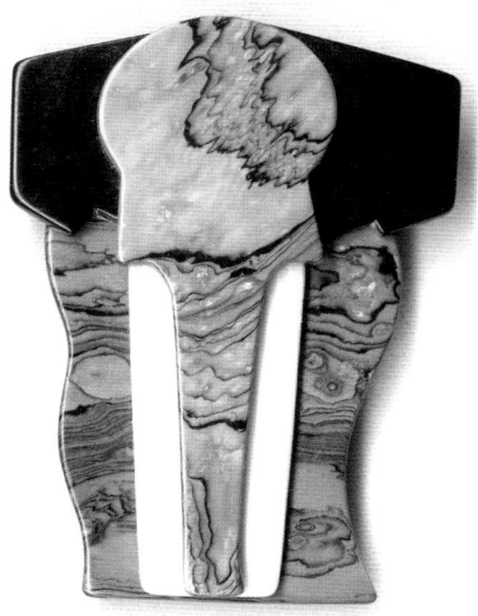

Gray Elephant, very rare; attributed to Lea Stein, signed Agatha Paris; private collection.

Green Elephant, 1968-1981 to present, 2-1/8", **$68.**

Ladybird, 1968-1981, private collection.

Flower Pot, 1968-1981 to present, 2", **$85.**

Accordian, 1968-1981 to present , 1-3/16", **$57.**

Gomina Sleeping Cat, 1990 to present, 2-7/8", **$75.**

Letter, 1968-1981 to present, 1-3/8", **$57.**

Full Colorette, 1968-1981 to present, 2-1/4", **$85.**

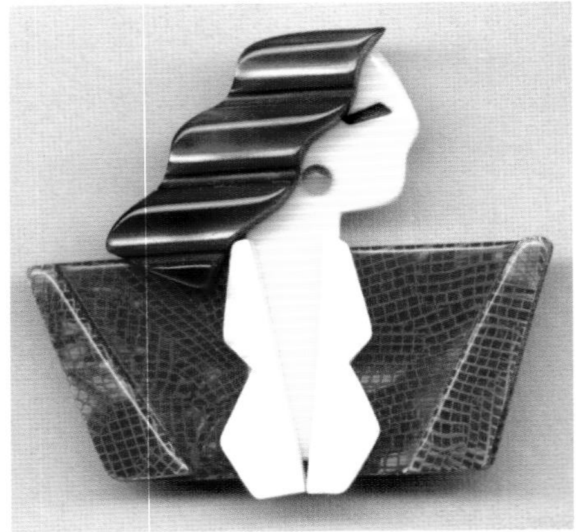

Carmen / Joan Crawford, 1968-1981 to present, 2", **$110.**

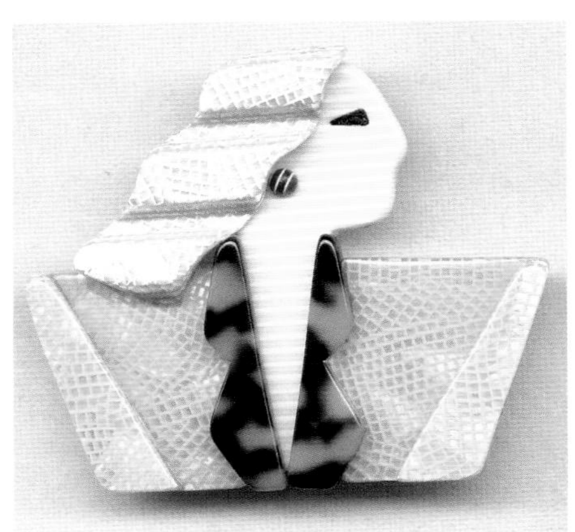

Carmen / Joan Crawford, 1968-1981 to present, 2", **$110.**

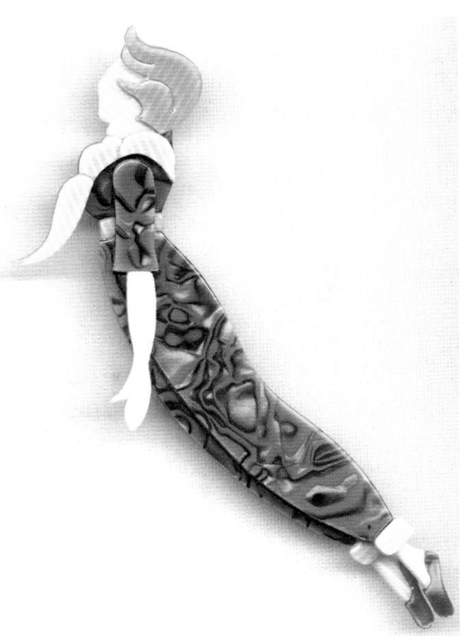

Tennis/Diving Woman, 1968-1981 to present, 4", **$190.**

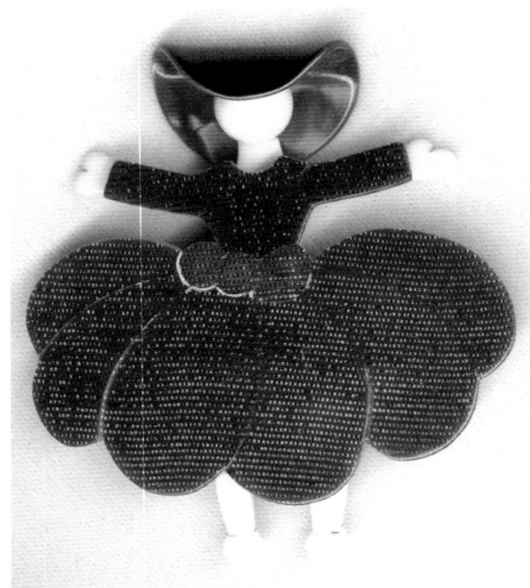

Scarlett O'Hara / Ballerina, 1968-1981 to present, 2-1/2", **$80.**

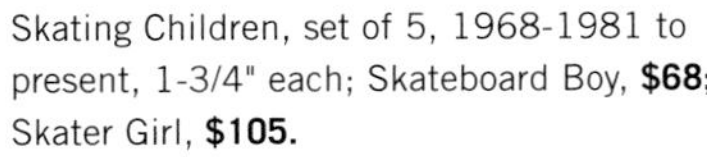

Skating Children, set of 5, 1968-1981 to present, 1-3/4" each; Skateboard Boy, **$68;** Skater Girl, **$105.**

Marie-Christine Pavone

Large Spiral Cat, 3-1/4" **$110.**

Pair of Long Cats, 4" each, **$110** each.

Ondulo the Dog, 2-1/4", **$125.**

Mirko the Cat, 3-1/2", **$110.**

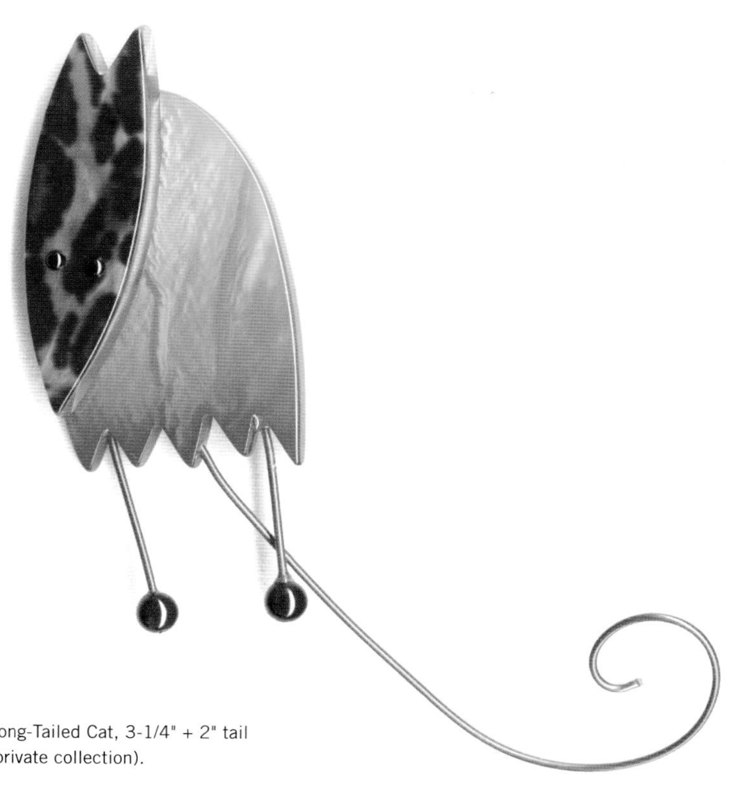

Long-Tailed Cat, 3-1/4" + 2" tail (private collection).

Inchworm, 3-1/8", **$110.**

Bobbie the Dog, 3-3/8", **$142.**

Sheep, 2-1/2", **$110.**

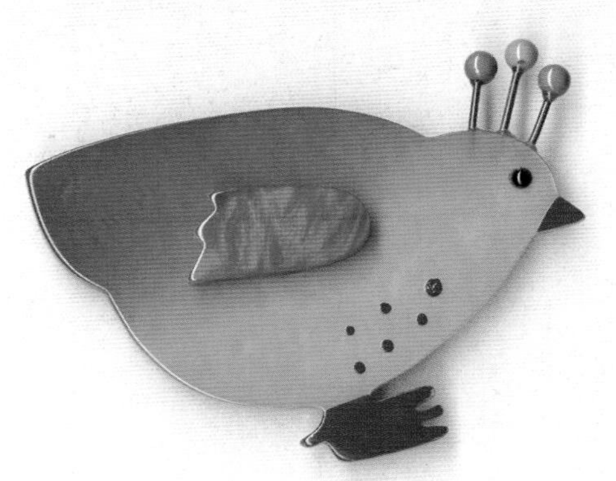

Chicken, 3", **$110.**

Parrot, 5", **$175.**

CHAPTER 24  FIGURALS AREN'T JUST FOR CHRISTMAS

Happy Holidays

The heart, symbol of Valentine lovers, is an early example of holiday jewelry. The first commercial Valentine cards were not sent until the 19th Century, but physicians believed the human heart was the organic center of love even in the 12th Century. Romantic sentiment especially suited the Victorians, who not only loved hearts, but also loved Cupid, the handsome young god with loads of sex appeal turned into a fat infant by the Vics. Both the heart and Cupid are major figural motifs in jewelry, as are lovebirds, the doves that mate for life. Some of the most beautiful hearts are from Trifari, with faux moonstones or fruit salad stones or pastel button cabochons. The number of Cupid pins is countless, from Coro Duettes to the whimsical Castlecliff scale weighing love (represented by Cupid), versus money (coin weights on the other side). As for lovebirds, many made them, but Boucher is behind some of the greatest beauties.

Just about every holiday has affiliated figural jewelry. Some women even collect clock pins to sport for the switch to Daylight Savings Time. Halloween has gotten particularly hot. The most well-known figural brooch related to All-Hallows Eve is the vintage Bakelite Pumpkin Head Man with straw-stuffing accent, so coveted and expensive, modern Bakelite artists have copied it. Scarecrows make a popular Halloween motif and also hark back to "The Wizard of Oz."

Other October themes collected in honor of the 31st include black cats, pumpkins and witches, one of which plays spooky haunted-house music when the switch in her back is pressed. Literally every Halloween theme has been captured in brand new jewelry coming out of China: ghosts, werewolves, bats and spiders spinning webs.

The rage in Christmas jewelry in the 1950s was the plastic Santa with battery-operated light-up nose, and Rudolph with the same. Reindeer in fact were a chosen subject for many jewelry companies even in the '30s and '40s, in gilded sterling or enameled base metals, the deer often with jewels dangling from antlers. Deer ranged from elegant works of art by Reja and Eisenberg to more cartoonish versions from Gerry's.

Spooky Musical Witch brooch, heavily black-enameled, gold-plated metal, witch dressed for Halloween beckoning children to come over for candy, plays scary haunted-house music, 1990s, signed AJC, 3", **$25**. The third figural in this series (not pictured) is a 3" Santa brooch that plays a medley of holiday tunes, also signed AJC.

As for Thanksgiving, two favored figurals serve to take the spotlight, the cornucopia or horn of plenty, spilling beads or rhinestones, and the turkey brooch, the most desirable and delicious of which is the rare Staret brand. If only collectors could call Butterball to learn how to find one.

Jaunty Leprechaun brooch, gold-plated metal, deep-metallic paint, puffing on pipe, holding three shamrocks (with a fourth in his green derby), tiny emerald eyes, unsigned, 1990s, 3", **$25.** This is one of three figurals in a series.

Thanksgiving Feast brooch, silver-plated metal horn with RS pave and variously sized brilliants, unsigned, 1950s, 3", **$50.**

Dangling Love brooch, carved wooden hearts dangle on leather strips from long wooden arrow, unsigned Elzac, 1940s, 4-1/8", **$75-$150.**

Cupid, Draw Back Your Bow fur clip, enamels, gold-plated metal, unsigned, 1938-42, 2-3/4", **$100.**

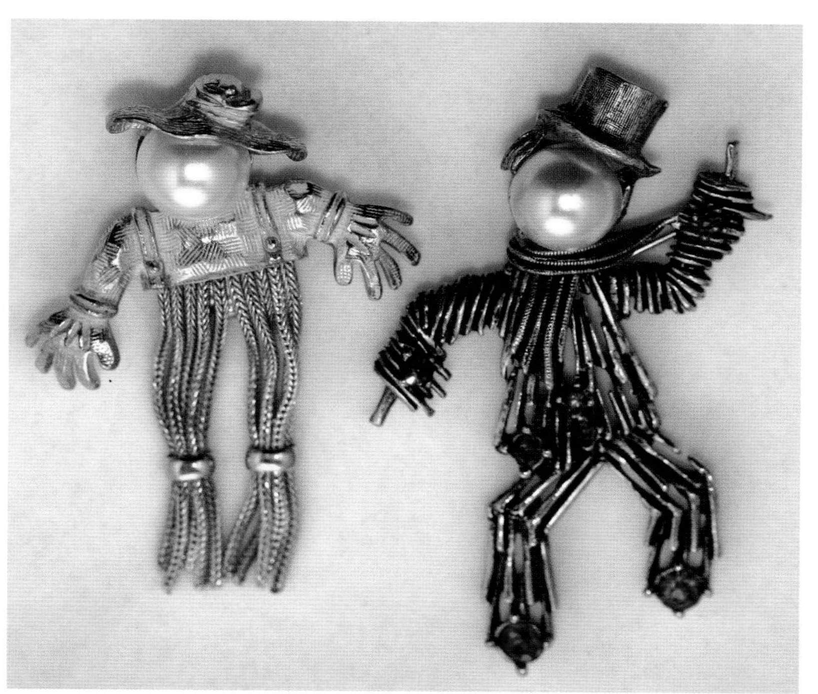

Fancy-pants scarecrow pin, left, gathered chains as trousers, white enamel shirt, hat, faux pearl face, unsigned, 1950s, $2-1/2", **$50**. Field hand in top hat pin, right, pearl head, antiqued gold-plated metal, multicolor RS accents, unsigned, 1960s, 2-3/4", **$50**.

Valentine Cherub fur clip, silvered pot-metal angel (rhodium reverse), pave-set RS curls, wings and arrow, black plastic simulated onyx heart, signed "12," 1935-42, 2-3/8", **$100-$150**. (May be an Eisenberg piece.)

Three Anti-Crow Dudes, from left: stick-figure pin, loose draping chain, high hat, very Nightmare Before Christmas Jack, signed Napier, 1950s, 3-1/8", **$150**; bow-tie boy pin, jade head, enamel bow tie, opaque jade and carnelian ovals, navettes, RS hat, unsigned, 1950s, 2-3/4", **$50-$100**; straw man pin, turquoise-color cabochons and RS, straw-cast gold-plated metal, unsigned, 1950s, 2-3/4", **$50-$75.**

Carnival horn pin, baroque pearls, carved carnival glass tulips, givre teardrops, pearlescent and opaline navettes, fruit salad mix, antiqued gold-plated metal, signed Florenza, 1950s, 2-3/4", **$100**.

Carved Bakelite cornucopia brooch, cherry-red fruit beads, unsigned, 1930s, 3-1/2", **$250**.

Bounty of Color pin, glittering polychrome RS chain, topaz horn, multi-shape fruits, signed Bauer, 1990s, 3", **$250**.

Horn of Plenty pin, antiqued golden metal with holly leaves and berries pouring from horn, unsigned, 1950s, 2-3/8", **$25**.

Caroling Girls pin, enameled gold-plated metal, trio of friends or sisters trills Yuletide tunes, unsigned Mylu design, 1970s, 2-1/2", **$25-$50.**

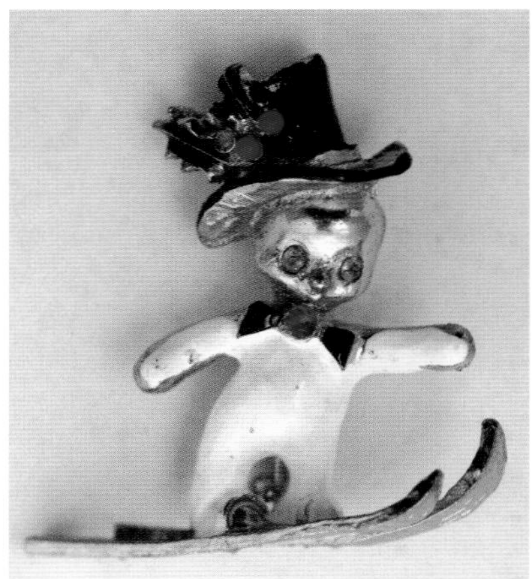

Snowman Skiing pin, top-hatted, enameled, gold-plated metal snowman takes to the slopes, unsigned Mylu design, 1960s, 2", **$10-$25.**

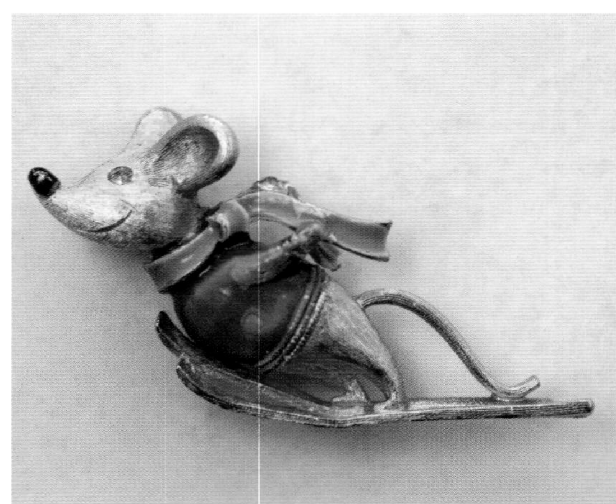

Skiing Rodent pin, enameled and gold-plated metal mouse slaloms downhill wearing fashion scarf, signed Gerry's, 1960s, 2", **$10-$25.**

CHAPTER 25  Taking Aim on Zodiac Signs

Age of Aquarius

What jewelry house could resist designing a line of Zodiac-themed pins, pendants and bracelets once the rock musical *Hair* broke records on Broadway in 1968, or when the 5th Dimension hit No. 1 on the charts in 1969 with the "Age of Aquarius/Let the Sunshine In?"

Many jewelry houses explored the astrological houses of the heavens related to this ancient science, but some did it long before the late-Sixties blockbuster put peace and understanding on everybody's lips. (One irony: The basic back-to-nature, simple-life message of the cast in *Hair* heralded the new Hippie Look and helped contribute to the doom of many jewelry companies. Glitter and glitz gave way to beads and leather and looks that did not even require simple gold plating.)

Zodiac-related memorabilia—postcards to piano music—dates back farther than related jewelry. Figural pins affiliated with astrology signs don't turn up much in the old materials, whether plastics such as Bakelite and celluloid, or carved wood. It's not easy finding gold and diamond pins either, although fish, archers, rams, crabs et al, in every medium, may be astrological in disguise. Art Deco artwork on the other hand is replete with Zodiacal references, and beautiful turn-of-the-century postcards illustrate elaborate renderings of the signs. Some 1903 piano sheet music is all about astrology, with song titles such as "You'll Have to Read the Answers in the Stars."

A partial list of companies that issued astrological jewelry includes Art, Beau, Carnegie, Cini, Coventry, DeNicola, Hobe, Joseff, Lang, Mamselle, PLM, Schrager, St. Labre, Tortolani and Trifari. The most recognizable and collectible pins are probably the colorful, wittily designed DeNicola star cast. Eye-catching hues and a fresh, dimensional rendering of familiar signs – as well as scarcity – make the DeNicolas pricey, with pins rarely priced under $150 each on the secondary market. That's decent for a pin made in the late 1950s. Two notes of interest about the DeNicola Zodiacs: A less splashy duplicate line in plain, antiqued gold with just a smattering of faux pearls and rhinestones also appeared later, no longer marked DeNicola. They may have been rehashed in the late Sixties in response to the madness for Aquarius. Second, by coincidence we had several DeNicolas in a group near unsigned resin figurals attributed to Hattie Carnegie and saw a clear relationship. The unmarked resin ram in faux turquoise, coral and ivory is a

Sagittarius the Archer pin, archer set into Moon with plastic resin panels, pave-set RS, signed DeNicola, 1960s, 1-3/4", **$175-$250.** *Courtesy Lisa Corcoran, Jazzle Dazzle, jazbot.com.*

twin to one version of the DeNicola ram. Throw a similarity to Kenneth J. Lane designs into that mix and we can trace the manufacturer to Gem-Craft under Alfeo Verrecchia and later his twin brother Gene Verri.

The Joseff and Cini sterling Zodiacs are special because so beautifully crafted, and the very *moderne* 1945 Carnegies, one of the oldest groupings (verified by design-patent information) are assigned to Hugo de Alteriis's astro series. One of the most coveted non-pin pieces is Tortolani's sign-crammed bracelet, with a full house of heavenly characters.

Taurus the Bull pin, 3-D faux-jade cast resin face, coral resin body, enamels, RS accents, ring through nose, signed DeNicola, 1960s, 1-7/8", **$175-$250.** *Courtesy Lisa Corcoran, Jazzle Dazzle, jazbot.com.*

Aries the Ram pin, brushed gold-plated metal, teal and orange metallic-enamels, pave-set RS, 3-D simulated-jade resin face, signed DeNicola, 1960s, 2-1/2", **$175-$250.** *Courtesy Lisa Corcoran, Jazzle Dazzle, jazbot.com.*

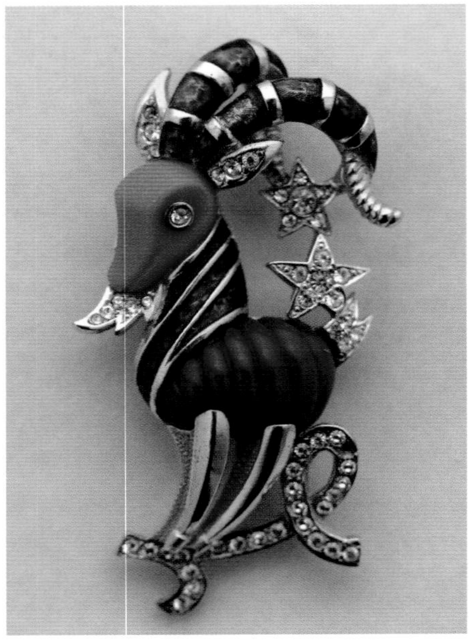

Capricorn the Goat pin, jade-resin body, coral resin face, gold-plated metal, polychrome enamels, RS accents, signed DeNicola, 1960s, 2-1/4", **$175-$250.** *Courtesy Lisa Corcoran, Jazzle Dazzle, jazbot.com.*

Crab on Shell pin, signature Joseff of Hollywood antiqued Russian gold-finished metal, claws holding faux pearl, signed Joseff, 1950s, 2-1/4", **$250.**

Antiqued Crab pin, gold-plated metal, seed-pearl and RS pave accents, unsigned DeNicola design, 1970s, 2-1/4", **$25.**

Sadge the Archer, gold-plated metal, simulated ruby eyes, signed Mamselle, 1960s, 2", **$25.**

Plain Crab pin, gold-plated metal, emerald RS eyes, signed Mamselle, 1960s, **$25.**

Scorpio Zodiac pin, antiqued gold-plated metal, seed-pearl and RS pave accents, unsigned DeNicola design, 1970s, 2-1/4", **$25.**

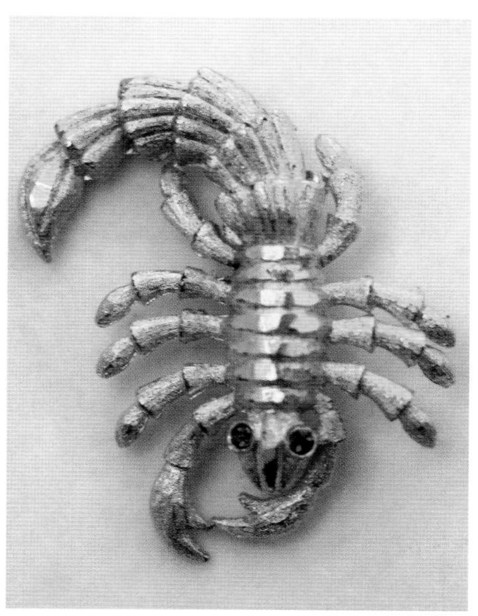

Scorpio the Scorpion pin, gold-plated metal, emerald RS eyes, signed Mamselle, 1960s, 1-5/8", **$25.**

Scorpio pin, gold-plated metal, pave-set crystals, coral-bead eyes, claws grasping Baroque pearlized resin cabochon, signed P.I.M., 1960s, 1-3/4", **$25.**

Aquarius the Water Bearer pin, brushed goldtone metal, signed Trifari, 1970s, 1-3/4", **$25.**

CHAPTER 26 Some Collections Are Heart-Healthy

Isn't It Romantic?

No, actually; it isn't always romantic. Many collectors hunt for hearts simply because the basic shape is aesthetically pleasing (think how often we doodle them)—and because designers apparently lavished extra attention on the classic icon of *amour*. The result: pieces of exceptional beauty and individuality. Says one hard-*coeur* devotee of a heart-healthy collection, "It's their beauty I love, their lines, designs, and all the periods they represent. It's been fun finding fine hearts from the Victorian, Art Nouveau, Art Deco, retro modern and '60s eras." This collector wears them to school for two weeks starting Feb. 1, just as she wears Christmas pins beginning the day after Thanksgiving. And while a rose may be a rose, a heart isn't always a good heart. "Most people think hearts are hearts, but their lines vary, and some aren't pleasing at all. I think my collection got started because I started seeing hearts with great lines."

Jewels of India fur clip, carved glass watermelon emeralds, drippy heart vine shape, ruby cab teardrops, gold-plated, four layers, signed Trifari, 1940s, 3", **$250.**

One that first grabbed her attention was a large, crystal-pave brooch with jewel-studded pastel shoe-button cabochons in atrocious condition. The design integrity of vintage costume jewelry is often so powerful, collectors see clearly the possibilities beneath the devastation. The heart cost $3, its restoration about $60. "Well worth it," she says. "It's one of my favorite pieces of vintage jewelry." Two other hearts found early on heightened her interest: a pair of big Trifari beauties. The pink-and-blue pastels creation shows up in other Trifari motifs (a treble clef, a question mark) as well, and the Trifari navy-and-white heart would prove irresistible to anyone.

A collection was born.

Fans of figurals know which stand out as favorite pins because they can gaze upon them endlessly. The most stare-worthy design for her is two large overlapping hearts in rose-gold and yellow-gold plated metal with topaz stone and rhinestone trim from the 1940s. Another features a background of black fabric with sequins: "I appreciate a Victorian brooch," she says, "because someone thought enough of it not to melt it down or discard it when it was out of style, so it still exists more than 100 years later."

In the book *Victorian Jewelry: Unexplored Treasures* by Ginny Redington Dawes and Corinne Davidov, the authors note that hearts fell out of favor in the late Victorian era, beginning in about 1885, as women grew more independent, active, and aware of the world around them. That was quite a change from the earlier 19th Century when everyone wore silver love brooches, padlocked hearts with miniature keys.

But no one can keep a good design down, especially one that represents a universal symbol. The heart is the classic locket shape, holding hair or photographs of beloveds. It is the motif of choice in sweetheart jewelry from the war years, whether done in red celluloid with sassy messages or wood hearts spilling from Lucite arrows. It is the favorite icon of romantics and Surrealists alike.

Love them for their shape or their meaning, either way, hearts are here to stay.

Midnight-blue masterpiece, plastic heart pin centerpiece with faux pearl and RS overlay motif attachment, diamond-shaped faceted sapphire RS and pearl accents surround, unsigned, 1940s, 3-1/8", **$300.**

Ruby twist rope pin-pendant, faceted glass heart, gilded metal frame and second frame of RS, 3-D, unsigned, 1950s, 2", **$50-$100.**

Multicolor pin, lacy enameled filigree openwork heart, polychrome jewels of various shapes, five decorative dangles inset with cabochons, unsigned, 1930s, 3", **$150.**

Retro overlapping double foliate brooch, large topaz RS oval, crystal pave, openwork goldplate metal, swirling leaf, unsigned, 1940s, 2-1/2", **$150.**

Romantic Pastels pin clip, gold-plated with RS pave swirls, flowers, pink and blue oval stones, signed Trifari and "23," 1940s, 1-3/4", **$250.**

Shoe-button chef d'oeuvre, pot metal, pave-set RS and pastel igloo cabochons studded with chatons, unsigned, 1940s, 3", **$250.**

Rich emerald stones pin-pendant with montana cabs, rhodium finish, plus twin second heart in ruby RS, each unsigned, 1940s, 2-1/4", **$100** each.

Rosy Heart pin, pink RS chain, gold-plated wire-vine frame, drippy enameled red hearts, signed Vendôme, 1950s, 2-1/2", **$150.**

Czech bead-tipped wood bells and flowers pin, floral seed beads, 1930s, unsigned, 2-1/8", **$50-$100.**

Triple pearls pin, baroque shapes surrounded by faux pearls, unsigned, 1950s, 2-1/2", **$50.**

Plastic flowers pin, posies wired onto filigree backing, unsigned, 1950s, 2-1/2", **$50.**

Layered teardrops pin-pendant, pale blue sapphire teardrops, marquises, ovals, blue-jeweled heart, gold-plated filigree swirls, celadon RS chain, peridot accents, deep, swedged layers, unsigned, 1950s, 2-3/4", **$150.**

True Grit hearts, 3-D Dorothy Bauer RS chain pins, signed Bauer, 1990s, 1" to 1-1/2", **$50-$100.**

Basket-weave brooch, Trifanium and baguettes, signed Trifari, 1940s, 1-1/2", **$150.**

Heart of darkness, jet black Lucite plastic, faceted and opaque unsigned, 1940s, 1-3/4", **$25.**

Victorian filigree brooch, wirework swirl frame and enhancer with heart dangles, MOP centerpiece, unsigned, 1910, 3-1/4", **$50-$100.**

Very Vic heart pin, French fabric and sequins Victorian pin, heart inset into twisted rope frame, tube clasp, unsigned, 1900, 1-1/2", **$100.**

Lucite double carved coeur pin, inset with rose cab button surrounded by channel-set crystals, unsigned, 1940s, 2", **$50.**

Flaming Heart brooch, prong-set Swarovski crystals in red, topaz, hyacinth and jonquil chaton cuts, hematite-plated base metal, von Walhof Creations, signed, 2000s, 2-1/4", **$155.**

Red and the Black pin, faux pearls and enamel, red-swirled glass-covered foil, unsigned, 1950s, 2", **$50-$75.**

  COLLECTORS LOVE PEOPLE PINS

Population Explosion

The earliest cast of characters to inhabit the world's wardrobes were probably St. George doing-in the dragon, Madonna (Mary, not Madge) holding child, various aquatic tritons, and popular goddesses such as Diana. Now, six centuries later, who hasn't been a brooch?

For fanciers of fashions by Chanel, Coco herself stands in pin form.

Dramatic Ballerina brooch, finely enameled face, arms and legs, delicately painted features, layered tutu of rhodium and gilded sterling, studded with simulated rubies and emeralds, unsigned, 1945-55, 3-1/4", **$650-$850.**

People (along with face figurals) are hands down the jewelry category with the highest quotient of variety and amusement. Whether they are anonymous works of art with wild specialty stones or simple metal castings of Elvis, surprises never stop in a search for fantastic folks.

Every expression has been captured in pins, even anger. Every hairdo has been coiffed, every ensemble worn. People pins dance, pose, ski, run, sit, skate, scowl, sneer, smile, play drums, play football, walk dogs, kiss, drink too much and jump for joy.

Coro's international chorus line of enameled characters includes French apache sluggers, Flamenco dancers and señoritas, Colonial Americans, Spanish swordsmen, English royals, Russian cossacks, Asian lantern lighters, African tribal natives, Cambodian water carriers, Mexican guitarists, Midwestern farmers.

The most basic people figural is a charming metal stick figure; at the other end of the spectrum is a tall, jewel-encrusted gladiator or big ballerina in glittering tutu, her hand-painted face lavished with rich enamels.

A shortlist of wanted characters so hard to capture they seem like fugitives would include the plastic Art Deco Josephine Baker and her jazz band; Coro Romeo and Juliet; Walter Lampl Chinese couple; DuJay marching band members; Boucher Siamese dancers; Hobe jeweled Thibetan netsuke; Chanel Novelty Punch and Judy; Eisenberg Original dancers (Can-Can, ballet, folkloric), maids, mermaids, ladies; fair Calvaire dames and debutantes; Har genies; KJL Sixties sea gods and goddesses; Elzac metal señorita with Lucite fan and headdress; Reja royals and Carnegie soldiers; DeRosa Indian woman; Trifari sailor girl and newspaper boy; Reinad native, Danecraft Scrooge. These are glorious gals and guys.

Collectors even know many people pins' names, from Ivan and Tania to Peter and Helen. And while most figural forms are apparently human, some aren't: Reja's stone-cold figural

Ballerina pin, pink faux moonstone face, channel-set baguettes and pave hem, gold-plated metal, 1950s, 2-1/4", **$100.**

Retro ballerina pin, twisted Boucher style, gold-plated limbs, oval aquamarine RS bodice, unsigned, 1940s, 3-1/4", **$150.**

Sterling ballerina pin (from parure of pin, pendant, necklace, clip earrings), cast silver, signed Napier, 1940s, 2-1/4" pin, **$350** parure.

Hobe Thibetan fur clip, elegantly jeweled hand-worked filigree frame holding ivorine netsuke-like Asian character, signed Hobe, 1930s, 2-3/4", **$250-$450.**

Vogue Oriental brooch, bronzed molded-ball grotto frame surrounding ivorine netsuke-like character, prong-set simulated rubies, signed Vogue Jlry (sic), 1940s, 3-1/2", **$250-$450.**

Frosted Netsuke pin, acrylic Asian figure on floral gold-plated frame holding jade leaves, base, and coral demi-cabochon, unsigned (possibly Swoboda), date unknown, 2-1/8", **$75-$125.**

Monkey Man brooch, elaborately festooned ivory simian netsuke with jungle surround of glass flowers and brilliant seed beads, signed Stanley Hagler N.Y.C. and Ian St. Gielar, 2000s, 4", **$200.**

Singin' in the Rain man pin, tipsy gent in formalwear dancing with light post, enameled, gilded metal, RS baguettes, unsigned, 1940s, 2-1/2", **$150.**

Art Deco "Bronze Statuette" pin, metal and enamel, stylized Deco icon, graceful-athletic nude in classic position, unsigned, age uncertain, 2-1/2", **$50-$100.**

Bellhop pins, enameled man carrying alligator bag, attached on reverse like a charm, unsigned, 1940s, 1-1/2", **$25-$50**; enameled pot metal, skirted lady with faceted emerald-cut luggage in pink and purple, unsigned, 1938-42, 2", **$50-$75.**

Palm Tree Bellhop or Traveling Lady pin, pot metal, RS accents, Technicolor metallic enamels, unsigned, 1940s, 2-3/4", **$50.**

Drum Major pins, enameled pot metal brooch and gilded, enameled metal fur clip, both with RS accents; larger brooch, unsigned, 1940s, 3-1/4", **$75-$100**; smaller fur clip, unsigned Urie Mandle, marked Patent Pend., 1940s, 2-1/4", **$100-$150.**

Spanish dancers fur clips, enameled pot metal, RS accents, 2-1/4", unsigned Coro designs, 1940s, **$50-$100.**

Musketeer, Lady and Romeo fur clips, enameled rhodium and pot metal, RS accents, 1-3/4", 2-1/8" and 1-3/4" respectively (left to right), unsigned, 1940s-50s, **$25-$100**. Three unrelated examples of enameled people pins from many backgrounds. Romantic musketeer likely was paired with his matching lady love; Romeo is missing his Juliet on balcony; courtly or Revolutionary-era lady belongs with a gentleman as well.

Beaded Soldier fur clip, bronzed metal, cobalt navettes, ovals, studded with multicolor seed beads, unsigned (resembles a rare Eisenberg piece, but this one is probably Czech), 2-1/2", **$100-$150.**

Ethnic Busts fur clips, metal with faceted RS and cabochon accents, unsigned, 1935-42, 1-5/8", **$50-$100** (clip on right is sometimes seen marked Eisenberg Original).

Two Soldiers fur clips, enameled, gilded metal, RS accents, one with flag, unsigned Hattie Carnegie, 1939, 2-3/8", **$250+.**

Thai Princess brooch, gilded sterling, jewel-tone navettes, unsigned Urie Mandle (earrings, not shown, duplicate Mandle's findings and circular sterling hallmark), 3", **$200-$250.**

Suffering Señora fur clip, pot metal set with jewel-tone chatons, signed Monet, 1940s, 2-1/4", **$50.**

Surprised Fisherman fur clip, 1-1/2", and Shoe-Toting Hitchhiker fur clip, 1-3/4", Black Americana, enameled pot metal, unsigned, 1938-42, **$100-$150** each. The fellow fishing obviously originally had something unusual at the end of the line.

Sailor & Shark pin, 3-D stick figure, enameled gold-plated metal, signed Industria Argentina, 1930s, 2-1/2", **$50.**

Ice Skater fur clip and Ice Skater pin, 1940s-50s, unsigned, 2", **$25.**

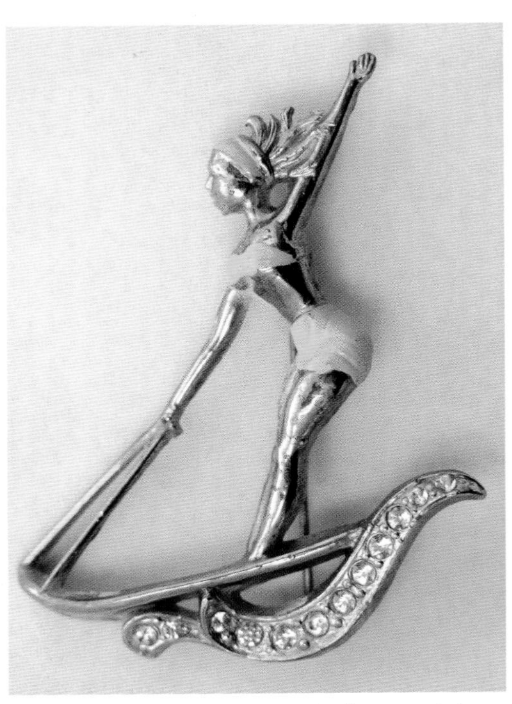

Tall Waterskiier pin, gold-plated metal, yellow enameled bikini, unsigned, 1950s, 3", **$50.**

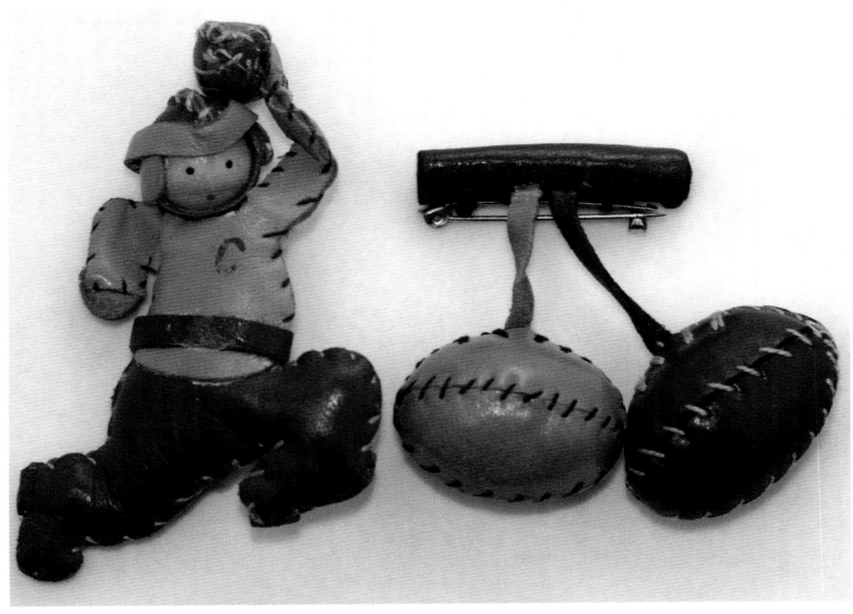

Leather football player and footballs pins, 1920s, unsigned, 2"-3", **$50+.**

Dutch Lady Pushing Flower Cart pin, enameled pot metal, RS accents, rotating wheel, unsigned, 1940s, 2", **$50-$75.**

Fan Dancer pin, 3-D stick figure whimsy novelty, enameled brass, signed Stern-Genzer, 1930s, 2-1/2", **$50.**

Languid Lady at Mirror brooch, pewter finish, reflective mirrors surface, signed AJC, 1980s, 4", **$50.**

Chic Lady in Scarf, pave-set RS, enamel accents, signed Polcini, 1960s, 2-1/4", **$50.**

Large Lady pins, colorful cast resin, vaguely reminiscent of artist Linda Carter Holman's women, unsigned, 1980s, 3", **$10-$25.**

People, People pin, 13 faces, silvery metal, unsigned, 1990s, 2-7/8", **$10-$25.**

Pearly Jester fur clip, enameled, gilded metal, multi-cut polychrome jewels, signed Calvaire, 2", **$75-$150.**

Smiling Jester pin, popular motif, gilded metal, RS accents, unsigned (Reja design), 1940-50s, 3-1/2", **$50+.**

CHAPTER 28  Fun With Fantasy Figurals

Myth & Magic

From the beginning of time human beings have been enamored with magical and mythical creatures, goddesses and everything imaginable above and below the earth, unseen yet still spell-binding. Fairies and mermaids enchant, wizards work magic, gods grant favors—or wreak havoc and allow men to blame anyone but themselves for their terrible travails. Inhabitants of earth simply love the other-worldly. And the allure of such lore, the escape from reality to fantasy, has always been an exciting adventure.

While Eisenberg is probably credited with the most valuable and coveted individual pieces from this broad category (its Verdura-like mermaid, pave-winged angel, and stern-faced King Neptune), no one in the jewelry world capitalized more on the universal fascination with magic and myth than Jonette Jewelry and Kirks Folly. The Merlin-like magicians and wizards of J.J., the winged creatures who scatter fairy dust for Kirk's Folly, populate untold collections.

In fact, Helen, Jenniefer, Elizabeth and George Kirk built a non-make-believe empire on fairy dust (or actually, Folly Dust. The company mottos are "Dreams really do come true" and "Believe in the magic.")

Successful immediately after marketing Helen's jeweled chopsticks as hair ornaments to Bloomingdale's in 1979, the Kirks eventually brought their flock of fairies and angels to QVC and sold out in less than an hour. The audience for the brand of consumer magic the Kirks spun was so large, theme cruises, parties, anniversary balls, live shows and fairy teas became regular events.

The family's menagerie of jeweled figurals includes characters such as Laila the Uptown Fairy, Fabula the Forum Fairy, Dixie the Pixie, Gandolf and Olorin the Wizards, Draco the Dragon, Forest Fairies and Sunset Astral Fairy, the Fairy Godmother, Archimedes, Pan, magic spiders, unicorns, castles, knights and even Fairy Wand brooches full of Folly Dust, all designed to bring the Kirk fantasy themes to life.

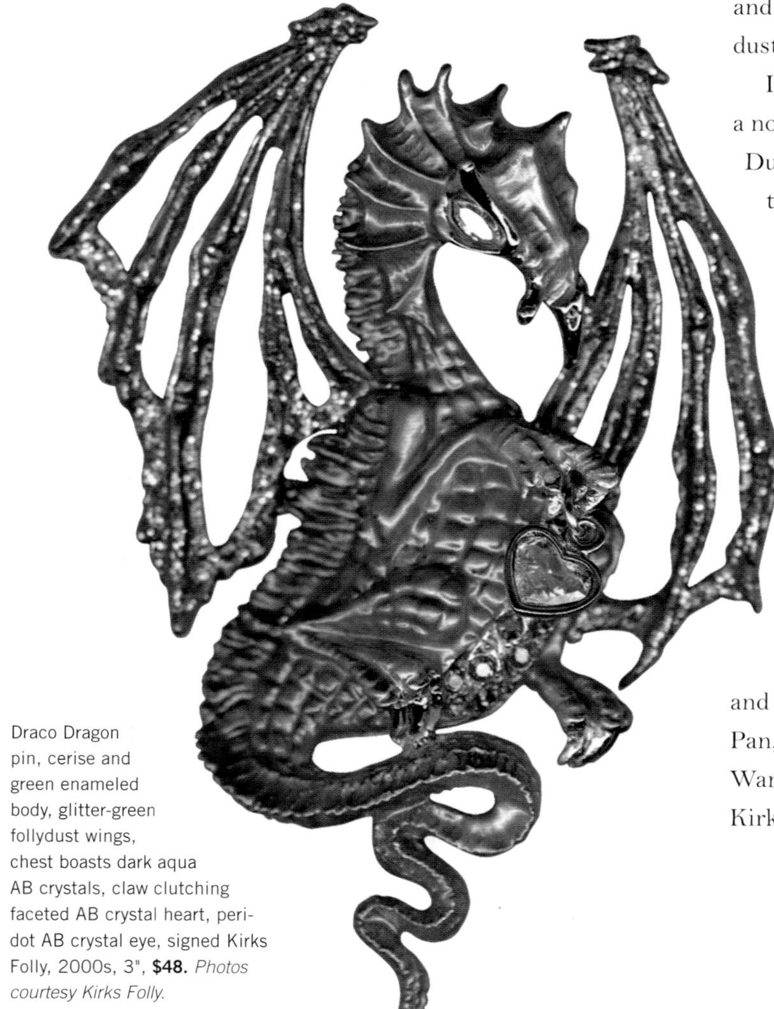

Draco Dragon pin, cerise and green enameled body, glitter-green follydust wings, chest boasts dark aqua AB crystals, claw clutching faceted AB crystal heart, peridot AB crystal eye, signed Kirks Folly, 2000s, 3", **$48.** *Photos courtesy Kirks Folly.*

Forest Fairy pin, pale blue dress and wings, sitting on branch to blend with bright teal-enameled leaves accented with AB crystals, signed Kirks Folly, 2000s, 3", **$31.50.**

Olorin Wizard pin, hand-enameled green and teal robe, one hand holding faceted AB globe, hourglass containing follydust in other hand, plus olivine ABs, teal and amethyst beads, golden star medallion around neck, owl at feet, signed Kirks Folly, 2000s, 2-1/2", **$36.**

Sunset Astral Fairy pin, one of Kirks Folly's most famous fairies, holding twinkling star with crystal stone, and with fiery pink and orange sunset colors reflected in wings and dress, signed Kirks Folly, 2000s, 3-1/4", **$31.50.**

Fairy Godmother II pin, updated Kirks Folly classic with elaborate AB crystal-encrusted butterfly wing, hands holding faceted AB wishing globe, embossed sash wrap with star and bead crystals, tresses dressed in crystal-centered star, signed Kirks Folly, 2000s, 3", **$52.**

Ship of Dreams pin, swan soaring from ship, follydusted wings wrapping ship's sides, moons and stars emblazon sails, trio of balloons carry ship above clouds, pinwheel spins, rudder moves, signed Kirks Folly, 2000s, 3", **$58.**

Knight in Shining Armor pin, dressed in crystal AB armor, hand enameled, embellished with rainbow of crystals, signed Kirks Folly, 2000s, 3", **$49.**

Woodland Fairy pin, unusual "boy" fairy with glass wings, riding dragonfly with green enamel wings filled with assortment of AB crystal stones, signed Kirks Folly, 3-1/4", **$40.**

Forget-Me-Not fairy pin-pendant, glass wings edged with follydust, hat and dress of lavender enamel sprinkled with follydust, carrying bundle of forget-me-nots, crystal bead hanging from bouquet, signed Kirks Folly, 2000s, 2-3/4", **$58.**

Ophelia Unicorn pin, encrusted with AB crystals, golden horn spirals upward, flowing mane hand-enameled in soft cream, dotted with bouquet of flowers in pink, buttercup, teal, signed Ophelia and Kirks Folly, 2000s, 2-3/4", **$40.**

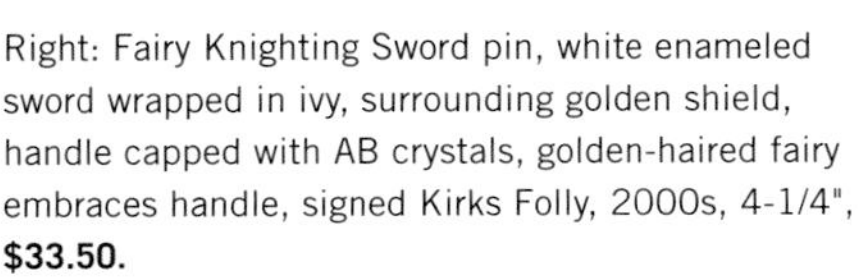

Right: Fairy Knighting Sword pin, white enameled sword wrapped in ivy, surrounding golden shield, handle capped with AB crystals, golden-haired fairy embraces handle, signed Kirks Folly, 2000s, 4-1/4", **$33.50.**

Billiken Head brooch, cast brass with six Oriental charms dangling on chains, unsigned, probably Reinad, 1938-42, 4-1/4", **$75-$150.** (Go SLUH!)

Crystal Gazer Wizard brooch, pewter finish metal, tiny RS, AB cabochon in hat, signed JJ, 2000s, 4", **$25-$50.**

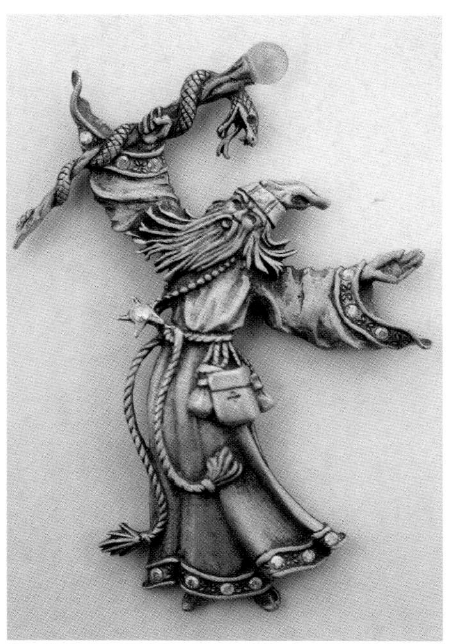

Storm Wizard pin, pewter-finish metal, RS accents, crystal ball atop raised snake-wrapped staff, signed JJ, 2000s, 3-1/4", **$25.**

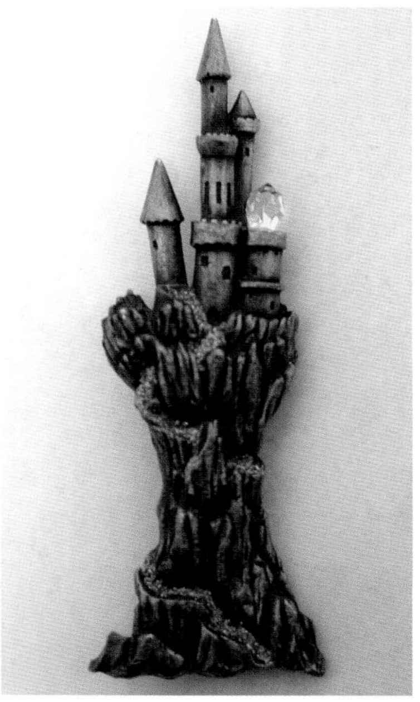

Golden Castle on Cliff pin, antiqued-gold cast metal, crystal atop one tower, glittery river running downhill from moat, signed JJ, 2000s, 3-3/4", **$25.**

Hunter Goddess Diana dress clip, pot metal, unsigned, 1935-42, 2-1/2", **$50.**

Dramatic Unicorn pin, gilded metal, blue cabochons, enamel accents, signed Reinad, 1940s, 3", **$500-$750.**

Glittery Mermaid pin, soldered rhinestone chain, unsigned, 2000s, 3", **$10-$20.**

Mermaids

Captivating aquatic sea maidens familiar to everyone as mermaids (half female, half fish) are widely popular, and that passion followed in figural jewelry. With flowing hair that undulates like waves, and curving, sinuous tails, focus has long been more on their beauty than the fact they legendarily lure men to their deaths, even if inadvertently.

Mermaid tales date back to about 1000 B.C.—and at least one philosopher thought it wasn't the ape from which we sprang, but sea creatures. Hans Christian Andersen's *The Little Mermaid* has lived on for 150-plus years, most notably with its reincarnation at the hands of Disney.

Not to mention Darryl Hannah's portrayal, which just might have helped her lure the ultimate he-man catch, John F. Kennedy Jr.

In jewelry, few figural aficionados resist adding one mermaid to their collectible seas.

Enchanting Fairy brooch and Mermaid Pin-Up Girl. Fairy, glittering prong-set polychrome Swarovski crystals, signed, Bettina von Walhof, 2000s, 3", **$120.** Mermaid, undersea beauty in classic pin-up pose, first-quality peridot, rose, sapphire, jet, siam red and pale topaz Swarovski crystals in round chaton and oval cuts, prong set by hand, hematite-plated base metal, part of von Walhof Creations' "Under the Sea" collection, signed, B&M von Walhof, 2000s, 2-3/4", **$120.**

Neptune pin, king of the seas wearing diadem, holding trident, RS jeweled collar and tail, large molded faux-jade glass belly, ruby RS eyes, well-cast gold-plated metal, unsigned, 1955-65, 3-1/8", **$150.**

Two-Tone Mermaid pin, mixed metals in gold and silver, signed UltraCraft, 1970s, 2-1/2", **$25.**

Bronzed Mermaid brooch, sculptural pewter, signed Drumm, 1970s, 3", **$50-$100.** Artist Don Drumm is known for his mythological creatures.

Merman Guide fur clip, appears to be pointing the way for a goldfish; enameled, gilded pot metal, RS accents, flowing tresses, unsigned, 1938-42,2-1/4", **$150.**

The Stuff of Life

Fifth Avenue Lamp Standard pin, gold-plated metal, jewel accents, plastic lamp globes, signed Mosell, 1950s, 3", **$300-$500.** (Brooch is the elaborate logo of the Frederic Mosell company.)

As Ecclesiastes, Pete Seeger and The Byrds said, To every thing...there is a season. In the world of figural pins, there are ice skates, beach sandals, pastel pumps and hiking boots. That pretty much covers the seasons, yet doesn't even scratch the surface.

Historically, the earliest figural "things" in jewelry portrayed crosses, ships and crowns. But what better way to discuss the vast variety of figural things in jewelry land than with a Top 50 list of the craziest commodities in pins we've ever laid eyes on.

No. 50. Ice cube with tongs **49.** Stereo speaker **48.** Shower stall **47.** Solar system **46.** Skull **45.** Lipstick **44.** Map of U.S. **43.** Pay phone **42.** Declaration of Independence **41.** Scissors **40.** Doghouse for man **39.** WWII gas mask fur clip **38.** Potbelly stove **37.** Blackboard **36.** Fishbowl **35.** Bookshelf **34.** Puppet show theatre **33.** Kiss timer **32.** Microphone **31.** Ear of corn **30.** Atomic explosion **29.** Surrey with fringe on top **28.** Jack in the box **27.** Ice-cream cone **26.** Symphony orchestra stage **25.** Weather house with in-out couple **24.** Cable car **23.** Ink pen nib **22.** Basket of cards **21.** Oil lamp **20.** Unicycle **19.** Pickle **18.** Comet **17.** Pearl Harbor **16.** Open window **15.** LP record album **14.** Typewriter **13.** Large mirror **12.** Japanese bomber plane **11.** Scales **10.** Fork full of jewels **9.** Belt **8.** Mechanical stoplight **7.** Framed mini-silhouettes **6.** Water buckets **5.** Cartridge ink pen **4.** Victrola **3.** Angry Christmas tree **2.** Hat rack of hats **1.** Fumigation apparatus.

Scales pin, 12k g.f., ruby RS, unsigned, 1940s, 2", **$50.**

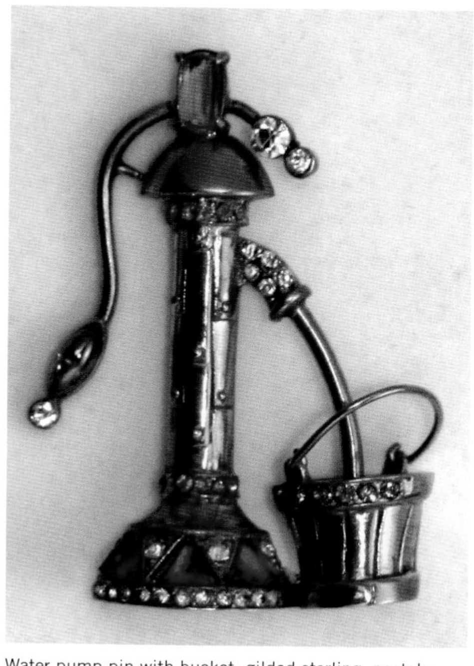

Water pump pin with bucket, gilded sterling, pastels, mixed cuts (emerald, triangle, navettes), ruby, sapphire, rose pink, pave diamante, sapphire cabochon, unsigned Aquilino, 1942, 2-1/4", **$250.**

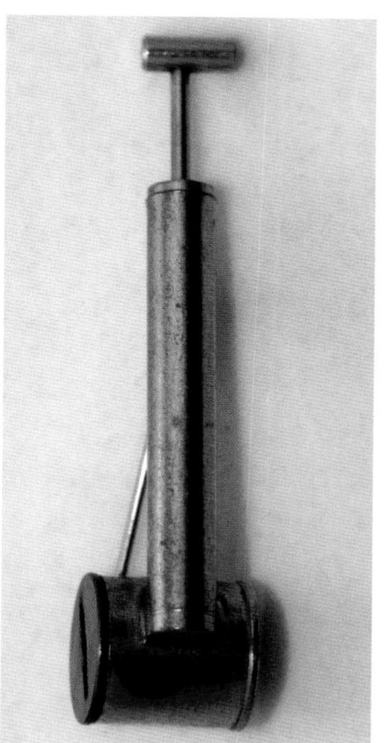

Fumigation device pin, rare, mechanical, brass, 1950s, unsigned, 2-3/8" to 3-1/8" open, **$50-$100.**

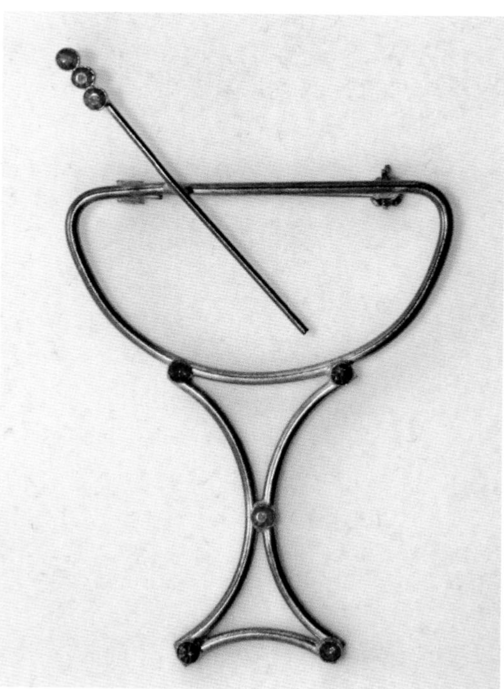

Cocktail glass brooch, brass metal wire perimeter, red RS accent olives, unsigned, 1940s, 3-5/8", **$50-$100.**

Top hat & walking stick brooch, gold-plated metal, aquamarine RS, large upside-down teardrop, unsigned, 1940s, 3-3/4", **$50-$100.**

Martini glass pin, pave-set RS, unsigned, 1950s, 2-1/4", **$50**. Cocktail glass pin, baguettes and chatons, unsigned, 1950s, 2", **$50.**

Jeweled Bow brooch, shades-of-blue simulated sapphires etc., openwork design, signed Schiaparelli, 1960s, 3", **$150-$200.**

Cinderella's carriage pin, jeweled and enameled four-horse coach, wheels spin, unsigned, 1930s, 3", **$100.** Model-T pin, baguettes and pave-set stones on car, unsigned, 1960s, 2", **$50.**

Gemmy Key brooch, jewel-encrusted, rhodium-plated key pin, pink and orchid faceted RS and fruit salad cabs, signed Trifari, 1950s, 3", **$75-$150.**

"Weather House" pin, pot metal, jeweled couple symbolizing fair or stormy weather move in or out of house on track, signed Coro, 1935-42, 1-7/8", **$100-$150.** Coro used a 3-D platform set-up for a number of motifs, including the stage for the Carnegie Hall series pin, a fenced garden scene, etc.

Jeweled Sword, heavily jeweled pot metal, unsigned Staret design, 1940s, 4", **$50-$100.**

Windmill pin, Iowa State Fair, 1983, 1-7/8", **$25.**

Grande Epée pin, large, decorative sword, faux jade cabs and pearls, signed CFW, 1950s, 4", **$50+.**

Question-Mark pin, large ABs in japanned setting, smaller and medium-sized brilliants, unsigned, 1950s, 3", **$50-$100.**

"Hello" Telephone pin, rotating dial, stamped gold-plated plastic, unsigned, 1950s, 2-3/4", **$25-$50.**

Fan fur clip, gold-plated metal with lemon-yellow cabochons, 1940s, unsigned, 2-1/2", **$50.**

Jeweled Artichoke pin, green enameling, RS accents, signed CFW, 1950s, 2", **$25-$50.**

Gourd pin, enameled, gold-plated metal, unsigned, 1960s, 2-3/4", **$50.** Artichoke pin, pea-green enamel on metal, signed Coro, 1960s, 2", **$50.** Carrots brooch, elegant orange enameling, signed Reja, 1950s, 3-1/4", **$150-$200.** Green pepper pin, green-enameled metal with red accent, signed Originals by Robert, 1960s, 1-1/2", **$50.**

Ear of corn pin, "Forbidden Veggies," multicolor and topaz RS on Lucite stalk, gold-plated husks, unsigned, 1940s, 2-3/8", **$75-$125.**

Clockwise from left: Strawberry pin, cherry oval cabochons, signed Swarovski (swan), 1980s, 1-7/8", **$75.** Strawberry Forbidden Fruits pin, red on red rhinestones/Lucite, enameled metal leaves and stem, unsigned, 1940s, 2", **$75.** Strawberry pin, pave-set RS florettes, enameled leaves, heavy gold-plated metal, 1960s, 2-1/4", **$50**. Strawberry pin, ruby RS in japanned metal setting, signed Weiss, 1970s, 1-1/2", **$50**. Strawberry pin, pave-set AB rhinestones, cast red and blue pinpoint light, unsigned, 1-7/8", **$50**.

Top left: Apple brooch, gilded sterling silver, mixed rhinestone cuts (navettes, baguettes, chatons, square cuts, ovals), signed CoroCraft Sterling, 1940s, 1-5/8", **$150.** Top right: Openwork apple pin, mixed stone cuts, cabochon and faceted square cuts, teardrops, navettes, cool blues and purples, signed Lia, 1990s, 1-5/8", **$25-$50.** Lower left: Apple pin, purple AB RS, gunmetal setting, pearlized beaded accents and givre navettes, unsigned, 1950s, 1-3/4", **$50.** Lower right: Bitten apple pin, Adam's apple, ruby and crystal RS where eaten, epoxy leaf, gold-plated metal, unsigned, 1990s, 1-3/4", **$25.**

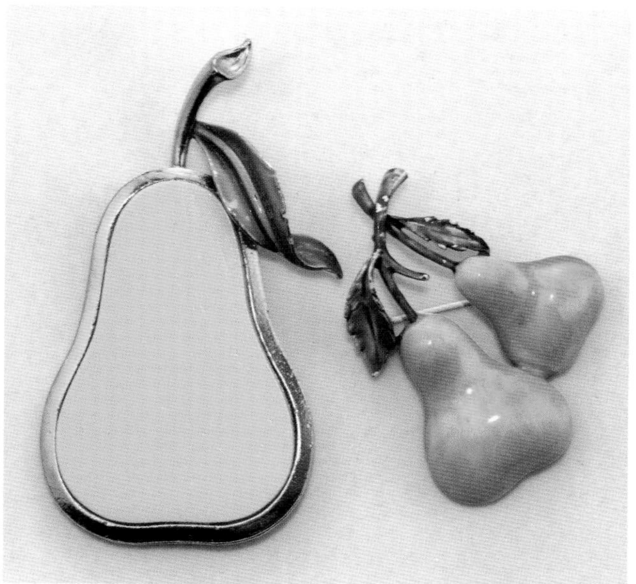

Pear pin, flat plastic yellow pear-shaped insert in metal frame, signed Lisner, 1950s, 3", **$75.** Pear pair pins, orange and yellow enamel, green enamel leaves, signed J.J., 1950s, 2", **$25.**

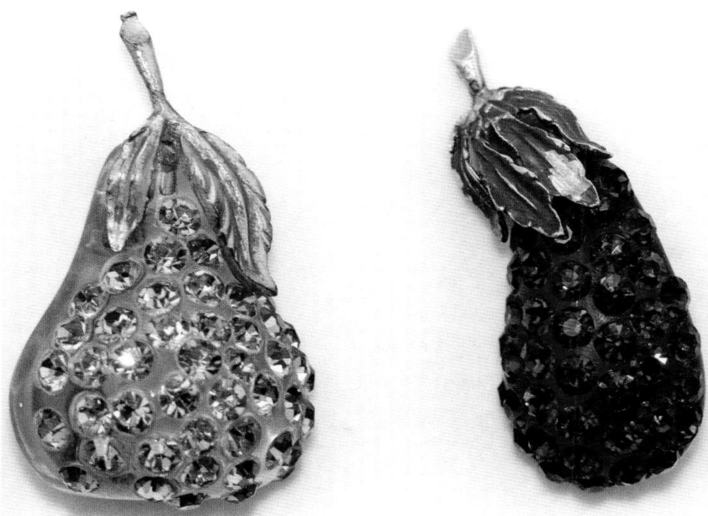

Pear pin, Forbidden Fruits, champagne-colored Lucite, topaz RS, unsigned, 1940s, 2-1/4", **$50-$100.** Eggplant pin, Forbidden Fruits, purple on purple (RS/Lucite), unsigned, 1940s, 2-3/8", **$75-$100.**

Pear pin, white milk-glass RS, white enameled leaves, gold-plated metal, signed BSK, 1960s, 2", **$25-$50.** Lemon pin, Forbidden Fruits, opaque white milk-glass RS on opaque lemon Lucite, unsigned, 1940s, 2-1/4", **$75.**

Peach pin, Forbidden Fruits (orange on orange, RS/Lucite), unsigned, 1940s, 1-7/8", **$50.** Onion pin, Forbidden Veggies, exact onion color, opaque, swirled Lucite with RS accents, unsigned, 1940s, 1-7/8", **$75-$100.**

Grapes brooch, blue ABs in japanned metal setting on leaves, iridescent lavender beads in two sizes with carnival glass effect, signed Thelma Deutsch, 1950s, 3", **$150.**

Grapes pin, beaded fruit and leaves, bead rope in purple, green, wired to bend, unsigned, 1930s, 3", **$100.** Grapes pin, blue glass beads wired to yarn-wrapped pinback, green glass leaves, unsigned, 1930s, 3", **$100.**

Grapes brooch, lavender flat-back cabochons and translucent fuchsia-hot pink RS; violet oval cabochons, pale fruit salad, RS tendril vines, pave-set RS, antiqued gold-plated metal, unsigned, 1940s, 2-7/8", **$250.**

Grapes pin, flat-back cabochons in four sizes and colors, montana, sapphire, ruby and emerald navettes, emerald leaves, unsigned, 1940s, 2-1/4", **$100.** Grapes pin, pearlized charcoal-gray beads, beaded copper leaves, unsigned, 1950s, 2-3/8", **$50.**

Sweet Lemons dress clip, dense, molded celluloid, pretty leaves, real-look branch stem, unsigned, 1940s, 2-3/8", **$75-$100.**

Lush Pears dress clip, dense celluloid fruit and leaves, real-look branch stem, unsigned, 1940s, 2-3/4", **$75-$100.**

Carved Pear dress clip, orange-red Bakelite, wood leaves, unsigned, 1940s, 2", **$75-$100.**

Cherries pin, Lucite ruby igloo cabochons, gunmetal stems, frosted fruit salad leaves, unsigned, 1950s, 2", **$50.**

Old-fashioned pay phone chatelaine pin, black enamel, separate receiver, unsigned, 1950s, 2", **$50.**

Raindrops umbrella pin, silver-plated metal with aquamarine RS teardrops, 1950s, unsigned, 2-3/4", **$50-$100.**

Tomato pin, metallic painted metal, signed B. Blumenthal & Co. Inc., 1935-42, 2", **$25-$50.**

Couple behind adjustable umbrella pin, painted celluloid, 1930s, unsigned, 2-1/2", **$50.**

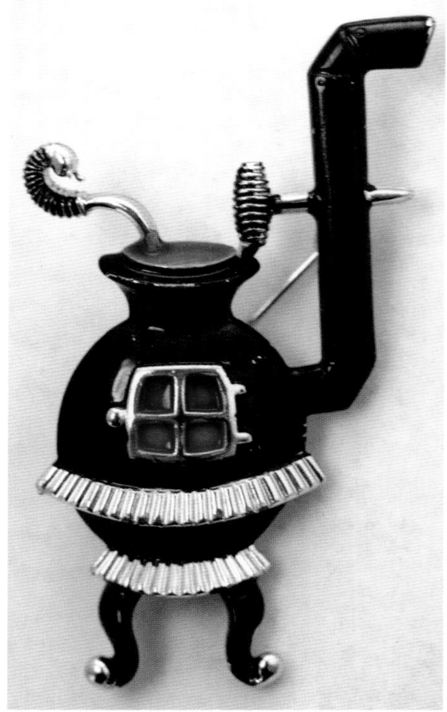

Pot Belly Stove, black enameled gold-plated metal, unsigned, 1960s, 2-1/2", **$10-$25**. Pot-belly stoves were a popular figural motif. Majority were signed Original by Robert; this one, unsigned, is surprisingly more detailed.

Raining cats and dogs umbrella pin, two-tone metal, signed UltraCraft, 1970s, 2-3/8", **$25.**

School blackboard pin, composition, Readin' Ritin' Rithmetic, unsigned, 1940s, 2-1/4", **$50.**

Lady with parasol pin, silver-plated metal, sapphire RS baguettes, unsigned, 2-1/4", **$50**. Lacy parasol pin, silverplate, crystal and aquamarine chatons, unsigned, 1950s, 2-1/4", **$25-$50.**

Ice-skate scatter pins, rhodium plating, pave-set brilliants, baguettes, unsigned, 1940s, 1-7/8", **$25-$50** each.

Floral Hat pin, mesh crown, enameled brim, unsigned, 1990s, 2", **$10-$20.**

Old-Fashioned Footwear fur clip, blue and black enameled gold-plated metal, unsigned, 1940s, 2", **$100-$150.**

Henry Higgins' Slippers pin, enameled, gold-plated metal, RS accents, signed BSK and My Fair Lady, 1950s, 1-7/8", **$25-$50.**

Open-Toe Shoe dress clip, celluloid painted black and red, unsigned, 1920s, 2-1/2", **$50.**

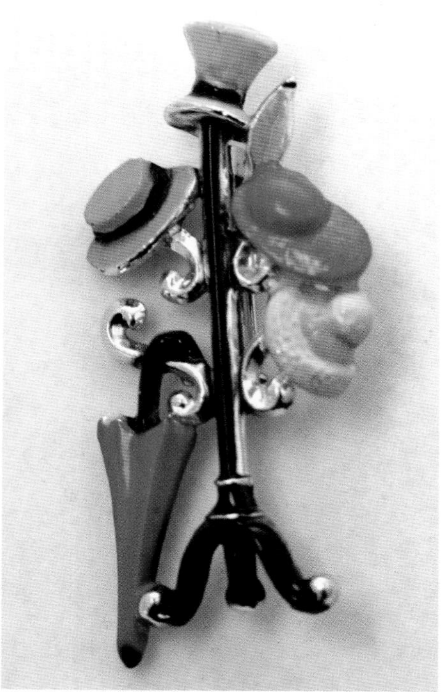

Hat-Rack pin, boldly enameled gold-plated metal, hat tree stand bearing variety of hats and an umbrella, unsigned, 1950s, 2-3/4", **$25.**

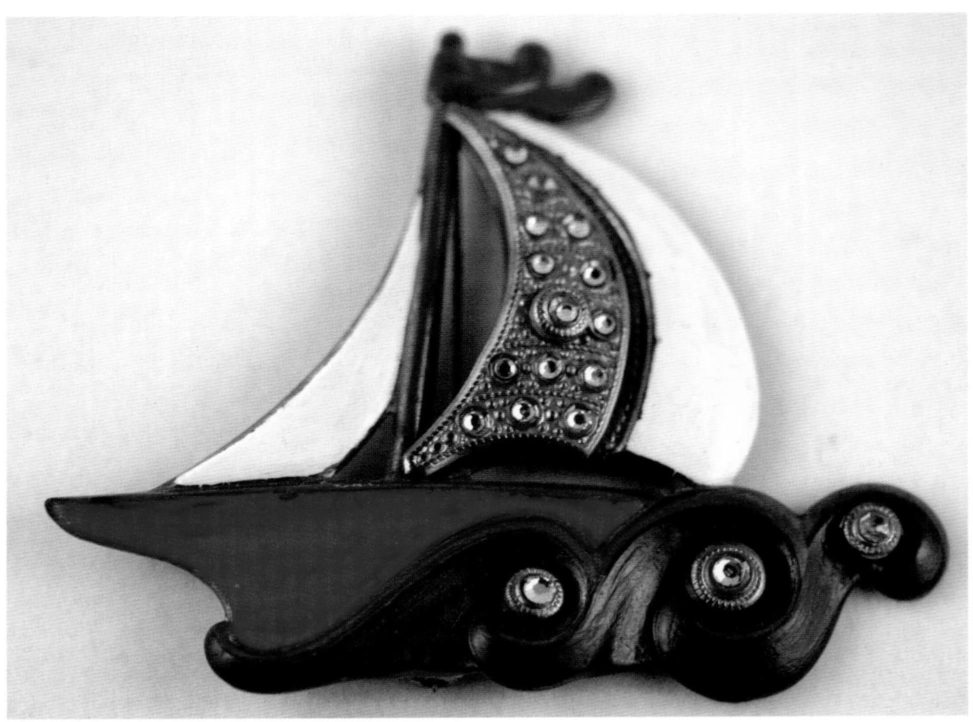

Sailboat brooch, brightly colored painted metal, faux marcasite, unsigned, 1950s, 2-1/2", **$10-$25.**

Sailboat pin, Damascene-patterned metal, marked Spain, 1970s, 2-1/2", **$10-$25.**

Sea Serpents Crown pin, enameled, gold-plated metal, signed MJ Ent., 1980s, 2", **$25.**

CHAPTER 30  MECHANICAL PINS WILL MOVE YOU

Open and Shut Case

Collectors are crazy about clever mechanical charms, so when that small size is tripled, quadrupled or quintupled, the result is a figural brooch that may be as valuable as it is mesmerizing.

Boucher is boss in this lofty domain. Admirers of figurals would give anything to find one of Boucher's incredible and rare "movables." Even knockoffs are notoriously coveted: pelicans with fish in their bills sell for $300 to $500, no comparison to the real thing. Boucher's puppet-like 1940 Cambodian and Punchinello clips have legs and arms that "fling" in and out at the pull of a delicate chain. Multiply Punchinello's original $10 price by 100 to 400 today, depending on who wants it (and how badly) when one becomes available. The enameled Boucher clown clip has a mechanical chin, while the masterpiece pink and cream pelican is a work of art with a fish trembling in his mouth that opens and closes via chain pull. The festively enameled 1940 Jester, originally $7.50, shakes his head and holds a finger up as if to say tut-tut (or shame-shame). Besides the beauty of the pieces themselves, their mechanical design engineering enhances intrinsic value and interest.

At the other end of the spectrum are mechanical jewelry pieces by J.J. and A.J.C. They are 1990-2000s movables, and while plainer and less complicated, they amuse. A snooty butler serves someone a grand dinner beneath a dome. Swing open the cover and find a lip-smacking cat who has already cleaned the fish entrée to the bone.

Some of the earliest mechanicals were celluloid pieces, hearts with knobs that turned for different messages, or traffic lights with chains that pulled up "stop" and "go" signs. An early Hattie Carnegie pin is a cop who, in a canopied stand, pops up to stop cars in their tracks. Another clip is an enameled clown who also seems police-like, with red and green rhinestones in either hand that alternately move up or down.

A typewriter's ribbon roller spins, airplane propellers turn, and in a Coro "weather house," the man or lady rotate out of the house to demonstrate meteorological conditions.

Two other well-known mechanicals are the Warner flower brooch that fully opens and closes via leaf, and of course Coro's Charlie McCarthy dummy pin clip, who appears to talk as his mouth opens and closes when a lever is manipulated.

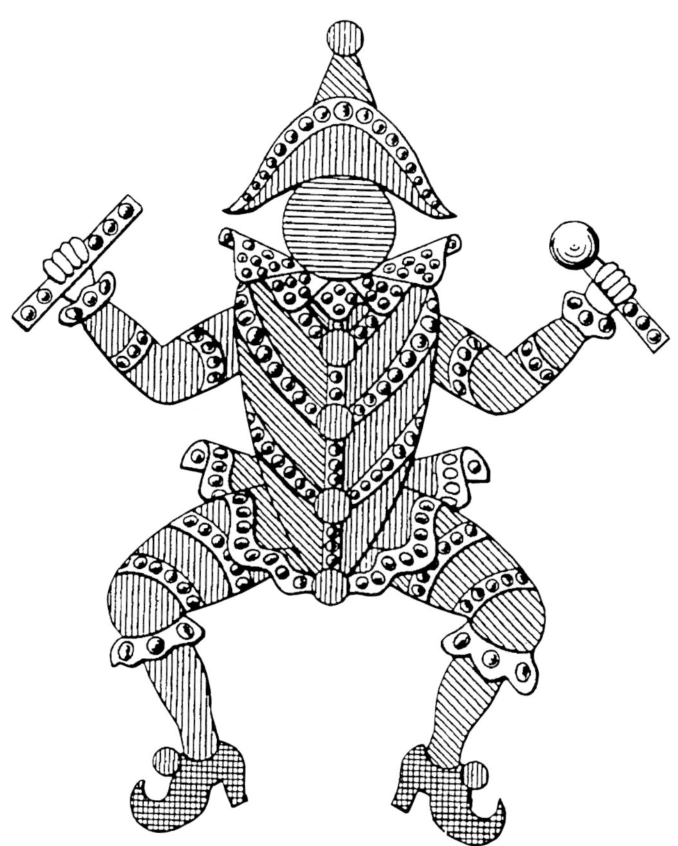

Boucher Moveable Punchinello, enameled, jeweled, rhodium-plated fur clip, mechanical appendages move when chain is pulled, signed MB, 1940, 3", **$5,000**. (See Angie Gordon's *Twentieth Century Costume Jewellery* for earlier specimen, possibly Boucher's own for Cartier?)

"Tricky Dick" Nixon flashing Victory signs, enameled metal, cut-out paper bag swings back to reveal Nixon's identity; unsigned, 1950, 1968 or 1972, 1-5/8", **$50-$150.** Several interpretations are apt. If a 1950s pin, possibly refers to the "Tricky Dick" monicker given Nixon by "The Pink Lady," Helen Gahagan Douglas, whose reputation political foe Nixon besmirched. If 1968, could represent the "New Nixon" comeback period, when he performed on "Laugh-In," or if 1972, shows someone flashing Peace signs but when Nixon's face is revealed, Peace signs become campaign victory sign instead.

Coveted Mechanicals

The seven mechanical 1940 brooches and clip pins by Boucher known as movables include:

- Clown
- Pelican
- Jester
- Cambodian
- Punchinello
- Cuckoo
- Buddha

Cowboy brooch, gold-plated metal: 10-gallon hat sits back off cowpoke's face, flips up to cover for a nap; signed Jeanne, 1950s, 2-1/4", **$50-$100.**

Traffic Cop Stop pin, painted tin: police officer hides under umbrella'd street stand, pops up with white-gloved hand in "Stop!" motion when lever is released, unsigned although seen marked HC for Hattie Carnegie, 1930s, 2-1/8", **$50-$100.**

"Dinner is Served" mechanical pin: Butler serves dinner; dome swings open revealing kitty and remains of large fish, signed A.J.C., 1990s, 2-1/8", **$25.**

Shower door pin, water turned on, towel over door, opens to reveal very surprised soapy naked lady, signed JJ in sans-serif italics, 1980s, 2-1/4", **$10-$25.**

 CHAPTER 31 Sea Life...to Sport on Land

Aquavita

It's a strange fact: Collecting interpretations of single-unique motifs is often more compelling than chasing broad-spectrum subjects. In other words, hundreds or thousands of *different* flowers grow in the real world, and each exists in jewelry form too.

But in the water world, only one basic seahorse glides through oceans—and this basic form must be creatively interpreted a thousand different ways in its jewelry manifestations. For some twisted reason, that is endlessly fascinating.

It's one reason so many people collect turtles, crustaceans, fish and the equine of the sea. They also make great canvases. The turtle's basic oval shell works well whether it's made of jade, Lucite, patterned metal or carved wood. Designers then decorated with many ornaments: rhinestone accents in a Trifari jelly belly, layers of beads in a Har version, Coro's swirling enamels mixed around pearls. One collector with an incredible bale of tortoises loves the figural because she rescues turtles and reptile wildlife, so the brooches allow her to wear her first love near her heart.

Aquavita have an intrinsic appeal because they are colorful and exotic creatures from mysterious, dark depths. The curling tail of a seahorse is a come-hither aesthetic hook. So many single fish are unique (and inexpensive), an entire school of smart fish is simple to build, followed by graduation to the next level for trophy catches such as CoroCraft's gilded sterling Rock fish or Trifari's baroque-pearl-bodied bubble blower.

Fish also have a following with Pisces people, just as Cancers dig crab pins. (Scorpios and scorpions, not so much.) Semi-hideous crabs and trembler-clawed lobsters, in fact, morph into some of the most spectacular specimens of aquavita in the jewelry world, but nothing's a bigger catch in the collectible seas than Boucher's cheerful pink octopus. That rarity sold most recently at auction for more than $14,000. No wonder so many women and men have gone fishin'.

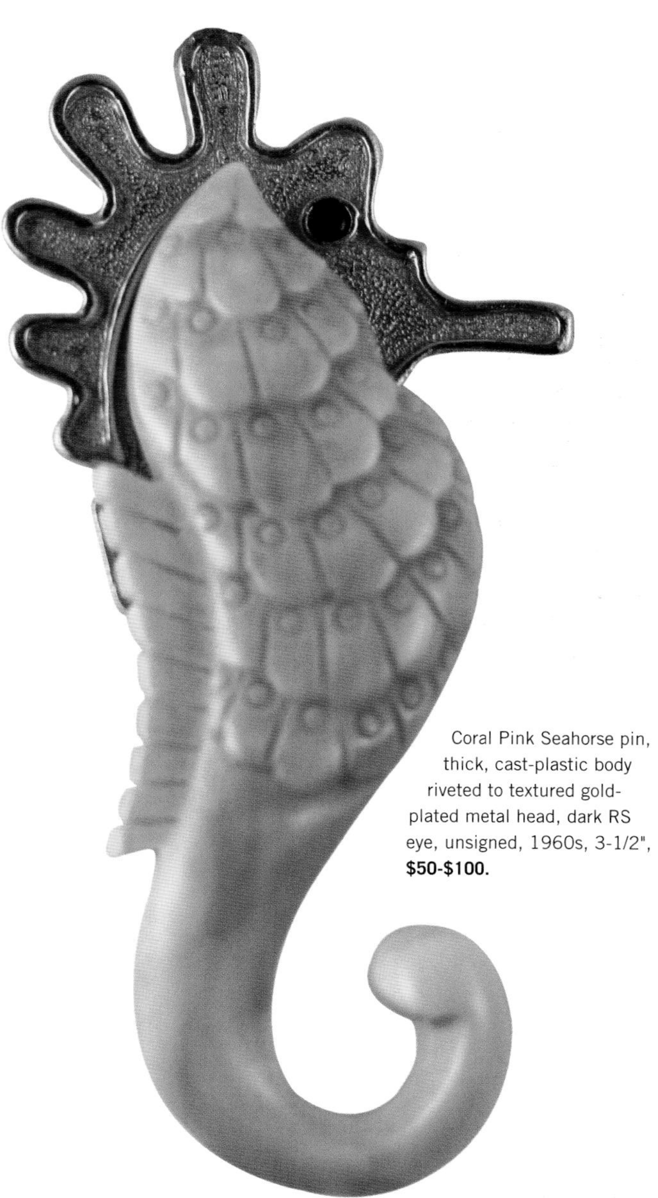

Coral Pink Seahorse pin, thick, cast-plastic body riveted to textured gold-plated metal head, dark RS eye, unsigned, 1960s, 3-1/2", **$50-$100.**

Seahorse Duette clip, lavish polychrome enamels on rhodium, cabochon eye, RS accents, signed Coro, 1940s, 3", **$250.** (Part of a two-piece fur clip set that attaches to brooch mechanism.)

Snow Seahorse pin, white-enameled, antiqued gold-plated metal, inset bead cabochons, beads dangling from chains on tail, unsigned, 1950s, 2-1/2", **$50.**

Beaded Seahorse pin, gilded, painted metallic green and purple polymer clay, unsigned Linda Goff, 2000, 4", **$75-$100.**

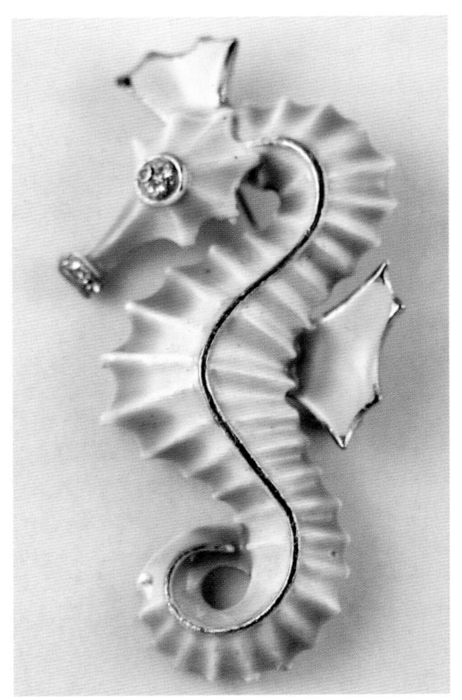

Elegant Seahorse pin, mint-green pastel enamel, RS accent, unsigned, 1950s, 2-3/4", **$50+.**

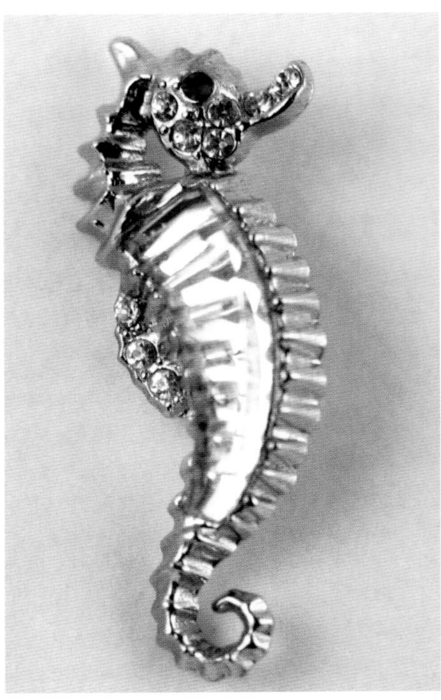

Aquamarine Seahorse pin, translucent carved glass, rhodium plating, jeweled accents, 1938-42, unsigned, 2-1/8", **$50-$100.**

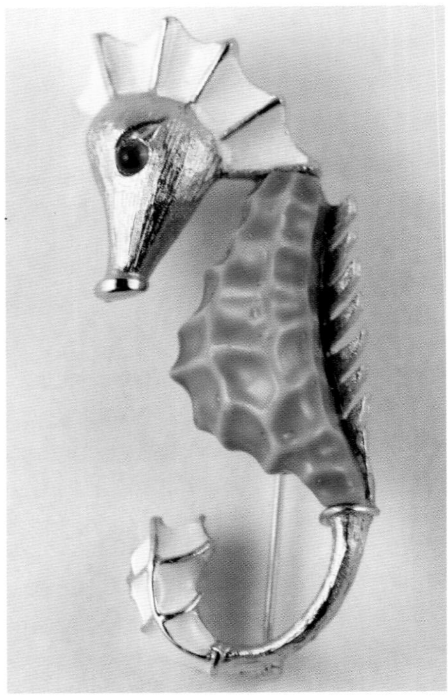

Patterned Seahorse pin, alligator'd sea-green plastic body, white-enameled, gold-plated metal, unsigned, 1950s, 2-5/8", **$50+.**

Jelly Belly seahorse pin, polychrome enamel on gold-plated metal, Lucite center, signed Coro, 1940s, 2", **$50-$75.**

Pearl-Bodied Seahorse pin, faux pearl-encrusted body, gold-plated face and body, unsigned, 1950s, 2-1/2", **$25-$50.**

Tortoise Seahorse brooch, root beer Bakelite, RS accent, unsigned, 1930-40s, 3", **$75-$150.**

Jade Seahorse pin, gilded sterling, jade belly, carnelian eye, signed AC, 1950s, 1-1/2", **$25-$50.**

Seahorse Duo fur clips, enameled red faces, openwork antiqued silver-plated metal, sapphire RS, unsigned, 1938-42, 2" and 1-1/2", **$250** pair.

Starfish pin (or could be a jellyfish), well-cast gold-plated metal, RS accents, green and white marbled resin, signed Corocraft, 1960s, 2-1/2", **$50.**

Spectacular turtle dress clip, jeweled baguettes and square cuts, pave-set RS head and feet, pot metal, arrow mark, 2-3/4", **$250-$300.**

Grand Turtle pin, Russian-gold metal, deep casting, pink glass cabochon, faceted lead crystals, unsigned Czech or Miriam Haskell, 1930s, 2-1/4", **$75-$150.**

Metal Turtle pin, elaborate construction, silver metal, quilt-patterned top shell swedged-riveted to base, dimensional, unsigned, 1960s, 4", **$150.**

Seal pin, inset with square and igloo multicolored cabochons, unsigned, 1970s, 3", **$50-$75.**

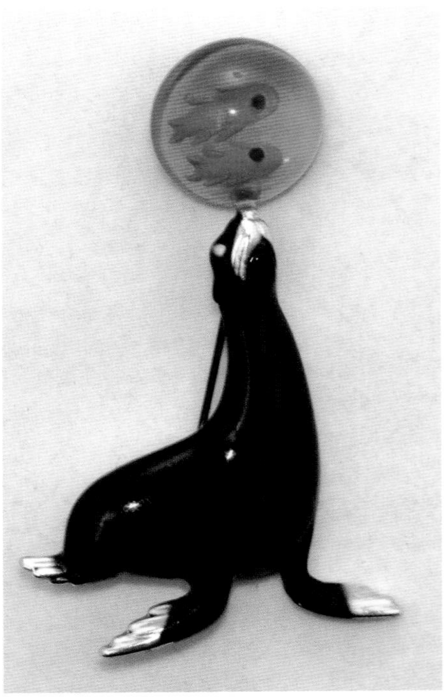

Seal pin, black enamel, with amber Lucite igloo bowl with fish, signed AJMC, 2000s, 3", **$25-$50.**

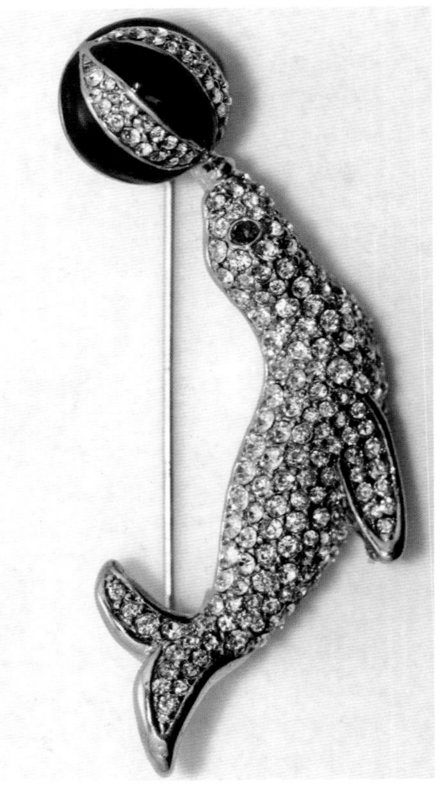

Seal pin, RS pave crystals with pave and black ball, green eye, unsigned, 2000s, 3", **$25-$50.**

Black jelly belly, clear Lucite and black enamel, goldplate, tiny antennae beads tip, unsigned, 1950, 2-1/4", **$250.**

Crystal-bellied crawler, gold-plated metal, large, faceted blunted, 1-1/2" navette, unsigned, 1940s, 2-5/8", **$150.**

Moonstone Belly Crab pin, gold-plated antennae and claws, pave trim, unsigned, 1940, 2-1/2", **$250.**

Colorful Crab brooch, multicolor hand-set Swarovski faceted stones, signed B&M Von Walhof, 2000s, 2-1/2", **$65.**

Splattered Crab fur clip, enameled red, pot metal, "Jackson Pollack," unsigned, 1940s, 2-1/4", **$150-$250.**

Fancy Rockfish pin, heavy, gilded silver, large diamante jewel accents, large simulated aquamarine in mouth, pink-rose faceted crystal eyes, exceptional casting, 1940s, signed CoroCraft Sterling, 3", **$250.**

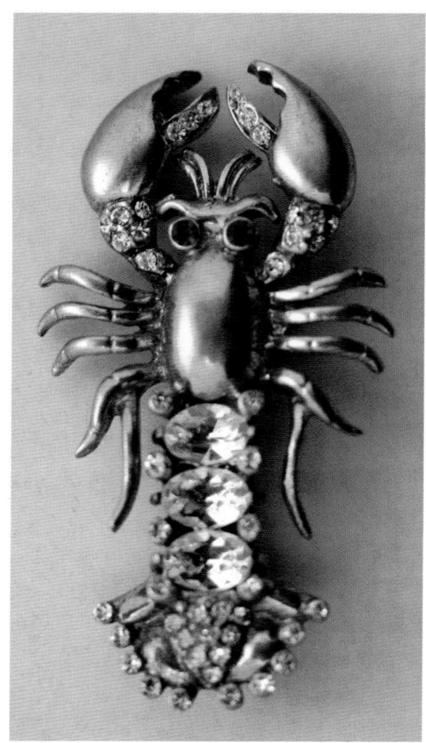

Glamorous Lobster pin, gilded silver, raised bezel-set simulated diamonds, tiny chatons for lacy effect, signed CoroCraft Sterling, 1940s, 2-1/2", **$150-$200.**

Lobster on Half Shell brooch, coral and glass, plastic red lobster on shell, signed Stanley Hagler N.Y.C. and Ian St. Gielar, 2000s, 4", **$200.**

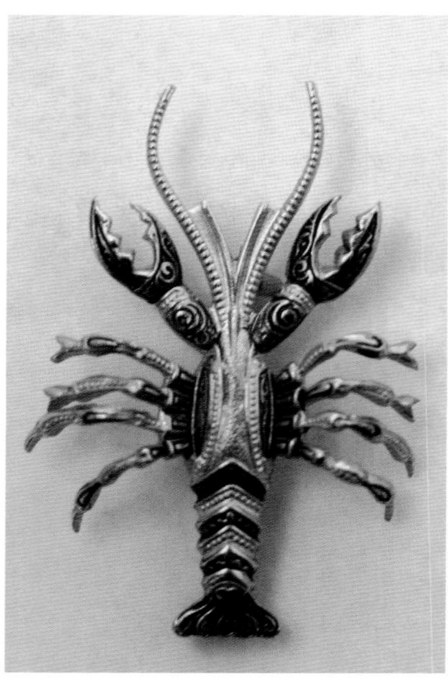

Damascene Lobster pin, patterned metal and enamel, marked Spain, 1960s, 2-1/4", **$10-$25.**

Frog on Lucite Lilypad pin, pewter and plastic frog, unsigned, date unknown, 3-1/2", **$50.**

Frog Among Waterlilies brooch, multicolor hand-set Swarovksi crystals, B&M Von Walhof Creations, 3", **$80.**

Fish pin-pendant, cast-amber resin acrylic, pave-set RS, unsigned, 1980s, 3-1/8", **$100-$150.**

Google-eyed fish, painted carved wood, unsigned Elzac, 1940s, 3-3/4", **$50.**

Damascene Fish pin, patterned metal and enamel, marked Spain, 1960s, 2", **$10-$25.**

Angel Fish brooch, 2-1/2", **$120,** and Pretty Prawn pin, 5", **$950,** trembler, each with hand-set first-quality Swarovski jewels, signed Bettina Von Walhof, 2000s.

Petite Tortoise pin, silver-plated metal, mixed crystal RS in diamante and topaz, signed CFW, 1950s, 1-5/8", **$25-$50.**

CHAPTER 32

Great Painters Made Jewelry Too

Art in Translation

Fifty years ago, Americans adored France, period. Everyone wanted to experience Paris, and back then, the 21st-Century-style snide jibes targeting our sophisticated *amis* across the Atlantic were no where on people's tongues. All things French were *It*, so a savvy company like Coro would of course want to capitalize on the spirit of that *joie de vivre.* Such chic was epitomized in Coro's Vendôme division, charged with capturing the *je ne sais quoi* of Gallic style.

The woman whose purview Vendôme was, head designer Helen Marion, surely traveled regularly to Paris to translate French fashion into *la mode Américaine.* One series of Vendôme brooches in particular also makes it clear Marion took in the blockbuster 1963 exhibit at the Musée de Louvre, *Métamorphoses: Cent Bijoux de Georges Braque.* Presented in the last year of the Cubist artist's life, the solo show caused a sensation, so exquisite were the 100-plus pieces of jewelry. Seeing Braque's lapidary works of art, Helen Marion was wise enough to distill their essence into a series of six costume-jewelry brooches, each marked Vendôme. She chose well, smartly incorporating Braque's favorite themes into the colorful pins, including birds, nature, human profiles and even cigarettes.

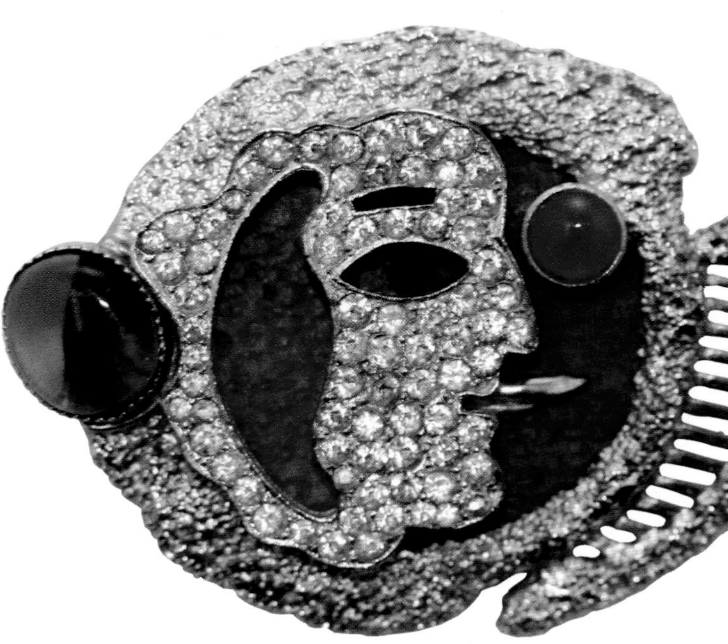

"Le Fumeur" brooch (imitating the work of Georges Braque, Cubist French artist whose jewelry was exhibited in Paris in 1963 at a major show in the Louvre), textured gold-plated metal frame, layers of color and materials, face in profile soldered above pools of lapis and carnelian enamels, bezel-set unfoiled translucent cabochons, signed Vendôme, 1963-65, 2-1/2", **$600.**

The Helen Marion costume jewelry interpretation of Braque's *Birds* sells almost 45 years after it was manufactured for approximately $500, which becomes a bargain souvenir when compared with the real thing. At the Tadema Gallery in London, Braque's *Birds,* composed of gold, diamonds and pink topaz, requires a few pounds over $85,000 in order to bring this important work home to roost.

The heady thrill of collecting jewelry by great artists is a realm most collectors cannot enter, but it's one to dream about. A shortlist of major artists who designed jewelry includes Picasso, Erté, Calder, Dali and Man Ray. If it is surprising to learn Braque's bijoux are made of gold and precious gems, that's probably because artists are usually associated with being bohemian, egalitarian types who would choose the humblest of materials to incorporate into their wearable art. Some did feel that way. Others viewed gold and diamonds literally as precious because they came from the earth. In other words, they wanted to work with natural materials. It becomes more understandable when viewed that way, but not more affordable. We ran into a 2005 appraisal of a woman's metal necklace with lion faces on bronze medallions, a work of art whose design provenance reportedly was Picasso's own hands. The appraiser said it was difficult to ascertain if Picasso's artistry was in fact at work without examining it in person, but if provenance were verified, valued it at about $20,000.

One big news story in Picasso jewelry broke in 1998, when up for auction came numerous pieces (marcasite portrait medallion, enameled floral portrait brooch, mechanical rings, etc.) previously unknown even to serious students of Pablo. The treasure trove belonged to his lover of nine years, Dora Maar, who kept the precious keepsakes of her long love affair stashed all over their Paris residence. The surprise to Picassophiles was that he made jewelry in the 1930s, pre-dating a commercial collaboration in the 1950s and '60s. Typically, predicted sale prices for the auction, especially the jewelry, were low. The New York *Times* reported that Maar's estate, which included paintings and drawings as well as the jewelry, wound up selling for $30 million—almost *le chump change* when one portrait of Maar herself sold in 2006 for more than $95 million.

The solution for impoverished lovers of Cubist figurals is the wide spectrum of Picasso-like jewelry available on the market: Eisenberg Enamels from the 1970s, unmarked plastics from the Philippines, and mad-mad stuff from as long ago as the '20s. (This book's author also took a crack at how Picasso might have designed a Christmas tree pin if anyone had worked up the nerve to ask him.)

Two other intriguing artists who made jewelry are Dali and Erté. Dali began his jewelry odyssey in 1949 with jeweled Surreal themes that vibrated from his paintings, portraying eyes, lips, bleeding hearts and melting motifs from nature. Almost half a decade elapsed before his estate gave its blessing to the reproduction of his creations in costume versions. While we could find no original jewelry of Dali's available on the market, as many as three permutations of one figural brooch, *Tristan and Isolde*, were being sold: a costume version with the estate's imprimatur, $159; an unsigned knockoff for $75; and a precious-gems version by Henry Kaston (a jeweler who reportedly worked with Dali), an 18k brooch with diamonds and rubies, originally $10,000 on sale for $5,000.

Erté's "wearable art" jewelry, on the other hand, is unmistakably Art Deco. Two particularly striking figural brooches are his sky-scraper-and-sunrays *Manhattan*, 14k gold and sterling silver with diamonds, about $7,000; and the charming *Love's Screen*, a pair of lovers behind an umbrella, 14k gold and sterling silver with seed pearls and MOP, $2,200.

Besides making a decision to go with precious versus common materials, artists had to decide if their work would be painterly, like brushstrokes but with metals and stones, or sculptural and dimensional, more like true jewelry. Some of Dali's jewelry is particularly sculptural.

The other category in figural jewelry for collectors fond of artistic geniuses but looking for a bargain is the metal brooch that copies exactly an artist's work of art. Look for Andy Warhol's work in this lineup.

Will the Real Artist Please Stand Up?

Best known as Picasso, Dali and Erté, the names behind the masterpieces were different from the signatures. Once again, what's in a name?

Dali: *Salvador Felipe Jacinto Dali I Domenech*

Erté: *Romain de Tirtoff*

Picasso: *Pablo Diego José Francisco de Paulo Juan Nepomuceno María de los Remedios Crispin Crispiniano de la Santísima Trinidad Ruiz y Picasso*

"Cubist Face" stick pin (matching earrings not shown; part of a great-artists series), 18k gold-plated metal and enamel, signed EISENBERG, carded Eisenberg Ice, tagged Artist Enamels, 1973-74, 3" inc. pin, **$100.**

The Men Behind the Men

Many artists who moved in the jewelry world designed it—and left the taxing execution up to gem-cutters and lapidary pros who could make their flights of fancy a reality. Some of the great artists' partners in jewelry making included:

***Baron Heger de Loewenfeld** for Georges Braque*

***François Hugo** for Pablo Picasso*

***Carlos Bernardo Alemany** for Salvador Dali*

"Tristan & Isolde" brooch (authentic authorized copy of 1940s pin by Salvador Dali, Spanish Surrealist artist), gold-plated cast metal and translucent red epoxy for wine goblet, RS accents, signed Dali (front and reverse), 2001, 2-1/2", **$100-$200.**

"Tristan & Isolde" pin, gold-plated metal and green epoxy, unauthorized copy of a Dali design, unsigned, 2000s, 2-1/4", **$25-$50.**

"Marilyn" pin, heavy gold-plated metal and enamel cloisonnné "painting" of famous Andy Warhol Pop Art work, signed Warhol, 1964, 2-3/4", **$50-$100.**

"Cubist Faces" pin, Picassoesque-style visages, enamel cloisonnné gold-plated metal, unsigned, 1960-70s, 1-3/8", **$25-$50.**

CHAPTER 33  Motifs from Lands Collectors Love

Exotica

Our love of mysterious, distant lands and fascination with exotic cultures are reflected in jewelry designs, but sometimes sparked by specific events: hit Broadway shows, popular movies or art exhibitions. Three culture-related design trends in vintage figural jewelry were African, Oriental and Latin themes. Foreign influences affected so many fashions, who knows exactly what the various jewelry houses and designers saw to prompt them to create Mexican men and tribal natives and colorful Chinoiserie, but here are some pertinent happenings in the Thirties, Forties and Fifties.

The 1927-28 Archie Leach Broadway musical vehicle "Golden Dawn" was mentioned in an earlier chapter. Reportedly it was a reprehensible piece of racist mockery, but proved popular during its run, was set in Africa and was made into a movie in 1930. "King Kong," which opens in Africa, hit screens three years later. In 1935 a blockbuster exhibition of African sculpture opened at the Museum of Modern Art in Manhattan. And December 1940 marked the 75th anniversary of the Thirteenth Amendment, abolishing slavery in America, celebrated with major concert series and exhibits of books, paintings and other works of art. In the 1930s, great jazz music accompanied theatrical cartoons that now, to modern viewers, are so racist, they are not televised. As for ratings, the hit television show "American Idol" could only dream of the radio audience enjoyed by "Amos 'n' Andy," starring two white men pretending to be black, in the 1930s: 40 million people tuned in to each episode. All such events and productions put black culture and Africa in Americans' minds. It was translated into jewelry ranging from beautiful masks and African natives to racist caricatures to novelty pins such as a "white man" being carried in a boiling pot by two cannibals. Key pieces from the era include Reja's *Africaner* series, with Nubian, Ubangi and Congo Belle pins, as well as the Rice-Weiner *Jungle Jewelry* of Zoltan Korda's *The Jungle Book*, from the exotic native woman's head to the young drummer boy, as well as Mazer Blackamoors, the Coro native head set and Ubangi.

An extremely well-received 1939 Gene Autry film, "South of the Border," was followed by Autry's 1941 "Down Mexico Way," both captivating audiences with Spanish missions, Native American culture and colonial heritage, old ruins and lovely senioritas. Carmen Miranda was a major Latin influence in America, and Cuban émigré Desi Arnaz introduced the Conga line dance of Carnivale to his adopted country, where it was the rage. (Arnaz, obviously best known for "I Love Lucy," starred in "Cuban Pete" (1946), "Jitterumba" (1947) and "Holiday in Havana" (1949).

"Guys and Dolls" moved from Broadway in 1950 to the silver screen in 1955, and the contrast of Sister Sara's but-

Exotic African Head, gold-plated metal with multicolor RS collar, crystal pave feather flourish, unsigned, 1938-42, 3-1/2", **$100-$150.**

toned-up self to the frenzied dance frolics when Sara and Sky travel to Havana couldn't have been more drastic, showing Cubans as sensuous and free-living. Noted pieces of jewelry in this realm include Chanel-Reinad's Mexican in a palm tree, Boucher's many colorful Mexican personnages of the 1940s, especially the sleeping Mexican man resting against a cactus; Coro's toreador-bull chatelaine, Mexican woman with child. An entire Elzac jewelry line in 1946 was called *Tiempo de Fiestas.*

Grinning Chinaman dress clip, pot metal, Reinad for (signed) B. Blumenthal & Co. Inc., 1940-42, 2-1/4", **$100-$150.**

Some '30s exhibits at the Chicago Art Institute included Chinese and Japanese Color Prints in 1936, and Chinese Porcelains and Jades in 1938-39. During these years and beyond, four different "Charlie Chan" series were broadcast on four different networks. The comic strip ran from 1938-42, post publication of the E.D. Biggers Charlie Chan novels, 1925-32. "A Chinese Honeymoon" was a huge Shubert hit in 1902, but most people are more familiar with movies dating from about 1930 to roughly 1944, criticized not only for their racist Asian portrayals but likewise the picture they painted of characters of African heritage. *Teahouse of the August Moon* was a hit in 1953, and Belgian-Chinese doctor-novelist Han Suyin wrote *A Many-Splendoured Thing* in 1952, which became a hit Academy-Award-winning film in 1955.

Some have commented that America's overly romanticized view of China caused complications after WWII.

Asian-influenced jewelry of note includes Reja's Chinese Mandarin and Cambodian Dancer, Coro's Fujiman, Chinaman, emperor and empress Duette; the Boucher Mandarin and Chinese couple, Chinese dragon and huge dwarf tree; Trifari's Ming line, Hobe's Thibetans and Bandora jeweled Netsuke, Sandor's Balinese head, and Nettie Rosenstein's Chinese couple.

Whether the come-home message of "You Belong to Me" or Sinatra's '53 recording of "Come Fly with Me," Americans knew what wanderlust was. If they couldn't go there, they could wear a virtual souvenir on their collars.

Tribal Queen dress clip, pot metal with chains, Reinad for (signed) Blumenthal, 1940-42, 3-3/4", **$50-$100.**

"Fujiman" Chinese Warlord fur clip, pot metal, signed Coro, 1942, 3", **$100-$150.**

Sleepy Señor on Donkey fur clip, enameled pot metal, unsigned, 1938-42, 2", **$50-$100.**

Lantern bearer Chinaman, enameled pot metal, art glass beads, unsigned, Rice-Weiner design, 1941, 3", **$50-$100.**

Mexican Sombrero Man hunter brooch, crossbar dangling charms of duck, Billiken, art beads, chickens, etc., unsigned, 1940s, 3", **$50-$100.**

Napping Native Man pin, enameled, gold-plated metal and Bakelite, unsigned, Worth design, 1955-65, 2", **$25-$50.**

Primping Native Woman pin, enameled, gold-plated metal and Bakelite, unsigned, Worth design, 1955-65, 2", **$50-$100.**

Chinese maiden fur clip, enameled gold-plated metal, RS accents, unsigned, marked Patent Pend., patent No. 120,462 by Walter Lampl, 1940, 2", **$250.**

Ethnic Tribal Court dress clip, brass with turquoise etc. beads, dimensional, unsigned, 1950s, 3", **$50-$100.**

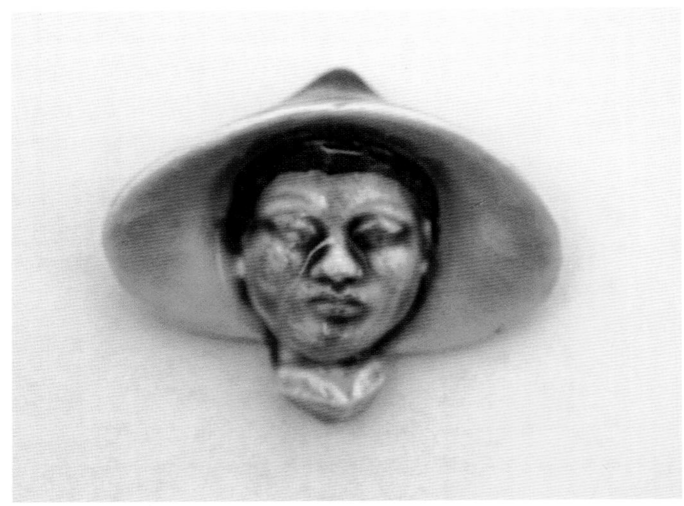

"Good Earth" Chinese lady, ceramic version of Coro pin, unsigned, 1940, 2-1/2", **$10-$25.**

CHAPTER 34 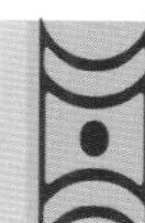 CHATELAINES ARE CLEVER CONNECTIONS TO THE PAST

Chain Gang

Compared with the domestic Victorian models ladies of the house carried around the home to keep small tools and accessories handy, these decorative chatelaines have no utilitarian function. But pins and clips with chain liaisons could at least keep a bull from wandering away from a matador. While figural pins joined by links aren't chatelaines strictly speaking, they've come to be called that.

Jewelry chatelaines of the 1920s through 1950s may be amusing or even elaborate. And when one end has "gone missing," the hunt is on for the fugitive, if its identity is known. If not, only style and imagination will tell. For instance, a tall, heavily jeweled gladiator (see P. 202) is missing his other half—and the full chatelaine does not appear in any book.

To what was he attached? A chariot, a lion or a second gladiator?

Older Eisenberg connected-clips featured fairly heavy double chains and in most cases, when the clips turn up, they no longer have the chains. Few collectors even realize the pin clips were once connected. Check them for bale-like loops. The king and queen and a number of flowers grow in this category, but many more may be as well. Chain champion Reinad was partial to chatelaine jewelry, so some pre-1942 Eisenberg linked pins may have a Reinad provenance. Finally, the triplets by Chanel (Reinad) are series of three animals connected by chains, usually in graduated sizes.

Some of the best known chatelaine jewelry includes the Leo Glass string of birds; unsigned Art Deco crystal rhinestone people walking dogs and father-son animal motifs (plus similar gold-plated whimsy figurals); Fashionart crowns; eagle and drums; Chanel and Blumenthal penguins; unsigned chatelaines attributed to Coro: heart and key, toreador and bull, cupids, horses, Mr. And Mrs. Pig, Mr. & Mrs. Bird; Nettie Rosenstein frogs; mother and baby swans; Star-Art sterling clocks.

Art Deco Dog & Walker pins, ridged-glass simulating baguettes in geometric 2-1/8" dog; 2-1/2" man has all-navette body and fruit-salad head, marked 238, 1930s, **$100.**

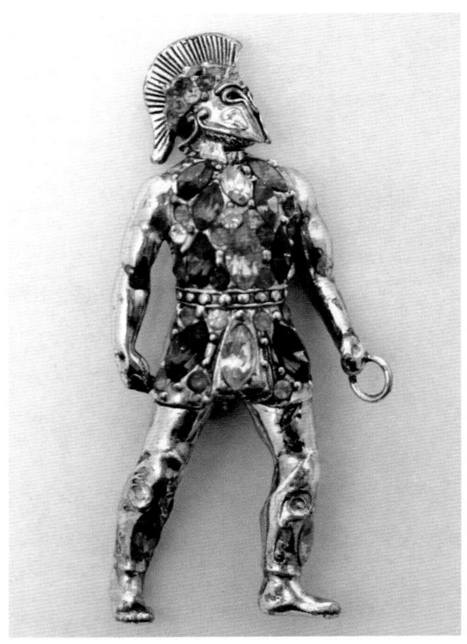

Lonely Gladiator brooch, gilded base metal, encrusted polychrome faceted navettes and chatons, unsigned, 1950s, 3-3/8", **$150.** Highly detailed (toes visible on bare feet, tiny facial features and beard cast in metal beneath helmet). Chain and partner pin missing, so mystery remains: To what was gladiator attached? Chariot, lion ... ?

Clown & Accoutrements brooches, 3-D metal clown head in rose-gold-plated finish wears top hat, oversized bow tie, wired-bead eyes, red nose; attached to second top hat with cane, unsigned, 1930s; 2-5/8" head, 2-1/2" cane, **$150.**

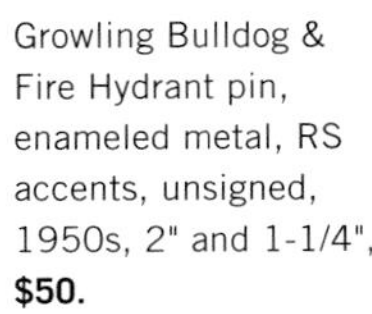

Growling Bulldog & Fire Hydrant pin, enameled metal, RS accents, unsigned, 1950s, 2" and 1-1/4", **$50.**

Jeweled Key & Crowned Lock pins, antiqued gold metal, large simulated aquamarine stones, polychrome cabochons, triple-strand connector chain, unsigned, 1947-52, 3-3/8" key, 1-3/4" lock, **$75-$150.**

Double Horse brooches, pennant flags, jeweled manes and eyes, gilded metal, unsigned Reja design, 1940s, 2-3/4" each, **$100-$150.**

Gun & Holster pins, pistol fits into 3-D holster, gold-plated metal, simulated diamonds and emeralds, unsigned, 1947-52, 3-1/2" pistol, 2-3/8" holster, **$75-$150.**

CHAPTER 35 Guys in Costumes

Send in the Clowns

Like clowns or not, their history is a wild ride. And the innate fear Cosmo Kramer, for instance, felt toward clowns wasn't unfounded. As they tumbled down through history from their origin in ancient Egypt, clowns, fools or court jesters were feared for many reasons. Physical deformities or mental shortcomings that relegated them to fool or clown class in the first place made them outcasts and required them to dress in loud stripes. And because they enjoyed or were allowed the "free speech" of the insane, they seemed to operate outside societal restrictions. In the extreme, people even viewed clowns as devils. No wonder European clowns often appear more sinister—an attitude that translated to jewelry. The Charles F. Worth company designed clown figurals for Har (probably Harrods) that appear almost satanic. When dealers describe the clowns on Har charm bracelets, they typically say the charms include devils, but that the clowns are much creepier.

Americans are most familiar with whiteface circus-type clowns such as Clarabelle, and character-clown hobos Red Skelton and Emmett Kelly, or tramps such as Chaplin. Clown categories are actually much more nuanced than that, and if you take the clown out of the costume, it's said the classic clown relationship is clear in trios from Moe, Larry and Curly to Jerry, George and Kramer, each playing a specific role in the comic triangle. One of the most "foolish" factoids is that Uncle Sam is based on a clown, perhaps the greatest of all, an American named Dan Rice (né Daniel McLaren), the most inventive and versatile circus performer ever—who, with name recognition better than Lincoln's, also ran for the office of president of the United States.

In jewelry, the black-and-white-faced Pierrot, born out of the Commedia dell'Arte, is common, whether ceramic or rendered in gold-tone metal. The ubiquitous nature of inexpensive clowns has cheapened the category, which, like some clowns, is sad. Most funny-boy brooches are garish as expected, since the costumes and face paint are part of the polychrome package.

But because clowns, from anonymous red-haired acrobats to Emmett Kelly lookalikes, are so common, the unexpected treasures get overlooked because no one's looking. Mechanicals—the mouth-moving Boucher masterpiece, unsigned

Distinguished Clown pin, sculptural, deeply cast antiqued gold-plated metal, tiny pastes, faux pearl buttons, signed Crislu, 1960s, 2", **$50-$75.**

swivel-head fellows with two faces, jesters with moving legs and arms—are smart collectibles. The Ivorine "whiteface" and the "auguste" (bright colors but no whiteface) clown lineup Kenneth Lane created for Hattie Carnegie (and later used himself) are works of art in plastic and metal, especially the large heads. His designs are still being made today, copied in China. Crislu has its mark on a simple vintage bust of antiqued-gold metal, with tiny crystal rhinestones, that looks like a small sculpture. As for harlequins and jesters, the variety's enough to make any collector grin, but Calvaire and Reja have some of the best-known and most desirable of all fools.

Perhaps clown jewelry will enjoy a renaissance, as its real-life counterparts have. Celeb clowns are circus's biggest marketing tool, used by ringmasters from The Big Apple and Ringling Brothers to Cirque du Soleil.

Mechanical Cop Clown fur clip, arms raise and lower, enameled-gilded metal, RS accents in hands, 2-1/8", 1930s, **$100-$150.**

Bragging Clown pin, pantomimes "The One That Got Away," enameled metal, signed CFW (sometimes signed HAR), 1955-65, 1-7/8", **$25-$50.**

Acrobatic Clown pin series, all versions of original design by Kenneth J. Lane for Hattie Carnegie; unsigned, range from 1970s to 1990s, each 2-1/8", **$15-$25** each.

CHAPTER 36  Flowers, Flowers, Everywear

A Garden of Jewelry Delights

Corsages, real and fake, were *de rigueur* fashion accessories for events and holidays, especially in the 1930s-50s. A swell suit, coat or gown was naked if worn unadorned to a football game, country-club dance, Christmas Day Mass, Easter parade or Mother's Day breakfast without a pin-on bouquet covering lapel or wrist.

No wonder floral brooches are the most overgrown of all figural categories. Less cumbersome than corsages and more durable than crispy petals, flower pins also had the advantage of sparkle when needed. Every color for every ensemble in a wardrobe could easily fit into a jewelry box, allowing ladies the freedom to file flattened corsages between the leaves of a book.

"Quivering Camellia" fur clip, enameled pot metal and simulated gems, trembler, signed Coro, 1938, 2-1/4", **$25-$50.** This is the oldest version, one section of a Coro Duette brooch.

Jewelry makers kept those cherished corsages in mind, though, for some pins are as big and bounteous as blooms.

Floral styles covered every conceivable mode and mood, daytime to evening: large Lucite and wood blossoms by Elzac; elaborately enameled beauties by Chanel Novelty (aka Reinad, long mistakenly assumed to be French, from the house of Chanel); delicious Lisner pastels with jelly belly petals; spectacularly stoned Coro confections, including every color of wiggling camellia; the dimensional triumphs of Trifari art, equivalent in workmanship to the finest precious jewelry; lavish Miriam Haskell beaded clips spilling leaves and flowers in asymmetrical abandon; gigantic holiday poinsettia; Ming's Sterling marvelous painted-ivory Bird of Paradise flora in brilliant yellows; Monet's densely enameled floral fur clips; Weiss and Hollycraft's antiqued-gold pastels defining Fifties finery; Eisenberg's mammoth metal-and-jewel corsages; Boucher's elegant, soigne flora; Hattie Carnegie's woven bouquets of seed-bead loops; DeRosa's lavish vases abloom with buds; Warner's open-close mechanical posey; Staret's glossy hands grasping jeweled lilies, and 500 dozen others.

These don't even include the countless figurals that *include* flowers in their design: baskets, carts, planters, flowergirls, ballerinas with floral tutus, gents proffering posies ...

In terms of pop culture, an example of historically significant flora would be the masses of Flower Power specimens of the Sixties-Seventies, mostly enamel paints on metal, which sprung up out of anti-war sentiment.

Actress Vivien Leigh wears a floral brooch and bracelet in this vintage portrait.

If You Only Buy One Flower Pin ...

Dealing with the broad spectrum of symbols and significance in florigraphy is too vast and complicated a study to undertake in a jewelry book. But anyone who wants to buy one flower with meaning can consider either the flower routinely assigned to their birth sign (shown first, below) or have fun with new-age affiliations associating flowers with Zodiac type. We filled in the specific jewelry choices in the categories.

Capricorn: Deja or Trifari jelly belly **Carnation** (fascination); Hobe, Kramer, Leo Glass, Vendôme or Nettie Rosenstein **pansy**, Coro Quivering **camellia**

Aquarius: Castlecliff trembler **Iris** (faith and hope); Ming's Ivory **bird of paradise**, Cini **orchid**

Pisces: Trifari **Daffodil** (rejuvenation); Mosell or Sandor **waterlily**, Robert **poppy**, Trifari **willow tree**, trembler **lilac**

Aries: Chanel Novelty or Eisenberg **Daisy** (innocence); DeRosa or Har **thistle**, Oscar de la Renta **lily**

Taurus: Boucher **Lily** (purity); Trifari **poppy**, Chanel Novelty **palm** tree, Silson **apple** tree, Calvaire or BSK **violets**

Gemini: Iradj Moini, Leo Glass, Chanel Novelty, DuJay, CoroCraft, Mazer, l'Atelier de Verre, Nettie Rosenstein or DeRosa **Rose** (love); Chanel Novelty Trifari or Gripoix **lily of the valley**, Stanley Hagler, Ugo Coreanni or Rice-Weiner (Zoltan Korda) "Jungle Jewelry" *Jungle Book* **orchid**

Cancer: **Larkspur** (levity) Vendôme **morning glory**, Schreiner **jonquil**

Leo: **Gladiolus** (strength); Reja, Cristobal or Weiss **sunflower**, Dior **passion flower**

Virgo: **Aster** (daintiness); Gripoix, Boucher (or Trifari Japanese) **cherry**, Coro **acorn nut tree**

Libra: **Marigold** (affection); Blumenthal, Calvaire or BSK **hydrangea**, Pennino **blue** flowers, DuJay or Reja **strawberries**

Scorpio: Ming's Ivory **Chrysanthemum** (cheerfulness); Attwood-Sawyer **holly**, Lucite **black-eyed Susan**, Tortolani **cactus**

Sagittarius: Trifari, Gerry's, Stanley Hagler **Poinsettia** (success); Trifari or Blumenthal **peony**, Joseff of Hollywood **oak** leaves.

Garden of "Quivering Camellia" fur clips, eight examples in different chromatic enamels, signed Coro, 1938-, 2-1/4", **$25-$75** each.

Jelly Petals Flower pin, enameled metal, pink Lucite petals, signed Lisner, 1940s, 2-1/2", **$50-$75.**

Drippy Glass fur clip, cast pot metal flower spilling profusion of poured glass candies attached to refined chains, unsigned Reinad (probably for Eisenberg), 1938-41, 6", **$500.**

Trembling Bells brooch, white celluloid flowers wired into gold-plated metal cups, fuchsia RS pistils/stamen, green metallic wash on golden leaves, unsigned, 1938-42, 3-3/4", **$250-$350.**

Porcelain Roses brooch, antique Czech porcelain flowers, glass posies, beaded petals in spring-color seed beads (greens, pink, teal, blue) hand-wired onto filigree base, prong-set RS accents, signed Stanley Hagler N.Y.C. and Ian St. Gielar, 2006, 3-7/8", **$200.**

Givre Jelly brooch, bicolor (turquoise and amethyst) Lucite oval petals, faceted royal blue RS, carved-effect amethyst glass, crystal RS accents in simulated pot metal, signed Jelli Belli, date unknown, 4", **$50-$150.** Interesting piece due to large size, extreme showiness, and point of masquerading as vintage. Also, what appeared to be a tiny scratch on reverse turned out to be the mark, "Jelli Belli."

Orchid Aflutter brooch, gritty, textured seed beads surrounding tropical bloom, signed Stanley Hagler N.Y.C. and Ian St. Gielar, 2006, 3-7/8", **$150.**

Jewel Bounty fur clips, two examples, each with eight pearl-centered faceted-glass flower petals in ruby and sapphire, 1938-42, unsigned, sometimes attributed to Trifari or DeRosa, 4", **$75-$150** each.

Tall Spray pin, three stems with enameled metal and multicolor RS, unsigned, tagged by dealer as "new Haskell," 2000s, 5", **$50.**

Pond Flower pin, pale yellow ceramic button center, fuchsia Lucite petals, unsigned Elzac, 1940s, 3", **$50.**

Sunflower pin, enameled pot metal, lemon-yellow molded glass discs, signed B. Blumenthal Inc., 1938-42, 3", **$100-$150.**

Lava Balls dress clip, enameled pot metal, textured glass beads, unsigned, 1930s, 3-1/2", **$150.**

Fruit Floral dress clip, jeweled Lucite shoe-button cabochons, navy-blue enameled pot metal leaves, unsigned, Trifari design, 2-3/8", **$50-$100.**

Stylized Deco Triple Bloom pin, plastic flowers, unsigned, 1930s, 4", **$50.**

Lustrous Acorns dress clip, green silk cord, chocolate Bakelite nuts, unsigned Miriam Haskell, 1942-45, 2-3/8", **$75-$150.**

Pearl Beads Flower pin, curling golden leaves with metallic paints, large color-washed faux pearls, signed B. Blumenthal, 1930s, 4", **$50-$100.**

Springtime Vase fur clip, enameled posies, leaves, stems attach to ribbon banner spelling cheerful "Tra La," stiff wire wraps horizontally for vase effect, unsigned, 1935-42, 2-1/4", **$50.**

Fruit Bloom fur clip, cherry cabochons and RS mixed with crystals, bronzed pot metal, unsigned, looks like pre-signature Eisenberg, 1930s, 4", **$100.**

Pussy Willow pin, brushed gold-tone metal, encrusted faux pearls, signed Emmons, 1962, 2-1/2", **$25-$50.**

Dark Flower pin, pearl drops wired onto gunmetal flowers, signed Reinad, 1941, 3", **$50-$100.**

Lush Leaf fur clip, two shades green enamel pot metal, RS trim, signed Coro, 1938-42, 3-1/8", **$50-$100.**

Wreathy dress clip, upper half translucent pink beads and clear seed beads thread-sewn onto perforated plastic base; lower half all metal flowers with centers of clear crystals or tipped pink beads wired onto plastic base, early unsigned Miriam Haskell, 1942-45, 2-1/8", **$75-$150.**

Triple Lily Bell flower fur clip, turquoise beads and unfoiled aquamarine crystal navettes and baguettes, signed Eisenberg Original and S, 1930s, 3-3/4", **$250** if perfect, $100 as is (with one jeweled stamen and two marquis-cut stones missing).

CHAPTER 37 THE CRÈME DE LA CRÈME

Masterpieces of Costume Jewelry

A frequent stop for jewelry buyers window shopping on the information superhighway is N&N Vintage Costume Jewellery at Jewelmuseum.com. It would be amusing to capture the looks on people's faces, as they do on rides at Walt Disney World, the first time they arrive at Jewelmuseum.

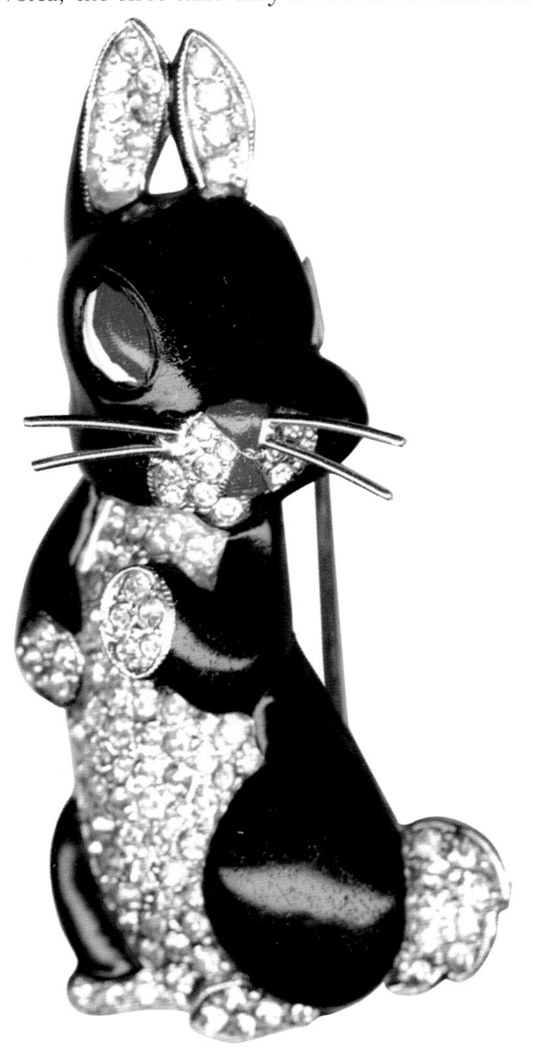

Black Rabbit with Silver Whiskers pin clip, 1938, rhodium-plated base metal, pave-set rhinestones, enamel, Trifari 'Alfred Philippe' with Crown, 34, 2-1/4", **$1,175.**

Most expressions would likely show awe mixed with disbelief for here is the cream of the vintage costume jewelry crop. Natasha and Neil Cuddy, based in Toronto, Canada, opened the shop for business in January 1999. Dealing in jewelry for 25 years, they originally commenced in England. "In Canada, we specialized in the great costume jewelry of the classic period from the 1930s to the 1960s, when jewels made from glass were artistically more interesting and innovative than jewelry including precious stones," Cuddy says—"and equally well-made."

The realm they devote to masterpieces at Jewelmuseum showcases the rarest and greatest designs, reflected in taller prices. Even novices would quickly notice the masterpiece wing is top-heavy with Trifari and Boucher creations. "They are the finest pieces," Cuddy notes, "and the 1938-42 period is the classic period for their designs, and generally all other vintage costume jewelry."

The site (and the couple's collecting *modus operandi*) changed after they discovered what is commonly referred to among collectors as "the Italian book," 1997's *American costume jewelry* by the Brunialtis. "We learnt a lot about the history of pieces, and with Roberto Brunialti's permission and help, incorporated a lot of that info on the site," Cuddy explains. They continue to be surprised at the variety and quality of KTF Trifari pieces from 1934-37. "Virtually none were patented, so it is always a surprise to see new ones," Cuddy says.

Collectors can sit back, relax, and drink in the aesthetic pleasures of a handful of costume jewelry's masterpieces.

Strutting Rooster pin, ca. 1937, rhodium-plated base metal, pave rhinestones, black-and-red-striped enamel, Pat Pend, 34, KTF Trifari 'Alfred Philippe,' 2-1/2", **$975.**

Corn on the Cob pin, 1941, rhodium-plated base metal, rhinestones, metallic enamel, Boucher, MB (phrygian cap), Des Pat'd, 3-3/4", **$1,525.**
Photos courtesy Neil Cuddy.

Strawberries on a Branch pin clip, 1941, rhodium-plated base metal, rhinestones, enamel, Trifari with Crown, 'Alfred Philippe,' 3-1/8", **$1,675.**

Flower Vase with Ruby and Pave Flowers pin clip, 1942-47, rose and yellow gold-plated sterling, rhinestones, 'Alfred Philippe,' Trifari with Crown, Sterling, 2-1/4", **$965.**

Gooseberries on Branch with Ladybug pin clip, 1941, rhodium-plated base metal, rhinestones, enamel, Trifari with Crown, Pat Pend, 'Alfred Philippe,' 3-1/8", **$1,585.**

Giant Peacock pin, 1941, rhodium-plated base metal, pave rhinestones, MB (phrygian cap), designer Marcel Boucher, 5-1/2", **$925.**

Leaf Crest pin clip, 1942, rhodium- and gold-plated base metal, sterling, sapphire, emerald and ruby rhinestones, Trifari with Crown, Sterling, 'Alfred Philippe,' 2-1/2", **$465.**

Two Birds on Branches pin, 1942, rhodium-plated base metal, rhinestones, enamel, Trifari with Crown, Des Pat No 131365, 56, 'Alfred Philippe,' 2-1/2", **$1,450.**

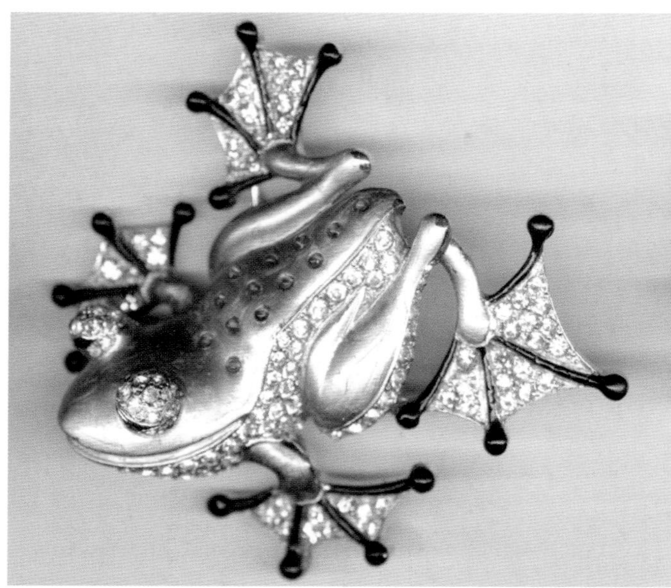

Tree Frog pin, rhodium-plated base metal, rhinestones, enamel, cabochons, Mark J (part of the MB Marcel Boucher metallic-enamel series of animals, birds and flowers from 1940-41, designer Marcel Boucher, 2-3/4", **$2,675.**

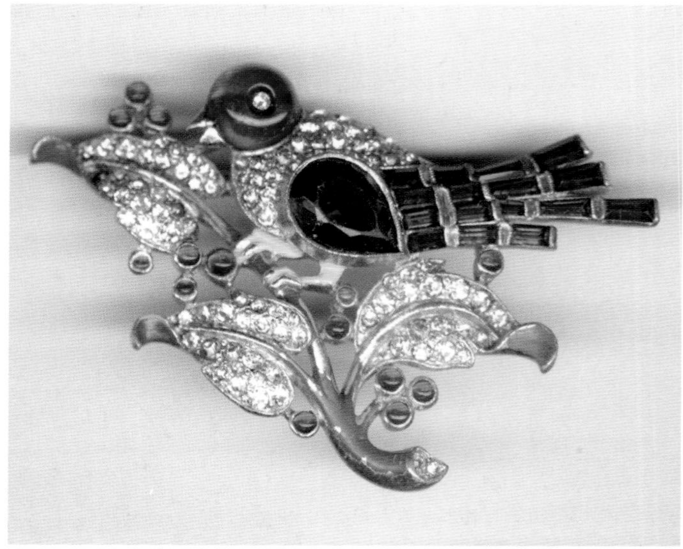

Shoebutton Bird on Branch pin, 1940, rhodium-plated base metal, rhinestones, enamel, tricolor cabochons, Trifari with Crown, Des Pat No 119456, 'Alfred Philippe,' 2-1/3", **$975.**

CHAPTER 38 The Aesthetic Appeal of Acrylics

Clearly Delicious: Jelly Bellies

Once Lucite was available to jewelry makers, it's interesting how differently they used it.

DuPont Plastics intro'd its version of polymethyl methacrylate, called Lucite, in 1937, two years post Plexiglass' invention. Elliot Handler of California was an early design engineer recognizing its possibilities, experimenting with it as early as 1938 and full time by 1939 at Elliot Handler Plastics. He had his first Lucite jewelry hit in 1940. Handler mostly employed it in clear, flat, carved design motifs (often combined with scrap wood), and then as spiraling, looping strips of high color Lucite with ceramic. It's quite a different use than that of the classic so-called "jelly belly," often thick, rounded, molded cabochon forms serving as the bodies of animals or petals of flowers. Elzac didn't produce a classic jelly belly until Handler himself was gone from the company, in 1945, with the sterling brooch called Freshie the College Boy Penguin. (This pin was first identified in *A Tribute to America* by the Brunialtis.) When founding partner Zachary Zemby left Elzac as well, and founded his own jewelry company, he reportedly used Lucite figural elements in his *metal* jewelry.

Alfred Philippe at Trifari and Adolph Katz at Coro (as well as others such as Sandor Goldberger/Fred Block, Leo Glass, Joseph Meyer/Norma, David Lisner) turned the plastic into clear cabochon-igloo works of art. (Interestingly, Marcel Boucher did not fall for Lucite and made no jelly bellies.)

But what began in the late '30s as an exciting new medium for jewelry ... became a necessary replacement for jewels during the war years, when imported strass was unavailable. The Brunialtis also point out that large-scale jewelry was fashionable at this time and plastic could provide size inexpensively, especially when combined with sterling silver, because the pricey metal could be used sparingly. By 1950, jelly bellies were mostly history.

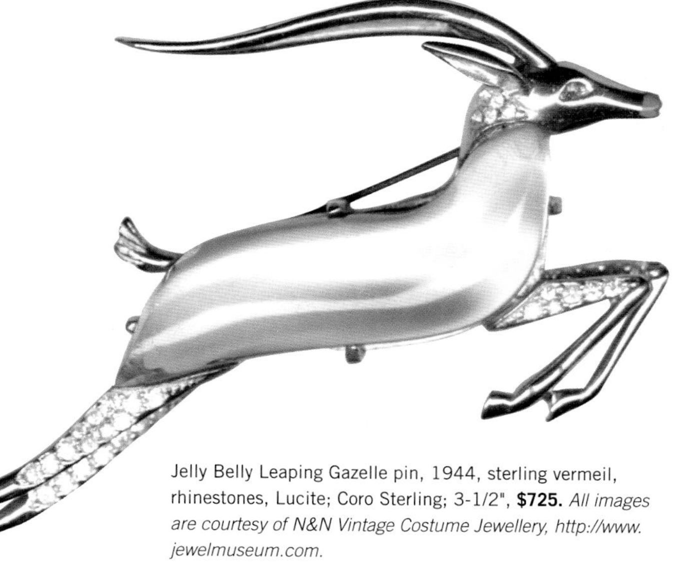

Jelly Belly Leaping Gazelle pin, 1944, sterling vermeil, rhinestones, Lucite; Coro Sterling; 3-1/2", **$725.** *All images are courtesy of N&N Vintage Costume Jewellery, http://www.jewelmuseum.com.*

Jelly Belly Man: Less is not Mir

The peripatetic costume-jewelry genius David Mir designed two of the most spectacular jelly bellies ever made. One is the masterful, crystal-clear seahorse with faux coral branch for Leo Glass, and the other is perhaps the rarest and most desirable jelly belly ever designed, the large, fierce Trifari bird with Lucite wings, perched on a baroque pearl. When one flew onto eBay, it sold at auction for more than $5,400.

Jelly Belly Hourglass pin, 1949, gold-washed base metal, rhinestones, Lucite; Trifari with Crown, Pat Pend, 'Alfred Philippe,' 1-3/4", **$875.**

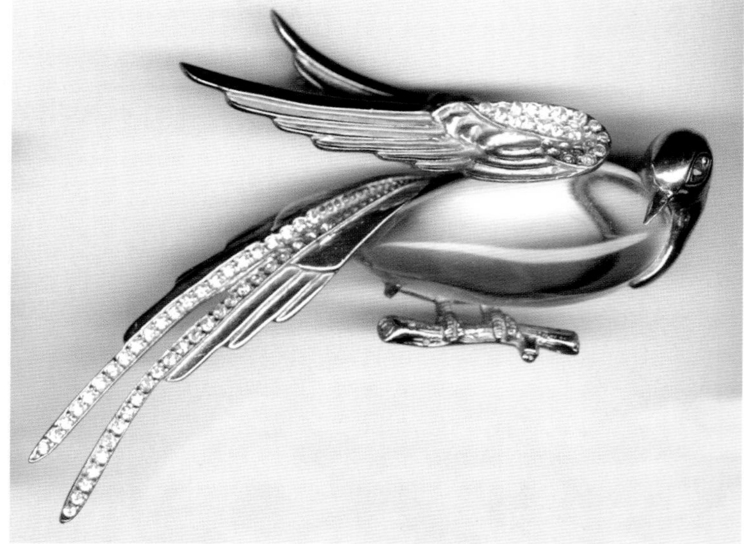

Jelly Belly Pheasant pin, 1944; gold plated sterling, rhinestones, Lucite, Corocraft Sterling with Pegasus; 'Adolph Katz,' 3-5/8", **$985.**

Jelly Belly Frog pin, 1943, sterling vermeil, rhinestones, cabochon eyes, Lucite belly, Trifari with Crown, Sterling, Des Pat No 135172; 'Alfred Philippe,' 2-7/8", **$695.**

Jelly Belly Crab pin, 1943-44, gold plated sterling, rhinestones, Lucite, Trifari with Crown, Sterling, Pat Pend, 'Alfred Philippe,' 2-3/4", **$795.**

Jelly Belly Lizard pin, 1944, sterling vermeil, rhinestones, Lucite, Trifari with Crown, Sterling, Pat Pend, 'Alfred Philippe,' 3-3/4", **$725.**

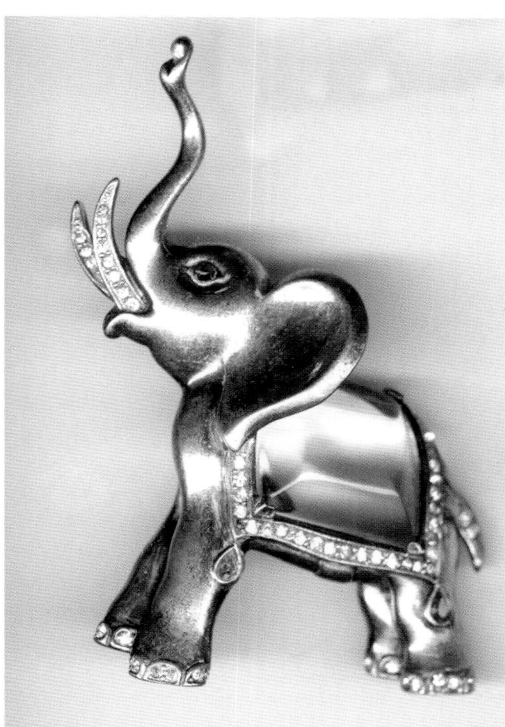

Jelly Belly Elephant pin, 1944, sterling vermeil, rhinestones, Lucite, Trifari with Crown, Sterling, Des Pat No 138202, 2-3/4", **$925.**

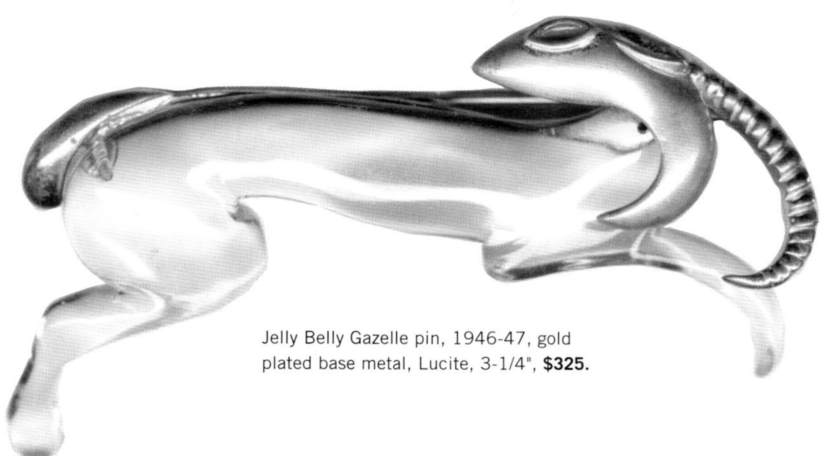

Jelly Belly Gazelle pin, 1946-47, gold plated base metal, Lucite, 3-1/4", **$325.**

Jelly Belly Horse Head pin clip, gold plated sterling, rhinestones, lucite Sterling Corocraft with Pegasus 1942, 2", **$925.**

Jelly Belly Rooster pin – "Chanticleer," 1944, sterling vermeil, rhinestones, Lucite, Trifari with Crown, Sterling, Des Pat No 137324, 'Alfred Philippe,' 2-1/2", **$675.**

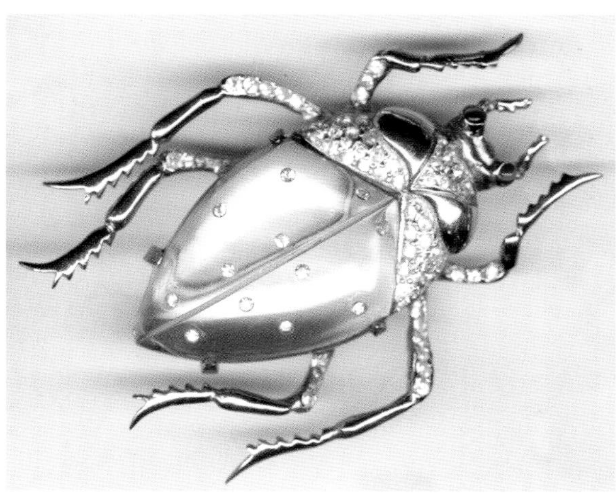

Jelly Belly Giant Beetle pin, gold plated sterling, rhinestones, Lucite, Corocraft Sterling, 1942, 2-3/4", **$1,175.**

Jelly Belly Swan pin, gold plated sterling, rhinestones, Lucite, Trifari with Crown, Sterling, Pat Pend, 1944, 2-1/2", **$875.**

Jelly Belly Swan pin clip, rhodium plated base metal, rhinestones, Lucite, enamelling, Trifari with Crown, Des Pat No 129164 Trifari "Norman Bel Geddes," 1941, 2-3/4", **$975.**

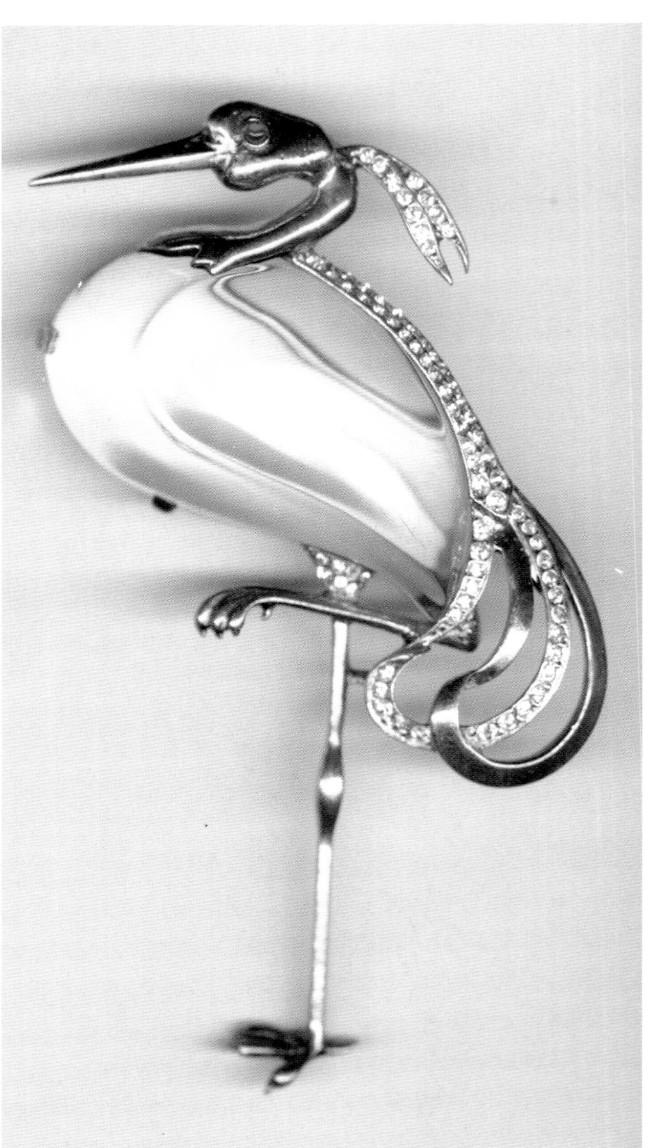

Jelly Belly Great Blue Heron pin, gold plated sterling, rhinestones, Lucite, Trifari with Crown, Sterling, 1943, 3-1/2", **$925.**

CHAPTER 39  SOUVENIRS OF TRAVELS, FAR AND NEAR

Going Places

Figural jewelry has a great sense of place, capturing a cozy corner of a room, a romantic niche in a park, or landmarks in the world's capitals. We all purchase souvenirs of our travels or lives, so how lucky that some of the best vintage costume jewelry brings those memories to mind, whether summertime's ice cream cart, a trip to California, or an evocative concert or film.

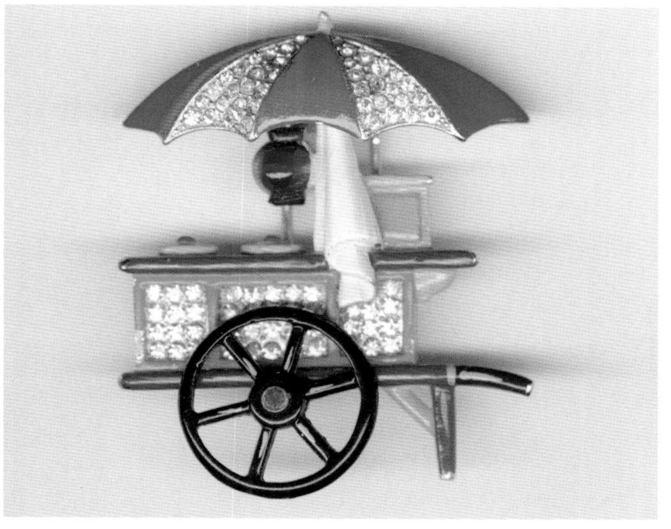

Ice Cream Cart with Umbrella pin clip; rhodium plated base metal, rhinestones, enameling, wheel rotates, Trifari "Alfred Philippe" with Crown, **$975.**

San Francisco Golden Gate International Exposition pin, 1939-40, Searchlights and Tower Art Deco Scene licensed souvenir; rhodium-plated base metal, rhinestones, enamel, marked: © G.G.I.E, LIC. 32C, 2-1/4", **$365.**

Orchestra on Stage with Proscenium Arch "Carnegie Hall" movie pin, gold-plated sterling, rhinestones, Corocraft "Adolph Katz" Sterling with Pegasus, 1947, 2", **$595.**

Punch and Judy Trembler Scene pin clip, gold- and rhodium-plated base metal, rhinestones, enamel, Puppets on springs, unsigned, mid- to late 1930s, 2-1/4", **$785.**

WWII Allied Patriotic red, white and blue Eiffel Tower pin, gold-plated sterling, rhinestones, Coro Sterling, 1942-45, 2-3/4", **$275.**

U.S. Patriotic WWII "Remember Pearl Harbor" pin, gold-plated base metal, enamel, unsigned, 1942, Honolulu Community Chest promotional fundraiser brooch, 2-1/2", **$475.**

Baby Peeking Over Fence pin; gold plated base metal, enameling, Hattie Carnegie, 2", **$165.**

Girl at Window pin, gold-plated base metal, rhinestones, enamel, cabochons, Boucher 3250, Pat Pend, 1950, 1-7/8", **$165.**

Dutch Couple Windmill pin, gold-plated sterling, rhinestones, enamel, windmill rotates, marked Carman Sterling, 1942-49, 2-3/8", **$245.**

Golden Book shelf pin, gold-plated base metal, rhinestones, enamel, unsigned, 1948, 2-1/4", **$165.**

Scene Pins

Circus scene pin, 3-D, clown tightrope walking, balancing on ball, holding hoops, horses and elephant, crowd painted in background, unsigned, 1960s, 2", **$150.**

Western scene pin, 3-D, cowboy on fence holding lasso, saddle nearby, cactus growing, rising sun in background, unsigned, 1960s, 2", **$150.**

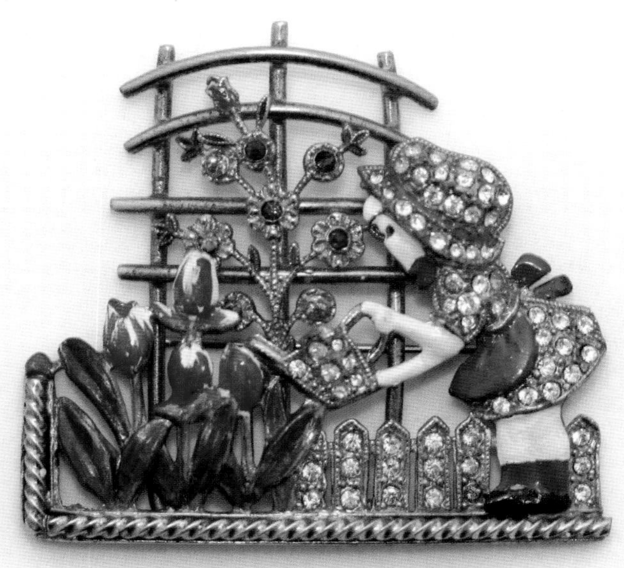

Mary, Mary garden pins, two different colorations, heavy gold plate versus gilded pot metal, elaborate, dimensional, pave-set RS and enameled tulips, trellis, fence, unsigned, 1940s, 2-1/8", **$150** each.

Class Menagerie

The field of animal figurals is so vast it could sink an ark. Limit a collection to a species and it would still require considerable time to amass all the horses, giraffes, cats, rabbits or even elephants who live in that jungle known as the jewelry world.

Animal series would be one satisfying direction to go in, attempting to amass varieties of fauna from specific lines and groupings. Possible candidates that prove to be worthy prey include:

Trifari Alfred Philippe jelly bellies with pave, gilt sterling and Lucite

Trifari exotic faux-carved jade-belly Ming line

CoroCraft Sterling enameled wildlife with single, oversized jewels

Reja gilded-sterling retro-deco jeweled menagerie

Charles F. Worth seed-pearl species

Kenneth J. Lane Renaissance fantasy figural brood

Marcel Boucher metallic-enamel animal beauties

Nettie Rosenstein pretty pave pals

Elsa Schiaparelli circus performers

Eisenberg lively mammal livery

Coro chatelaines and polychrome critters

Rebajes copper crush

Razza brawny compo crew

Schreiner featured creatures

Chanel (Reinad) zooey whimsies

Elzac ceramic Lucite flock

Staret gem-encrusted livestock

That list includes all vintage pieces. When the horizon is widened to study animals by contemporary designers such as Bettina von Walhof, Ian St. Gielar and Iradj Moini, the zoo grows by leaps and bounds.

Many unremarkable, unsigned animals also enrich collections. Their novel designs are the result of both well-known and unknown imaginations that took the time to create unique jeweled creatures, cute pets to ferocious wild things.

Elegant cat face, openwork pot metal, pave RS trim, emerald navette eyes, upside-down glass cabochon heart as mouth, signed Vitoge, 1940s, 2", **$250.**

Whiskered cat face, carved wood, straw whiskers, unsigned, 1940s, 2-1/2", **$50-$100.**

Tortoise cat pin, 3-D, tortoise-effect resin, gold-plated ball, green RS eyes, gold metal details with whiskers and tail, unsigned, 2000s, 2-1/2", **$50.**

Black Cat Puss pin, feline face with whiskers, jet RS in japanned metal setting, eyes stand out with red stones, teardrop ears, unsigned, 1960s, 1-1/2", **$25-$50.**

Psycho Kitty pin, alabaster and multicolor Swarovski crystals in hematite metal setting, signed B&M von Walhof, 2000s, 2-1/4", **$85.**

L'il Herman Kitty and Bashful Puppy pins, brilliant multicolor Swarovski crystals, signed Bettina von Walhof, 2000s, 4" each, **$385** each.

Dazzling Dog Pound, includes pins of American Eskimo, Brussells Griffon, Boston Terrier, Collie, Airedale Terrier, all hand-set first-quality Swarovski crystals, signed B&M Von Walhof, 2000s, 2", **$106.**

African Safari brooch, zebra centerpiece surrounded by jungle colors in all-glass beads and flowers, signed Stanley Hagler N.Y.C. and Ian St. Gielar, 2000s, 4", **$125.**

Glossy Squirrel fur clip, polychrome gray, brown and cream enamels, gilded sterling, RS pave-set head, tail and branches, ruby RS navette fruits, signed CoroCraft Sterling, 1940s, 3-1/8", **$250-$400.**

Fancy Squirrel with Acorn pin, Black Diamond Swarovski crystals, signed B&M von Walhof, 2000s, 2-1/2", **$68.**

Lambiekins fur clip, silver-plated metal with jonquil and turquoise enamels, bell charm dangling from collar, signed Monet, 1940s, 2-1/2", **$50-$100.**

Horse Head pin, satin finish coppertone metal, available in varying sizes, unsigned Trifari design, 1970s, 1-1/2", **$10-$25.**

Busy Squirrel dress clip, carved green Bakelite, unsigned, 1930s, 2-1/4", **$50-$100.**

Grit-Tailed Squirrel pin, holds faux-pearl nut, textured metal tail and accents, unsigned, 1960s, 2", **$10-$25.**

CHAPTER 41  Looking for One of Every Kind

Version Obsession

This category can be joked about as a kind of sickness, but it's an amusing addiction.

Basically, two kinds of version obsessions befall a collector. One is maker's mark madness, in which one popular design is discovered with many different signature attributions. The other is a successful figural design that's been found in different colors, materials or slight variations.

In the first category, Reinad is at ground zero on the strength of its Asian Princess and "Josephine Baker" clips alone. Because Reinad designed and manufactured work for so many big-name jewelry houses, it also recycled its creative output (and in some instances, apparently helped itself to others' work). Reinad marked identical figurals at different times as Eisenberg Original, HC / Hattie Carnegie, Mazer, Blumenthal, Chanel, Reinad and possibly MB / Boucher. The rare, upturned exotic head pin clip nicknamed Josephine Baker recently was discovered in reverse and signed Edward Stempa. Did Reinad make a reversed design *for* Stempa or did Reinad originally reverse Stempa's design for its own use? That question will have to be answered another day.

Other mark varieties on identical pieces include Mazer and Reinad's "R" on the large, extravagantly bejeweled comet or shooting star brooch; Blumenthal and Chanel on the trio-series animals; Hattie Carnegie and Eisenberg on large-scale showgirls in profile (and in instances of slight design variations, other marks as well); Hattie Carnegie and Reinad on the large jeweled unicorn, which is especially confusing and thorny because Ruth Kamke says it was her design at F&K.

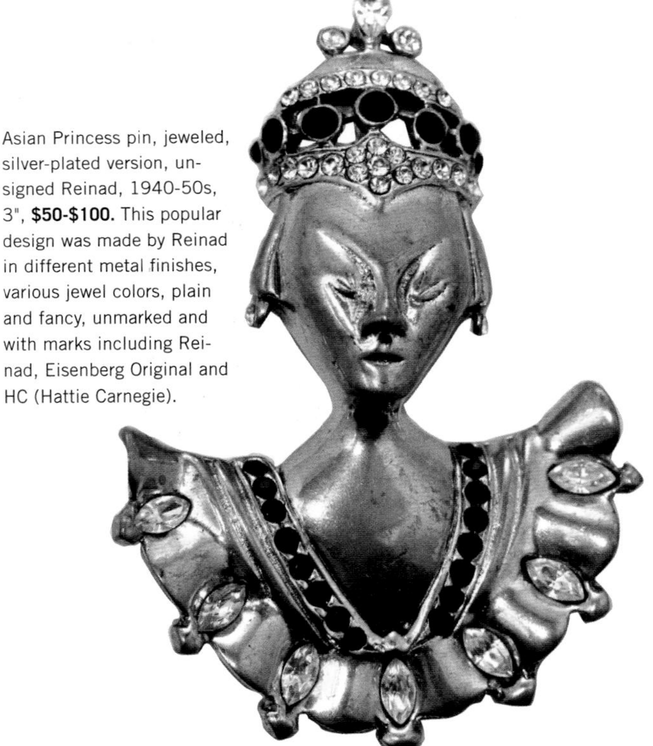

Asian Princess pin, jeweled, silver-plated version, unsigned Reinad, 1940-50s, 3", **$50-$100.** This popular design was made by Reinad in different metal finishes, various jewel colors, plain and fancy, unmarked and with marks including Reinad, Eisenberg Original and HC (Hattie Carnegie).

The Price of a Princess

Reinad's Asian Princess makes a fascinating study when it comes to sizing up sales venues. This large figural pin clip is not uncommon, so must have been popular at original retail. (As noted earlier, many versions appear, either unsigned or marked with major names.) On the Internet, it is now taken for granted to the point that it sold on eBay in February 2007 for an all-time low of $23. The same clip, less well-known in live-auction settings, sold in January 2007 for $185 to a high bidder in Pittsburgh. The moral of the story is, if collectors are not doing business on the Internet, many more figurals retain their rank as exotic rarities.

A sunflowers brooch in enameled gold-plated metal is found marked Eisenberg and Avon. Identical plastic and metal clowns and animals may be found with both Kenneth Lane and Hattie Carnegie marks (because they are Lane's designs). Hollywood/Hollycraft, Weiss and Pakula overlap in identical Christmas tree pin designs.

In the second category of versions, one of the most interesting groups is plastic, wood or composition versions of famous Boucher designs, such as the lavish Mexican man with jeweled sombrero, who turns up in both wood and composition—duplicates of the metal Boucher piece. Superstitious Aloysius was made in a plastic version. A wood version of the aforementioned Showgirl-in-Profile mimics the many versions of that pin. The Rice-Weiner Chinaman Water Carrier is also done in an all-wood version.

Numerous versions of the Calvaire Debutante exist (blonde, brunette, golden-haired; blue skirted and gold-skirted), but these are closer to copies or reproductions of the same era. (See Chapter 43 on reproductions.)

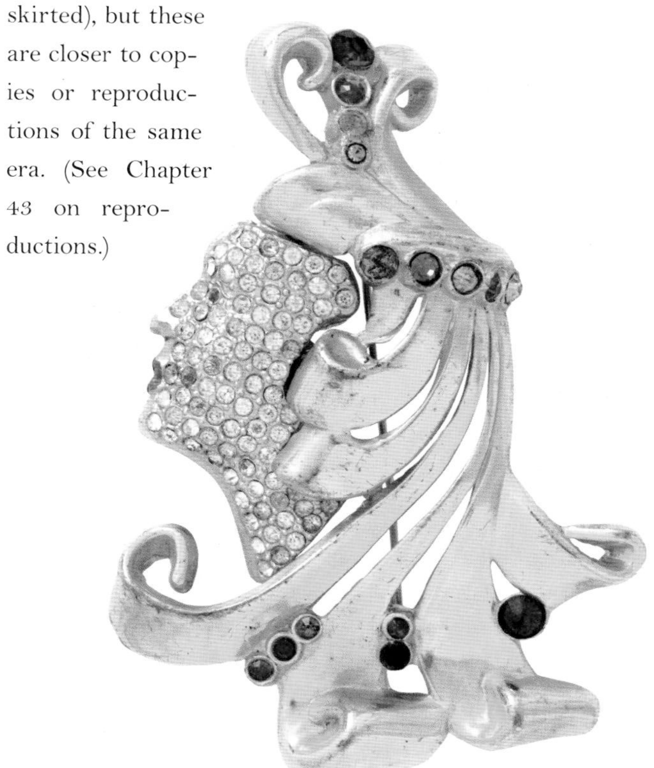

The "Showgirl Profile" was clearly a very popular design: countless versions were created, with long, wavy, usually bejeweled tresses. The most coveted and desirable version is Sandor's, with molded Lucite face, followed by the one top right and on the cover, her face all tiny pave-set crystals. (This one bears all the tell-tale signs of Reinad.) And one excellent take on the theme is actually signed Eisenberg Original. Some are one-piece castings, while others are two separate metal parts in different finishes, riveted or swedged together. Some are fur clips, others brooches. Because of its size and aesthetic appeal, the "Showgirl" is a satisfying motif to collect in its many permutations, including the wood version. The company provenance of this carved wooden brooch remains a mystery, as do most wood and composition renditions, but the amateurish placement of emerald rhinestones on the girl here almost suggests a do-it-yourself kit project. Is it possible the great costume jewelry designs of the Thirties and Forties were rendered in wood for jewelry-making at home? Each piece is between 3" and 3-1/2" tall. Showgirl with gilded tresses and pave-set RS face, **$250-$350.** Wood version, **$150** (due to rarity). All gilded metal version, **$150.** Two-tone riveted metal versions, **$50-$100.** (Although beautiful, for some reason these are less popular on the secondary market.)

Another renowned Boucher design, the Mexican man in sombrero grande, is shown here in a heavy wood compo version adorned with brightly colored jewels. Did Boucher issue wood and compo versions of his designs during the war, or license his designs to makers of jewelry kits? The hombre is looking at a fellow wood-compo creation, the head of mischievous elf Rumpelstiltskin. It seems if a rhinestoned wood-compo pin exists in an intriguing design, the metal version likely does too. Anyone have a Rumpy fur clip? Each 1940s pin is 3", jeweled, and valued at **$150.**

Asian man fur clip seems to be based on Boucher's finger-waving "Buddha." This fellow turns up wearing robes of different colors, perfect example of "costume" jewelry to match a woman's evolving fashion choices. He is unsigned, 1940s, 2-1/4", **$100-$150.**

"Superstitious Aloyisus: 2-1/4" pin done in red plastic instead of metal; and a static, 2-5/8" plastic version of Boucher's mechanical finger-waving "Jester" unmarked, 1940s, **$25.**

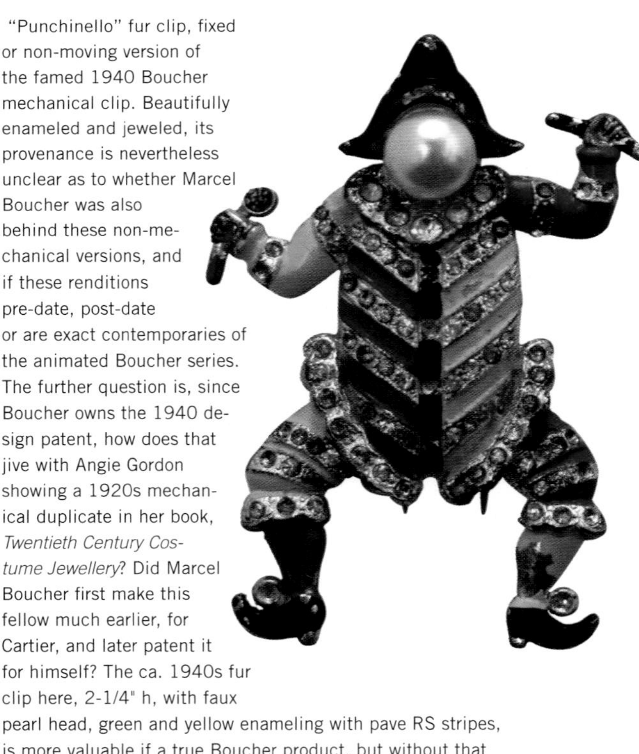

"Punchinello" fur clip, fixed or non-moving version of the famed 1940 Boucher mechanical clip. Beautifully enameled and jeweled, its provenance is nevertheless unclear as to whether Marcel Boucher was also behind these non-mechanical versions, and if these renditions pre-date, post-date or are exact contemporaries of the animated Boucher series. The further question is, since Boucher owns the 1940 design patent, how does that jive with Angie Gordon showing a 1920s mechanical duplicate in her book, *Twentieth Century Costume Jewellery*? Did Marcel Boucher first make this fellow much earlier, for Cartier, and later patent it for himself? The ca. 1940s fur clip here, 2-1/4" h, with faux pearl head, green and yellow enameling with pave RS stripes, is more valuable if a true Boucher product, but without that provenance, is valued at **$250-$450.**

The so-called 'Asian Princess' was obviously one of Reinad's most successful jewelry efforts. It is so plentiful on the market that its value on the Internet has plummeted. The opposite is true in live auctions among bidders present. This is because the design is so striking and substantial, anyone not over-exposed to it would naturally be wowed. Versions vary according to metal finish, jewel accents, pin mechanism and mark (including Reinad, Eisenberg Original, Hattie Carnegie, and some sans signature). Most versions are 3-7/8" tall, with the EO much taller because of long crystal chandelier briolettes; 1938-50s, **$50-$500** (depending on signature).

Unsigned versions of the Eisenberg Original king and queen. "La Reine" is a gilded-metal brooch with simulated topaz stones; "Le Roi" is a fur clip with antiqued silver finish and multi-color cabochons. Each is unsigned, 1940s, 2-3/4", **$150-$400.**

This take on the Eisenberg queen (left) features white-enameled hair; the queen next to her is a later model and has an unusual floral addition; unsigned, 1940s and 1970s, each 2-3/4", **$50-$100.**

"Calvaire Debutantes," enameled and jeweled gold-plated metal, 3-1/8". Fur clip on left is signed Calvaire; brooch on right is unsigned. Calvaire piece on left features bodice of invisibly set simulated emeralds, plus crystals at hem creating illusion of petticoat layer. Unsigned figural features enameled face, no hem detail. When Ray Calish's company, Calvaire, was finished with the 1930s design, its manufacturer or wholesaler obviously shared this fetching motif with other retailers or jewelry houses because she turns up in multiple renditions, including varied dress and hair colors. Signed fur clip, **$250+.** Unsigned brooch, **$150+.**

Wagon train driver cracking whip over steers; 3" gilded metal fur clip on left; 4" painted, carved wood version by Elzac on right; unsigned, 1940s, **$75-$150.**

Ceramic Bunnies by Elzac, portrays two of the many versions and uses of this rabbit: brooch with huge green Lucite background versus bunny button with trademark tail pompom, not to mention the exact rabbit design in metal motifs with enormous jeweled ears. Pin is 4-1/4", **$150;** button is 2-5/8", **$50-$75.**

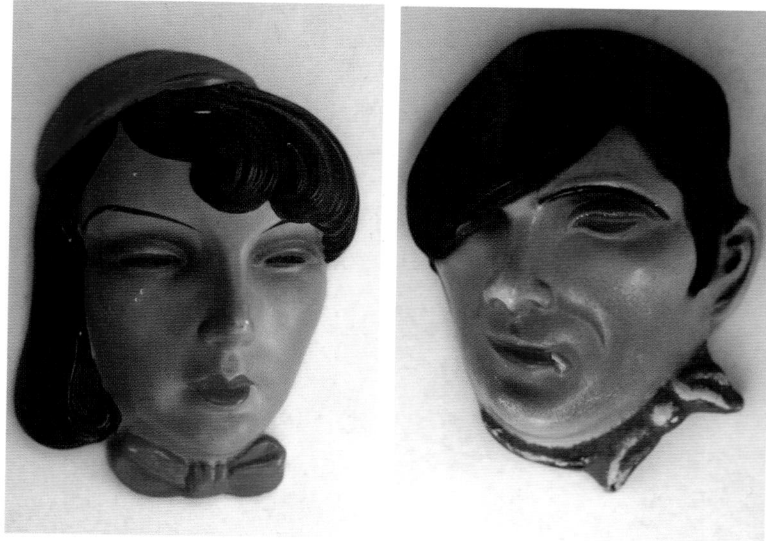

What came first, the fur clips or the decorative plaques? Here are Adolph Katz's famous Coro pair, Putain and Apache, done as hollow, 3-D painted composition plaques of 3-1/2". Fascinating, **$25-$50.**

Pop-Culture Eras

If a period of time strikes a collector as exciting, it's satisfying to follow the bliss to jewelry of the era as well. The zeitgeist of each different decade suits completely different jewelry lovers, and there is a time for every one of them.

Victorian: Delicate, small-scale, beautifully crafted and often very feminine pieces in such familiar forms as four-leaf clovers, horseshoes, shooting stars and comets, flowers, graceful hands and more. One collector says for starters she loves Victorian jewelry because it has managed to survive all these years, through so many changes in taste and fashion.

Art Deco: The jazz age's carefree insouciance suits some costume jewelry aficionados to a T. Brass, 3-D stick figures, some jeweled or enameled, playing golf or tennis, holding cocktails, jitterbug dancing or walking their Deco dogs, have a spare, cool sensibility that is as flip as a Flapper's wrist. Most specimens in this category are unmarked.

War and Peace: Collectors who can't get enough of *Foyle's War* DVDs are candidates for jewelry with military and patriotic themes illustrating doughboys and GIs, sailors, ships, eagles and everything affiliated with *les guerres.* The very same collector might also love the symbols of peace, from doves and sweethearts to flower-power brooches and the classic peace sign. In the latter group, two interesting pieces are Van S Authentics' massive fur-clip dove and a wonderful Christmas tree pin with peace-sign star made by a Coro designer who launched her own line at Gem-Craft.

Atomic: This category could be moved into wartime as a sub-section too. The Atomic Age inspired many jewelry houses to create some version of brooches bursting with beads or stones on a profusion of protruding wires, most of them explosive looking, some mimicking the atom. Some are particularly beautiful, such as a Reja set and an Original by Robert set.

Rock 'n' Roll: Baby Boomer's delight, encompassing couples dancing the hot numbers of the Fifties and Sixties, Elvis-related pins such as a large hound dog strumming a guitar, record-album pins and charms, Beatles jewelry, etc. Girls wearing Poodle skirts mark the early Fifties, while mice dressed in Granny gowns and glasses, by companies such as Gerry's, Mamselle and Jonette, stand at the opposite end of the classic rock era.

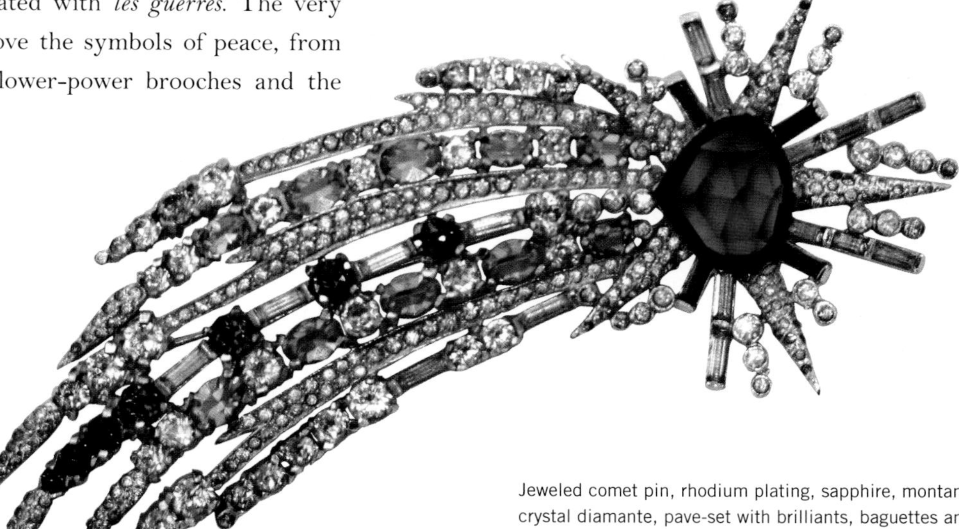

Jeweled comet pin, rhodium plating, sapphire, montana, crystal diamante, pave-set with brilliants, baguettes and ovals, mixed colors, each strand unique in tail, signed R (for Reinad; also seen marked Mazer), 1940s, 4-7/8", **$500.**

Delicate Hands brooches, Victorian to Fifties, 2" to 3", **$50-$150.**

Retro Space-Age Robots & Rockets pins, von Walhof Creations, signed, pave-set multi-cut Swarovksi crystals in colors including Black Diamond, Siam Red and Jonquil, 2006, 2-1/2", **$60.**

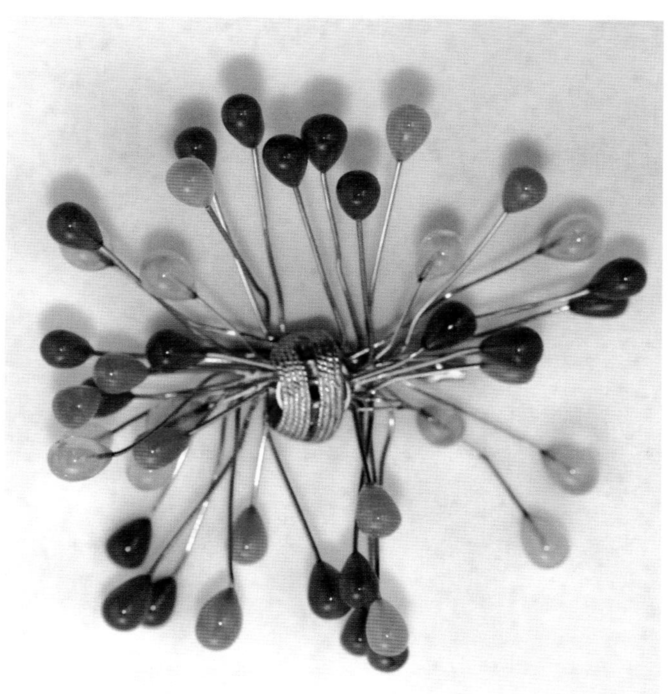

Atomic Age brooches, 1946-55, 2"-3", **$50-$150.**

Space-Age Sputnik pin, gold-plated metal with multi-cut pronged and bezel-set stones, well cast, unsigned, 1962-65, 2-3/4", **$150.** The pop hit "Telstar," named after AT&T's communications satellite, was high on the music charts for 16 weeks in 1962, including a stay at No. 1.

Retro Space-Age Robots & Rockets pins, von Walhof Creations, signed, pave-set multi-cut Swarovksi crystals in colors including Black Diamond, Siam Red and Jonquil, 2006, 2-1/2", **$60.**

CHAPTER 43 The Good, The Bad, and The Ugly

Reproductions

"Good" reproductions are fully disclosed remakes of rare pieces of costume jewelry. They allow collectors to enjoy the crème de la crème of vintage masterpieces—figurals we all have a slim chance of owning or even seeing. Some examples that have been made and admitted are the Staret Grinning Clown and Liberty Torch, the Eisenberg Naiad Mermaid, Trifari Sipping Stork, Boucher Grasshopper. (But examples of these also exist that are intended to trick. (See Deb Kosnett's Web site pages http://www.rhinestonerainbow.com/realfake.htm for up-close looks at authentic and copied pieces of famous figural jewelry.)

Other repros that can in one sense be categorized as "good" are same-era unsigned copies inspired by successful jewelry creations of that same time period. These can be fun to collect and are historically interesting. And some "of-the-era copies" are re-used originals made by or for the first company. Still other acceptable copies are later retreads of pin designs by the original company.

"Bad" reproductions include copies intentionally made to fool the public: signed copies of any era made strictly to dupe buyers and make money for manufacturers and sellers.

"Ugly" reproductions are ones that become so widespread and infiltrate the jewelry world so deeply, they at least temporarily tarnish great names. Prices on vintage Eisenberg weakened tremendously from a long rash of repros and didn't fully rebound until 2006.

The chilling effect is cast when no one feels certain real is real, and the Internet, which provides a virtual view rather than the real feel only in-person encounters provide, makes matters worse in terms of spread. It got very messy in the Weiss arena beginning with fraudulent Christmas tree pins (brand new, faked to be older), and continues still. New Weiss pieces of every stripe and type (so-called glitz, as well as figurals outside trees) are so prevalent in antiques malls, and some of the signatures so shockingly poor looking, it's hard to imagine production will ever come to an end.

"Ugly" is when new collectors rush to purchase beautiful Christmas tree pins, paying a lot because they believe they are rare and vintage when in fact they are being cranked out by the thousands and should be priced at $10. Ugly is when fakes fool so many of the people so much of the time, authors put the fakes in their

Copy of Eisenberg Mermaid or Naiad brooch, white metal, RS accents, large ginger-ale glass belly, faceted ginger-ale beads, signed Eisenberg Original, purchased from CornerGem, 2000s, 4", **$150.**

jewelry books and confuse thousands more collectors. Ugly is when hard-working designers, contemporary and past, have their intellectual property ripped off, fast and furious, cheapening the original design. If you have a jewelry Web site, you have received email from factories in China offering to copy anything and everything for unbelievably low prices, as long as they get to sell copies of the designs, too.

Reproductions can be a kick … or a source of heavy heartache. Smart collectors make sure they know what a real original looks like down to the last detail before plunking down serious money for a masterpiece that may only be a master counterfeit.

Copy of Eisenberg Cleaning lady fur clip (copy is a pin), signed Eisenberg, age unknown, origin unknown, 3", **$200.**

Copy of Calvaire Woman pin, gold-plated metal with RS accents, unsigned, origin unknown, 1990s, 3", **$50-$100.**

Copy of Staret Liberty Torch, enameled gold-plated metal, RS encrusted torch accented with simulated sapphires, unsigned, 3-1/4", **$50-$100.**

Copy of Coro Native Woman pin (matching earrings not shown), enameled gold-plated metal, pave-set RS accents, unsigned, 1990s, 3", **$50**/set.

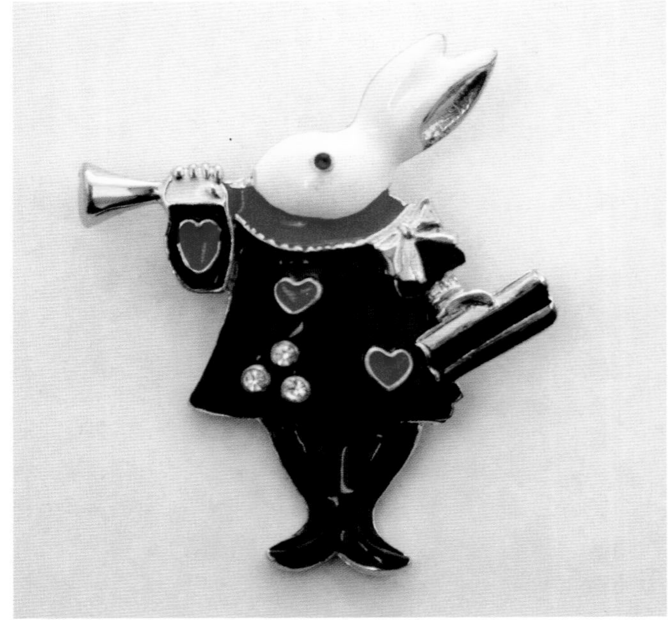

Copy of vintage *Alice in Wonderland* White Rabbit, 1-7/8" signed MMA, 1994, and 2-1/2" unsigned, 1990s, **$10-$25** each.

CHAPTER 44 RECOGNIZABLE FLAIR

Signature Styles

Even collectors whose hearts are exclusively ensconced in the enclave of vintage costume jewelry make exceptions for certain contemporary designers, such as Hanna Bernhard, Bettina Von Walhof, Iradj Moini, David Mandel, Robert Sorrell and Ian St. Gielar, whose creations are considered investment pieces.

Hanna Bernhard Paris

From France comes designer Hanna Bernhard, who is also known the world over for her NatParis Boutique. Collectors have gone slightly mad for these highly dimensional figural designs, some so sculptural and *gigantique* they have stands. "I always loved *les gros bijoux*," says Nathalie "Hanna" Bernhard, who was equally smitten, from a young age, with antiques and the intricacies of handwork. Her mother was a dedicated collector who took daughter along to antiques fairs; her father, a teacher, helped introduce her to crafts techniques and an appreciation of color artistry.

Hanna fell in love at first sight with an enormous pineapple brooch while browsing a flea market in the 1980s. The vendor, noting her enthusiasm, explained he worked at a wholesale jewelry factory, and he introduced Hanna to the head of Anceline, a jewelry design studio for major fashion houses such as Nina Ricci. Hanna and Pierre, the director, became friends, and she found herself frequently at the atelier learning jewelry-making techniques.

Several years later Hanna fatefully met her husband Fernand, a specialist in dental prostheses who had spent his childhood in colorful Corsica and enjoyed his free time observing the country's flora and fauna. Could there have been a more ideal mate for Bernhard, someone not only with an appreciation for color and nature, but perfect three-dimensional vision as well. She taught him everything she knew about jewelry technique; he combined it with dental prosthetic techniques. That led him to sculpt what became his first, famous animal-head brooches. "They are incontestably his most beautiful and sought-after pieces," Hanna says.

The two complemented in another fashion: Hanna had an extravagant design sense and unquenchable thirst for combining colors, while Fernand preferred capturing or rendering realism. They designed their first collection together in the early '90s for Fabrice, a jewelry shop in Paris' Saint-Germain-des-Prés district, well-known to American collectors. Parisian couture shows and private customers followed, especially those who had appreciated the earlier work of Roger Jean-Pierre, Scemama and Schiaparelli.

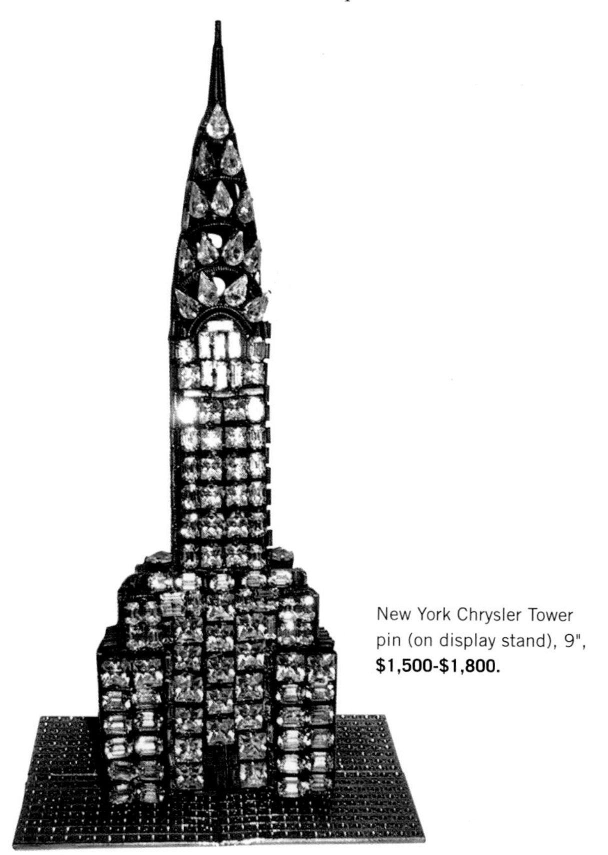

New York Chrysler Tower pin (on display stand), 9", **$1,500-$1,800.**

Each HB piece is one of a kind; most stones employed are vintage Swarovski crystal, old paste, glass elements and semi-precious stones. Old stampings and sometimes enameling are used; metal is hand-soldered. Fernand and Hanna usually make what moves them at the time, but also work by special request. They chose to retain the "Hanna Bernhard Paris" tag Nathalie designed before meeting Fernand.

In more recent years, the rage in Hanna Bernhard bijoux is the special display created to present the pieces, an environment such as a tree display for a koala bear. "Collectors can enjoy their jewelry as decorative works of art when they are not wearing them," Hanna explains.

The photos of Hanna Bernhard brooches on Pages 237-239 are from the NatParis Boutique, http://stores.ebay.com/NATPARIS-BOUTIQUE. Prices listed are retail. Photos courtesy Nathalie Bernhard.

Ostrich pin, 14", **$2,500-$3,000.**

Butterfly necklace pin, 6-1/2", **$1,600-$1,800.**

Koala bear head pin, 4-1/2", **$1,300-$1,500.**

Butterfly with trembler wings on flower pin, 6", an early piece, **$1,200-1,300.**

Peacock head pin (on display stand), 7-1/2", **$1,500-$1,800.**

Mr. Peanut pin, 8-1/2", **$800-$1,000.**

Shell pin (and display), 6-1/2", **$1,500-$1,800.**

Snake pin (clear Swarovski), 9", **$800-$1,000.**

Sea turtle pin (and display), 5-1/2", **$1,400-$1,600.**

Photos courtesy Hanna Bernhard. (First three pins are from private collections.)

Aztec pin (enamel, semi-precious stones), 4-3/4", **$1,200-$1,500.**

Buddha pin/pendant (Swarovski plus jade), 4-1/2", **$1,200-$1,400.**

Ladybug pin (early piece from the '80s), 4", **$800.**

Eagle pin, 5-1/4", **$1,400-$1,600.**
Photo courtesy Erik Yang.

Snake pin and earrings set: pin, 5", **$1,400-$1,600;** earrings, **$500-$700.** This is the first pin Hanna made for her mother, Nicole. *Photo courtesy Nicole Bernhard.*

Hanna Bernhard jewelry photos this page courtesy of artist Henry Dale House.

Elephant necklace, **$1,800-$2,000.**

Flamingo head pin, 4", **$1,400-$1,600.**

Horse pin on display, 4-1/2", **$1,400-$1,600.**

Shark pin, 8", **$1,300-$1,500.**

Jellyfish pin and display, 10", **$1,400-$1,600.**

Moon Santa pin, 6", **$1,400-$1,600.**

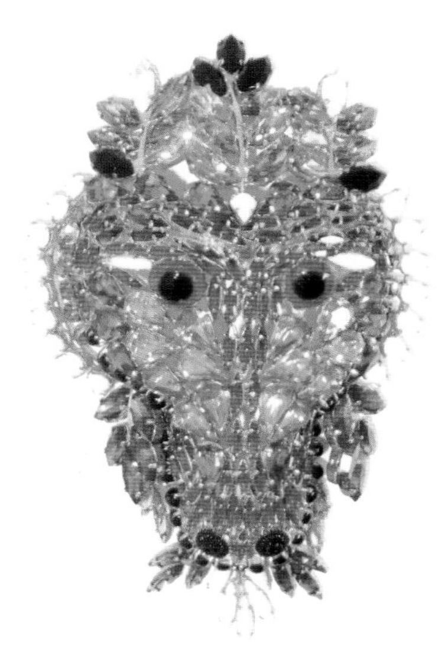

Mandrill monkey head pin, 4-1/2", **$1,400-$1,600.**

Hanna Bernhard jewelry photos on Pages 242 and 243 courtesy collector-designer-dealer Valerie B. Gedziun, who specializes in the work of leading contemporary American and French designers at www.valerieg.com.

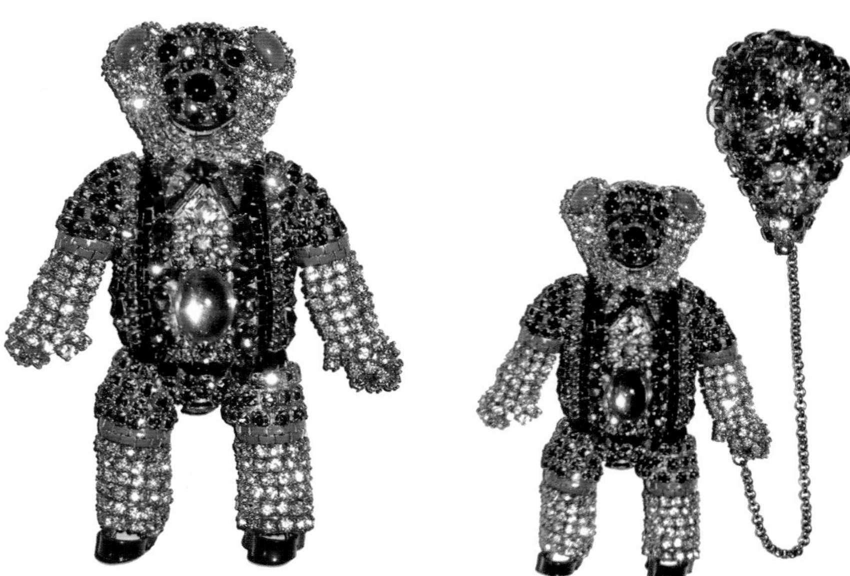

Teddy Bear Brooch with Balloon Pin (plus connecting chain), after Winnie-The-Pooh, 5" bear, 3" balloon, signed, **$1,500-$1,750.**

Pierrot, 4-1/4" x 4-1/2", **$1,500-$1,800.**

Phoenix, 5" x 2", **$1,200-$1,500.**

Butterfly, 3-1/2" x 3-1/2", **$900-$1,200.**

Lobster, 8" x 4", **$1,500-$1,800.**

Seahorse, 7" x 3-3/4", **$1,500-$1,800.**

Gazelle, 7" x 3-1/2", **$1,500-$1,800.**

Giraffe, 4-1/2" x 3-1/2", **$1,500-$1,800.**

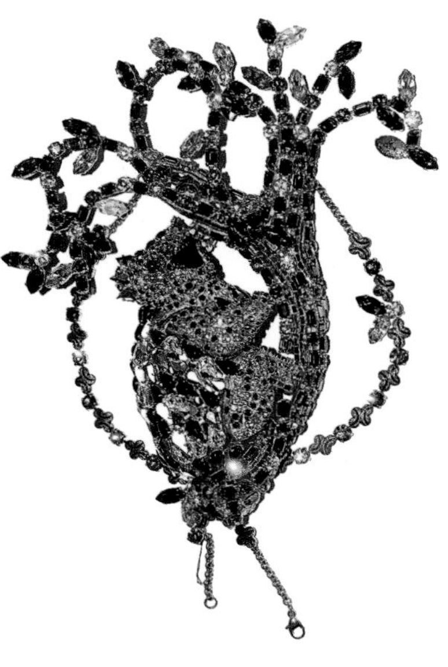

Koala necklace and brooch, 8" x 7", **$2,200-$2,500.**

Flamingo, 4" x 5-1/4", **$1,500-$1,800.**

Crocodile, 8" x 3-1/2", **$1,200-$1,500.**

Lizard, 7" x 2-1/2", **$1,200-$1,500.**

Dallas dealer-collector Dianna Flanigan likes Hanna Bernhard creations almost as much as her fabulous feline menagerie. Flanigan owns 10 Bernhard pieces–and four kitties. No doubt the first brooch here is her favorite?

Cat Face Brooch, 3-3/4", **$800.**

White Christmas Tree, 4-1/4", **$800.**

Curvy Christmas Tree, 4-1/8", **$800.** (Note the acid-etched floral design in base.)

Jeweled Christmas Tree, 4-3/4", **$700.**

Hummingbird & Flower with Display, 4" to 5", **$1,800.** (Brooches may be set into fenced flower-garden stand.)

Pink Poodle Pin, 5", **$900.** *Courtesy Jane Massey.*

Von Walhof Creations
Bettina Von Walhof, Michelle Von Walhof

Some collectors look for the early 1997 pieces Bettina von Walhof made when she first became a jewelry designer a decade ago, when her creations were charmingly primitive. The German-born jewelry dealer's first famous collection was a flock of fanciful Y2K bug brooches marking the Millennium, as well as celebratory motifs such as champagne glasses. Because von Walhof's pieces are showy and colorful, it's no surprise one woman attracted to the styles early on was Clinton-administration Secretary of State Madeleine Albright, rarely seen without a decorative pin on her lapel. First Lady, then senator and presidential candidate Hillary Rodham Clinton is also a fan. Von Walhof's partiality to nature and wildlife themes is a perfect expression of her background: the former young "Jungle Girl" got an early start training wild animals for film and the circus. (In America, she settled in Sarasota, Florida, naturally.) The jewelry company became a family firm when daughter Michelle von Walhof joined the business. The Von Walhof team creates each retro-look piece by hand, using top-quality Swarovski crystals and vintage findings. They design whimsical motifs for all the holidays, and specialize in exotic animal, dog and cat pieces, accepting special orders for uncommon breeds. The Von Walhof "wearable art pieces" are made in extremely limited numbers; many are one-of-a-kind. The effect of their elaborately set crystals, mixing gorgeous hues of chaton and baguette cuts in hematite metal settings, is practically painterly. Many of the creatures are "wigglers," their heads, tails, legs shimmying because set *en tremblant.*

Michelle's shop is at www.rubylane.com/shops/thecuriosityshop2.

Each jeweled brooch ranges in size from 3 inches to 8 inches:

Leonine Largesse, **$3,800.**

Jewel-Encrusted Crab, **$2,200.**

Sparkling Scorpion, **$2,200.**

Luscious Lobster, **$2,200.**

Precocious Pelican, **$350.**

Madame Ant, **$950.**

Kitty on the Moon, **$385.**

Mr. Lucky Halloween Cat, **$385.**

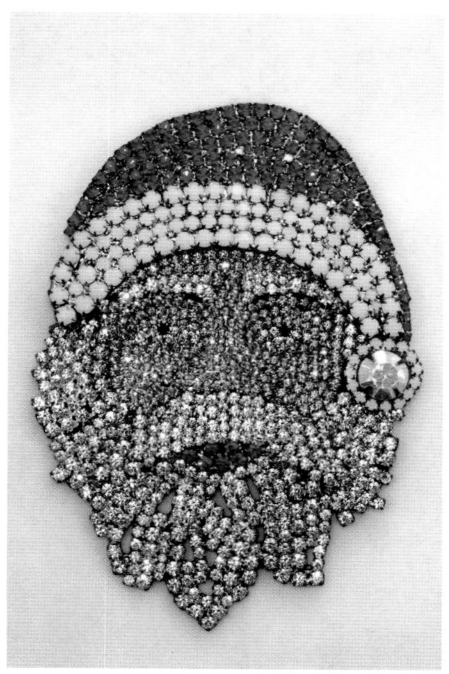

St. Nikolaus, **$485.**

Very Merry Christmas Tree, **$385.**

Stand-Tall Christmas Tree, **$850.**

Elephantine Elegance, **$650.**

Zazzie the Stallion, **$385.**

Miss Priss Poodle, **$385.**

David Mandel

David Mandel's oversized, theatrical pieces, fittingly signed "The Show Must Go On!" are recognized around the world. Because of his background in sculpture, Mandel approaches each creation as an *objet d'art.* His work graces desks, dressing tables and étageres almost as often as lapels. Each piece is crafted by Mandel in very limited editions.

Working Lights Trembler Tree, emerald-ice mix of pearlescent creme de menthe teardrops and shards-of-glass navettes for a tropical effect, large-jewel gift beneath tree set en tremblant, tied with springy, loose metal ribbon, lights up, signed The Show Must Go On, 1999, 5-3/4", **$375.**

Robert Sorrell

Anyone wowed by the bijoux in the movie "To Wong Foo, Thanks for Everything, Julie Newmar," already knows Robert Sorrell, renowned for wildly unique and interesting takes on ordinary objects. Sorrell's work is often large scale, featuring stunning stone work used to great effect in hand-crafted pieces. Sorrell designs for the Paris haute couture collection of Thierry Muegler, as well as the Cirque du Soleil.

Candle in the Wind, White Chiclet baguettes and milk-glass rhinestone chain (effecting dripping wax) compose a dramatic candle fit for a particular Princess. Liquidy emerald navettes and chartreuse stones plus multicolor paste accents are outdone only by the flaming jagged orange stones flickering atop the *bougie*; signed Sorrell Originals, 1999, 5-1/4", **$250.**

Iradj Moini

Known for bejeweled masterpieces worn and collected by some of the world's most elite aficionados of fashion and design, Iradj Moini long ago became the couture jeweler for Oscar de la Renta, making memorable tropical creations (such as his famous parrot) for the 500th anniversary party celebrating de la Renta's birthplace, the Dominican Republic. Moini's work is handmade of brass and copper wire with imported glass stones individually hand set into his highly coveted works of art.

Images here and on P. 250 courtesy Iradj Moini and Valerie Gedziun.

Mandel, Sorrell and Moini jewelry is at www.valerieg.com.

Orchid brooch, citrine, carnelian, emerald, peridot and tourmaline, 6" round, **$2,090.**

Cross brooch, citrine, emerald and ruby, 6", **$1,870.**

Iradj Moini

Butterfly brooch, green aventurine, citrine and carnelian, 5", **$1,230.**

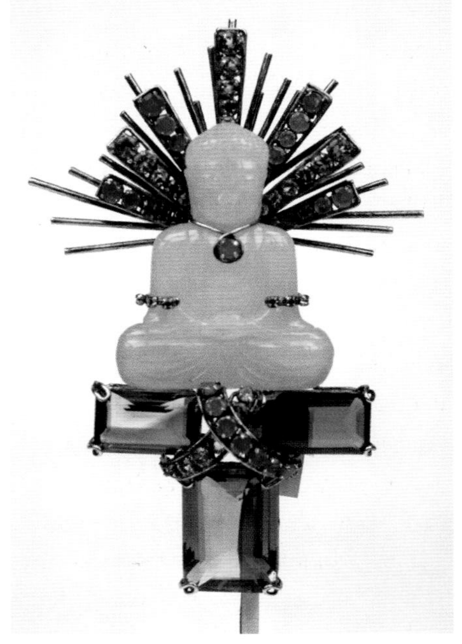

Brilliant Buddha brooch, chalcedony, citrine and emerald, 6", **$1,230.**

White Blossoms, **$1,500-$1,800.**

Orchid, **$1,500-$1,800.**

Peacock, **$2,400-$2,700.**

Crystal Pearl Spray, **$1,200-$1,500.**

Ian St. Gielar for Stanley Hagler

One of the most colorful and passionate jewelry artists died unexpectedly in March 2007. Polish-born Ian St. Gielar came to his craft through a series of American serendipities. Working in the Florida hotel industry in 1986, he met high-profile jewelry designer Stanley Hagler, who had relocated to Florida from New York. There, for three decades, he famously produced jewelry perhaps best described as "highly accomplished large-scale pieces of brilliant hand-wired pastes set amid the muted pearlescent hues of faux seed pearls."

St. Gielar began working as an independent contractor for Hagler, becoming his protégé in 1989. That was the year many figurals collectors first became aware of the pair, due to an initial foray into brooches with a holiday theme. One customer's commission of Christmas arbors in 1989 prompted the same reaction many sophisticated, artistic designers have when such novelties are first broached: They wonder if the form is too corny or mundane to take on. The first Yuletide trees special-ordered were such a success, though, they never doubted the motif's appeal again.

St. Gielar continued working in the signature idiom of elegantly hand-wired wraps and weavings after Hagler died in 1996. The biggest change to the classic look was that St. Gielar took it to Technicolor heights, whether employing vivid red glass strawberry beads from Europe or delicate porcelain flowers among settings of neon beading. St. Gielar's work is to be carried on by his wife, Velentina, under the name "Ian Gielar Studio."

The following brooches are 3 inches to 5 inches.

The Bees' Knees brooches, Golden Bee adorned with coral, left, and Queen Honey Bee in a tapestry of colorful beaded leaves and glass flower, **$150** each.

Parrot Tropicale brooch, Swarovski crystal parrot perched in a jungle of colorful glass flowers and beads, **$200.**

Scrumptious Strawberries brooch, antique strawberry beads with hand-wrapped leaves and flowers, **$175.**

Grandiose Rose Grapes, shimmering glass balls mimicking fat, juicy fruit, German vintage green leaves, **$150.**

Ocean Sea Turtles, Swarovski crystal turtles among seashells, coral and glass beads, **$150.**

Tutti Frutti Christmas Tree, one of a kind (all vintage materials used), including plentiful glass beads and fruit, **$200.**

Emerald Ice Christmas Tree, mammoth glass navettes like shards of green glass, red, white and green glass flowers and seed-beading, prong-set ruby RS, layered floral star including mirror-back stones, **$125.**

Bibliography

Brunialti, Roberto and Carla Ginelli. *American costume jewelry.* Edizione Mazzotta, 1997.

——. *A Tribute to America.* Edita, 2002.

Cannizzaro, Maria Teresa. *Brillanti Illusioni.* Dives Edizioni, 2002.

Cera, Deanna Farneti. *Amazing Gems.* Harry N. Abrams, 1997.

Dolan, Maryanne. *Collecting Rhinestone & Colored Jewelry,* 4th ed. Krause Publications, 1998.

Ettinger, Roseann. *Forties & Fifties Popular Jewelry.* Schiffer Publishing, 1994.

Flood, Kathy. *Things.* AuthorHouse, 2006.

Gordon, Angie. *Twentieth Century Costume Jewelry.* Adasia International, 1990.

Izard, Mary Jo. *Wooden Jewelry and Novelties.* Schiffer Publishing Ltd., 1998.

Lane, Kenneth J. and Harrice Simons Miller. *Faking It.* Harry N. Abrams, 1996.

Lanllier, Jean and Marie-Anne Pini. *Five Centuries of Jewelry.* Leon Amiel, 1983.

Lesher, Leigh. *Costume Jewelry.* Krause Publications, 2004.

Miller, Harrice Simons, *Costume Jewelry,* 2nd ed. Avon Books, 1994.

——. *Official Price Guide to Costume Jewelry,* 3rd ed. House of Collectibles, 2002.

Moro, Ginger. *European Designer Jewelry.* Schiffer Publishing Ltd., 1995.

Pitman, Ann Mitchell. *Inside the Jewelry Box.* Collector Books, 2004.

Romero, Christie. *Warman's Jewelry,* 2nd ed. Krause Publications, 1998.

Simonds, Cherri. *Collectible Costume Jewelry.* Collector Books, 1997.

Additional Resources

Interviews: Elliot Handler, Karl Eisenberg, Ruth Kamke, Robert Mandle, Kenneth J. Lane, Zachary Zemby and others.

Tollemache, Nick and Linda. "The Designs of Ruth Kamke." *Vintage Fashion & Costume Jewelry,* Vol. 10, No. 1, 2000.

Researching Costume Jewelry (www.illusionjewels.com/costumejewelrymarks.html).

Internet Movie Database (IMDb.com).

U.S Patent & Trademark Office Database (www.uspto.gov).

Encyclopedia Britannica.

Index